BARTHÉLEMY/GOODING/LUST/TOV

THE STORY OF DAVID AND GOLIATH

ORBIS BIBLICUS ET ORIENTALIS

Publié au nom de l'Institut Biblique
de l'Université de Fribourg Suisse,
du Seminar für biblische Zeitgeschichte
der Universität Münster i. W.
et de la Schweizerischen Gesellschaft
für orientalische Altertumswissenschaft
par Othmar Keel
avec la collaboration de
Erich Zenger et Albert de Pury

Sur les auteurs :

Emanuel Tov est professeur au Bible Department de la Hebrew University de
Jérusalem (Israël).
Johan Lust est professeur d'Exégèse de l'Ancien Testament à la Katholieke Uni-
versiteit de Leuven (Belgique).
David W. Gooding est professeur émérite au Department of Greek de la Queen's
University de Belfast (Irlande du Nord).
Dominique Barthélemy est professeur d'Exégèse de l'Ancien Testament à l'Uni-
versité de Fribourg (Suisse).
Tous quatre, chacun dans son domaine, ont déjà mené des recherches sur les
relations existant entre le Texte Massorétique et la Septante.

ORBIS BIBLICUS ET ORIENTALIS 73

DOMINIQUE BARTHÉLEMY
DAVID W. GOODING
JOHAN LUST
EMANUEL TOV

THE STORY
OF DAVID AND GOLIATH

Textual and Literary Criticism

Papers of a Joint Research Venture

ÉDITIONS UNIVERSITAIRES FRIBOURG SUISSE
VANDENHOECK & RUPRECHT GÖTTINGEN
1986

CIP-Kurztitelaufnahme der Deutschen Bibliothek

The story of David and Goliath: textual and literary criticism; papers of a joint research venture / Dominique Barthélemy... – Fribourg, Suisse: Editions Universitaires; Göttingen: Vandenhoeck und Ruprecht, 1986.

(Orbis biblicus et orientalis; 73)
ISBN 3-7278-0372-X (Ed. Univ.)
ISBN 3-525-53702-6 (Vandenhoeck und Ruprecht)
NE: Barthélemy, Dominique [Mitverf.]; GT

Publié avec l'aide du Conseil de l'Université Fribourg Suisse

ISBN 3-7278-0372-X (Editions Universitaires)
ISBN 3-525-53702-6 (Vandenhoeck & Ruprecht)

TABLE DES MATIERES

Vorwort (O. Keel) VII

Relation de la première étape du travail commun (D. Barthélemy) 1

INITIAL CONTRIBUTIONS

J. Lust : The Story of David and Goliath in Hebrew and in Greek. 5
E. Tov : The Nature of the Differences between MT and the LXX 19
D. Barthélemy : Trois niveaux d'analyse 47
D.W. Gooding : An Approach to the Literary and Textual Problems
    in the David-Goliath Story 55

RESPONSES

J. Lust. 87
E. Tov. 92
D. Barthélemy 95
D.W. Gooding. 99

Relation de la seconde étape du travail commun (D. Barthélemy) 107

Third stage by D.W. Gooding. 114
Methodological Remarks by J. Lust 121

CONCLUSIONS

E. Tov. 129
D. Barthélemy 138
D.W. Gooding. 145
J. Lust. 155

POSTFACE 157

Vorwort

Wir haben es hier mit einem ganz eigenen und, soweit ich sehe, einzigartigen Dokument zu tun. In seiner gewohnt unabhängigen und konstruktiven Art hat D. Barthélemy zusammen mit drei Kollegen zur Selbsthilfe gegriffen. Das Uebel kennt jeder. Die Vorträge an Kongressen rund um die Welt sind zu lang, die für Diskussionen vorgesehene Zeit wird in die Ecken gedrängt. Die Viertelstunde, die zur Verfügung bleibt, reicht für zwei, drei Informationsfragen, für die Rezitation von Kurzformeln des eigenen Glaubens, für psychohygienische Ventilierungen von Glücks- oder Unmutgefühlen.

In bewusstem Gegensatz zum munteren Marktplatz- und Selbstbedienungsbetrieb der grossen Kongresse haben die vier Autoren dieses Bandes ein langes, geduldiges und sorgfältiges Gespräch inszeniert. Das genaue Prozedere wird auf den Seiten 1-3 und 107-113 metikulös beschrieben. Die vier Autoren kommen nicht nur aus verschiedenen Ländern (Belgien, Israel, Nordirland, Schweiz), sondern vertreten auch verschiedene Arbeitsbereiche und Methoden, die J. Lust auf S. 155 kurz und freundlich beschreibt.

Inhaltlich liegt das Hauptinteresse des Bandes wahrscheinlich darin, dass hier vier Gelehrte, die in jahrzehntelangem Umgang mit vielen Texten, Erfahrungen gesammelt haben, im *terrain vague* zwischen Text- und Literarkritik Position beziehen. Die Fragen werden klar gestellt. Die Antworten machen deutlich, dass auch ein freundliches und einfühlsames Dialogisieren und ein exemplarisch sorgfältiges Abwägen aller Argumente die Wege von der einen Version zur andern nicht zwingend rekonstruieren können, da die menschliche Freiheit, um nicht zu sagen Willkür, durch bestimmte — wiederum erst zu rekonstruierende — Gegebenheiten und Anliegen zwar merklich eingeschränkt, aber nie aufgehoben wird.

Das ist eine schlichte Weisheit. Bei der Dominanz naturwissenschaftlicher Modelle droht sie ständig verdrängt zu werden. Es ist den vier Weisen zu danken, diese Weisheit — nebst vielem anderen — mit Bescheidenheit und Kompetenz exemplarisch praktiziert zu haben.

Der Herausgeber

RELATION DE LA PREMIERE ETAPE DU TRAVAIL COMMUN

(D. Barthélemy)

Le 6 octobre 1980, en accord avec Emanuel Tov (Jérusalem) et Johan Lust (Leuven), j'écrivis à David Gooding (Belfast) :

Lors du colloque organisé à Vienne par l'IOSCS, durant cet été, J. Lust, de Louvain, a fait une intéressante communication sur la Septante ancienne d'Ezéchiel (papyrus 967 d'Ez. et Vieille Latine), y voyant un texte bref (par rapport au TM), situation analogue à celle que l'on rencontre dans la Septante de Jérémie. On admet généralement que ces formes brèves sont plus primitives.

Discutant à trois, lui, Emanuel Tov et moi, nous pensions qu'il serait intéressant de faire un petit travail en commun sur un autre cas de "LXX brève", celui des récits de Goliath. Je considère en effet que, quoique y étant plus brève, la Septante y est secondaire par rapport au TM. Lust et Tov penseraient spontanément le contraire.

Ils m'ont chargé de vous demander si vous accepteriez de participer à ce travail avec nous trois.

Chacun de nous quatre rédigerait une petite contribution (de 10 à 25 pages) sur le même sujet : "Comment faut-il juger les grands 'moins' de la LXX en 1 Sam 17,12-31 et 17,55-18,5 ?" Il s'agit essentiellement de formuler et de peser des arguments. Dans une première étape, chacun m'enverrait sa contribution pour le 30 avril 1981, si la date est acceptable pour vous. Ensuite, je communiquerais à chacun les 3 autres contributions. Puis, chacun d'entre nous rédigerait une prise de position sur l'ensemble des contributions, en visant à dégager une méthode pour aborder les problèmes où interfèrent la critique littéraire et la critique textuelle. Nous échangerions ces prises de position en octobre prochain.

Nous verrions alors s'il est opportun de nous réunir pour un colloque de travail de deux jours, l'été suivant (1982) où je serais heureux de vous accueillir tous les trois. Nous verrions aussi s'il est utile de faire de ce travail commun l'objet d'une publication.

Cette initiative est motivée, de ma part, par une certaine déception à l'égard des colloques et congrès. Il serait intéressant de tenter, sur une échelle très restreinte, un travail en commun visant à des échanges aussi serrés que possible sur un sujet très précis.

Auriez-vous la bonté de me dire dès que possible si vous acceptez de travailler sur ce sujet avec nous trois et de proposer d'autres délais si ceux que je vous propose ne vous conviennent pas.

La date de fin-avril 1981 pour l'envoi des contributions initiales parut à tous trop rapprochée. De fait, celles-ci arrivèrent à Fribourg entre juillet 1981 et le

1

début de mai 1982 (DG ayant été retardé par des engagements antérieurs et par la situation difficile de l'Irlande du Nord). Le 11 de ce mois, j'écrivis à DG, JL et ET :

Je vous envoie les photocopies des quatre contributions dans l'état où je les ai reçues, c'est-à-dire — et j'ai moi aussi respecté la règle du jeu — sans qu'aucun de nous quatre ait eu connaissance en rédigeant sa contribution de celles des trois autres.

Le 8 avril dernier, J. Lust m'a demandé si je voyais un inconvénient à une éventuelle publication de sa contribution en ETL. Etant donné qu'il y avait déjà 9 mois qu'il me l'avait envoyée, il était compréhensible qu'il ait le désir d'en faire usage. Je lui ai répondu que chacun de nous gardait les droits de publication sur sa propre contribution, mais qu'il me semblait seulement que nous devions éviter de tenir compte (dans une publication) des contributions des autres membres de notre groupe; car nous réservons à notre décision commune une éventuelle publication d'ensemble, ou une publication de ce que nous pourrons tirer ensemble de ces quatre contributions.

Comme suite de notre travail, je vous suggère une deuxième étape où chacun étudiera l'ensemble des quatre contributions et formulera en quelques pages ses remarques sur les problèmes de méthode et les problèmes de fond posés par la comparaison de ces quatre études. Je suggère que chacun me communique avant la fin de cette année 1982 cette deuxième contribution qui devrait ne pas dépasser dix pages. Nous appliquerons la même règle : je n'ouvrirai les envois que lorsque les 4 seront rassemblés. Chacun aura donc réalisé indépendamment des 3 autres cette deuxième étape dont je communiquerai à tous simultanément le résultat.

A ce moment-là, il s'agira de voir si nous estimons utile de tenir ensemble un colloque (ici par exemple) ... ou si nous publions ensemble le résultat de ces deux "étapes" d'études ... ou si chacun tire personnellement de ce parcours réalisé ensemble les conséquences qu'il estime utiles.

Pourriez-vous m'écrire sans tarder vos réactions à ces propositions, et cela sous une enveloppe indépendante de celle qui contiendra votre éventuelle 2e contribution.

Le 25 décembre 1982, les quatre réponses étaient arrivées à Fribourg et, quatre jours plus tard, elles furent communiquées aux participants.

Nous publions ici les quatre contributions initiales et les quatre réponses dans l'état où ces documents de travail furent communiqués aux participants. Nous avons évité de faire après coup aucune correction de fond, afin que l'on puisse retracer avec exactitude la démarche de cette recherche commune. Seules quelques données bibliographiques ont été explicitées, quelques fautes de frappe ont été corrigées, les interréférences ont été adaptées et une ligne a été ajoutée (celle qui, à la p. 41 figure entre crochets).

Notons ici que deux des contributions initiales ont, sous une forme plus ou moins retravaillée, été déjà publiées :

Celle de JL, sous le titre : The Story of David and Goliath in Hebrew and Greek, *en ETL 59/1 (1983) 5-25.*

Celle de ET, sous le titre : The Composition of 1 Sam 17-18 in the Light of the

Evidence of the Septuagint Version, *en* : J. Tigay (ed.), Empirical Models for the Development of the Hebrew Bible, Philadelphia 1985.
Après la publication de ces documents de travail, je relaterai, aux pp. 107-113 la seconde étape de notre travail commun.

,

THE STORY OF DAVID AND GOLIATH IN HEBREW AND IN GREEK

As far as the Books of Samuel are concerned, the story of David and Goliath is by far the most important of the contexts in which several manuscripts of the Septuagint, among which the early majuscule B, differ considerably from the present Hebrew text. The Greek version in these manuscripts is much shorter than the Hebrew. It omits 1 Sam. 17,12-31.41.48b.50.55-18,6a.10-12.17-19.21b.30 [1].

Which text is to be preferred, the longer or the shorter one ? Which criteria allow us to make a proper choice ? Do we have to choose one text and discard the other or can we accept both versions as equally valuable ? A careful study of the data pleads in favor of the latter solution [2]. Before we proceed to a survey of the argumentation leading to this conclusion it may be interesting to reconsider the dominant role attributed to J. Wellhausen in this matter.

The Authority of J. Wellhausen

According to the recent and excellent commentary of P. Kyle McCarter Jr., many critics have followed J. Wellhausen in supposing that the evidence of the LXX reflects a subsequent shortening of an original longer text in order to give the story balance and economy [3]. Similar affirmations can be found in J. Stoebe's commentary on 1 Samuel and in his article on the story of David and Goliath [4]. While both authors refer to J. Wellhausen as an authority, they do not accept his views. Earlier introductions and commentaries often proceed along the same lines [5].

These repeated assertions make one wonder what J. Wellhausen really wrote. P. Kyle McCarter does not tell where in J. Wellhausen's *oeuvre* he found a basis for his statement [6]. J. Stoebe is more explicit. In his commentary he refers to J. Wellhausen's *Die Composition des Hexateuchs und der historischen Bücher des A.T.*, 3. Aufl., Berlin, 1899, p. 247. However, when one looks up the reference, one soon finds out that J. Wellhausen does not deal with the problem in question. He simply mentions : "The Septuagint omits these verses". For further comment he refers to his earlier monograph on the text of Samuel [7]. There, however, in his detailed analysis of the text, J. Wellhausen strongly affirms exactly the opposite : The Septuagint does not shorten the text, it rather corresponds to the original version which was later expanded upon by the Hebrew text.

When we turn to J. Stoebe's article on the topic, we find some more precise information. We have to consult the second edition of Wellhausen's *Composition*. There indeed we find briefly stated that : "When the Septuagint omits these verses, this seems to be harmonistic criticism" [8].

J. Wellhausen obviously changed his mind. This was already noted, for example, by Henry Preserved Smith [9] : "J. Wellhausen in his study on the text decided for the Septuagint, because harmonistic omissions imply a critical insight which we cannot suppose in the translators. This argument, though afterwards given up by J. Wellhausen himself, is still good".

Did J. Wellhausen change his mind a second time and return to his original standpoint ? The third edition of his *Composition* suggests that the answer should be affirmative. In this edition he no longer mentions the harmonising tendencies of the Septuagint brought up in the second edition. He merely refers the reader in a footnote to this earlier work : *Der Text der Bücher Samuelis.* The third edition certainly wishes to correct the foregoing one. One does not see where the correction could lie if not in a renewed acceptance of the thesis brought to the fore in *Der Text der Bücher Samuelis* [10].

The least one can conclude is that J. Wellhausen has hesitated. If one wishes to follow his authority, one may have to do the same. We did not yet evaluate his criteria. His arguments in favour of the Septuagint are more detailed than the ones in favour of the Hebrew text. We will have to deal with them in the following pages. We will proceed as follows : In a first section we will briefly survey the textual data. In a second, we will try to answer some questions of textual criticism. In a third, we will study the literary critical data and in a final section we will offer some tentative conclusions.

I. THE WITNESSES

1. The Greek Text

a. Direct Witnesses

As stated in the introduction, several Greek biblical manuscripts omit large sections of 1 Sam. 17-18. It should be noted however that not all of them omit all the sections mentioned in the introduction. The shortest text ist to be found in Manuscripts BV anvyb2 [11]. The longer text corresponding with the MT is given by manuscripts Ab + d + we. Other manuscripts have some of the omissions : cx fms ghija2. The relatively recently discovered fragment 815 written in Majuscules, probably in the fourth century (A.D.), has 1 Sam. 18,8-25 including vv. 17-19 but not vv. 10-11.21b.

The Greek text of the "pluses" in codex A, and in the other verses having the longer text, does not belong to the original LXX. They are inserts based on the MT. This is most obvious in codex A, where 17,11 is followed by the beginning of 17,32 : ϰαὶ εἶπεν δαυειδ and then by 17,12-31 [12]. Moreover, the Greek vocabulary and style of these "pluses" differ from the language and style of the surrounding sections. This must be due to the fact that these sections were translated separately, by a revisor. We do not have to elaborate the argumentation here, since this has been done sufficiently by other authors [13]. The same argumentation applies to the "pluses" in the Lucianic manuscripts. In this case the Lucianic codices certainly do not preserve any trace of the Old Greek [14].

All these data strongly suggest that the original Greek text did not have the "pluses" of the MT.

b. Indirect Witnesses

Some early indirect witnesses should be mentioned here. Josephus seems to have the shorter text, with the exception of 17,12-31, which he renders in his own style [15].

The *Sermo Hippolyti* might prove to be of special interest in this context. It is the earliest commentary on 1 Sam. 17,1-18,8, dating from the second century (A.D.). The text has been preserved in two Georgian manuscripts and in some fragments of an Armenian "catena". The Georgian version appears to be a translation of the Armenian text, which in turn is based on the Greek [16]. They are thus translations of translations. This may make it difficult to recover the original Greek wordings. Nevertheless, it appears possible to discern some important characteristics of the prehexaplaric Greek text.

Hippolytus quotes 1 Sam. 17,2-11 word for word (De David et Goliat 6,2-17). After a rather lengthy commentary on these verses, he quotes v. 17,32, omitting the verses inbetween (De David et Goliat 10,2-4). The dialogue between David and Saul in 17,33-37 is also given almost literally (De David et Goliat 10,16-11,18) whereas the following passages are rendered more freely, taken up in a running commentary. None of the passages omitted by LXXB are referred to. However, there is one exception. Towards the end of this homily, Hippolytus combines 17,54 with 18,1b.4 : When Jonathan sees David carrying the head of Goliath in his hand, he loves him. He thus omits 17,55-58, but not 18,1ff.

Hippolytus obviously uses a Greek text which was very close to LXXB [17]. He not only omits the same sections — with the exception of 18,1b.4 — he also has other characteristics in common with LXXB. In 1 Sam. 17,4 both give Goliath four cubits height instead of MT's six. In Goliath's taunt in 17,8 the Israelites are called "Hebrews" (עבר) instead of "servants" (עבד, MT). In his answer to Saul, in 17,32, David quietens "his Lord's" (אדוני) heart instead of "man's" (אדם). In 17,43 David is said to come to Goliath with "a stick" and with "stones" and not with "sticks" only (MT).

2. The Hebrew Text

Besides the Massoretic text we possess two minor fragments of 1 Sam. 17-18, discovered in Qumran. A first one is merely a scrap found in Cave 1. It is published and identified as part of 1 Sam. 18,17-18 [18]. If the identification is correct [19], the manuscripts to which the fragment belonged probably contained the longer text, since 1 Sam. 18,17-18 is missing in the shorter text.

The other fragment was hidden in Cave 4. It has not yet been published, but it is known from E. Ulrich's study on *The Qumran Text of Samuel and Josephus* [20]. The preserved text belongs to 1 Sam. 17,3-6. It displays one major variant when compared with MT : In verse 4 it reads "four" cubits instead of "six". It should be noted that the earliest witnesses of the short Greek version agree with the Qumranic fragment and also read "four" : i.e. ms. B, Josephus, the Sermo Hippolyti as well as the Lucianic manuscripts [21].

If we are to believe F.M. Cross and E. Ulrich, the fragment of 1 Sam. 17,3-6 belonged to a scroll 4 Q Sam. a, representing a non-MT-type of Hebrew manuscript agreeing in many points with the LXX [22]. This and other similar discoveries demonstrate "that the LXX's particularities are more likely to be based on Hebrew texts than we hitherto thought. However, they have not given us grounds for thinking that every single difference between the LXX and the MT presupposes that same difference in some Hebrew Vorlage" [23]. I quoted DG and agree with him. How does his statement apply to 1 Sam. 17-18 ? In my opinion, the agreement between 4 Q Sam. a, and the LXX 1 Sam. in general, and between the Qumranic and LXX versions of 1 Sam. 17,4 in particular, plead in favour of the possibility that 4 Q Sam. a offered the shorter text of 1 Sam. 17-18. This would imply that the shorter text of the LXX was based on a shorter Hebrew Vorlage. The different and longer MT would be based on a different and longer Hebrew Vorlage. However, "other possible causes of difference have not automatically been ruled out". We still need "to assess the comparative likelihood of the competing possibilities, before deciding which is the most probable" [24].

II. CORRUPTION OF THE TEXT ?

1. LXXB : A Shortened Text ?

Is the shorter Greek text a corrupted text ? Does it imply the shortening of a longer original ? In this hypothesis, two possibilities remain : the shortening may be either intentional or unintentional.

a. Unintentional Shortening

Unintentional shortening happens most often through *parablepsis* caused by *homoioteleuton* or *homoioarchton*. However, it is most unlikely that the whole of the omissions in LXXB could be explained in this way. Indeed, though there are omissions through *parablepsis* in 1 Sam. LXX [25], there are never as many as that in one chapter, nor such lengthy ones as 17,12-31 and 17,55-18,6a. Moreover, it is hard to find traces of a *homoioteleuton* in connection with the omissions in question. The only one which we can see is in 17,54; 18,6. The end of the report in the combat in 17,54 mentions that David took the head of the Philistine and brought it to Jerusalem. Several VL codices and ancient editions of the Latin text have a similar expression at the beginning of 18,6 : "When David returned from slaying the Philistine, bringing his head to Jerusalem..." [26]. The eye of the scribe may have wandered from 17,54 to 18,6. Such a lengthy omission may seem unusual in 1 Sam. However, it is perfectly possible that the Vorlage of our scribe did not have all the verses which we find in the MT. It is more likely that it had a couple of verses only, namely the ones referred to by Hippolytus in his homily. If this is correct, the original Greek text must have omitted 17,55-58 but not 18,1b.(3).4. The latter verses were omitted later on, through *parablepsis*.

A text shortened by accident may very well cause a discontinuity in the story. As far as the immediate context of 18,1b-4 is concerned, such cannot be detected. However, when considering the larger context, some kind of discontinuity may become apparent. Indeed, 1 Sam. 20,8 presupposes the *berît* between Jonathan and David related in 18,3. Actually, this is the main reason adduced in favour of the MT in 1 Sam. 17-18 by A. Kuenen [27]. According to him, the longer text must be the original one, since it is presupposed by its context. However, if one accepts, with A. Kuenen, that 18,1-4 is presupposed by 20,8, it does not follow that all the "pluses" of the MT are presupposed by 20,8. It is equally possible that the Old Greek had the short text, including 18,1b.(3).4. We saw indeed that the verses 18,1b.(3).4 may have been omitted through parablepsis [28].

b. Intentional Shortening

It is often said — and the saying has often been attributed to J. Wellhausen — that the LXX shortened the story intending to harmonise it. It is true that the narrative as it stands in the MT conveys some tensions both within itself and in respect of its relationship to the preceeding narrative. When one opts for the shorter text quite a few of these tensions disappear. Does this imply that the shorter text is a shortened version and thus corrupt ? We do not think so. With Kyle McCarter we may bring the following objections to the fore [29]. First, it is difficult to understand why an editor who was removing contradictions so boldly, would not remove them all and why he removed sections not containing major contradictions [30]. Second, and more damaging to the shortening hypothesis, is the lack of satisfactory parallels to such a phenomenon in 1 Sam.

According to P. Kyle McCarter, the major argument against the shortening hypothesis is that the "pluses" can be read as an independent story [31]. We have some doubts about the validity of this argument. It may be possible to prove that the MT version contains two independent versions of the battle between David and Goliath, or at least that its contradictory passages belong to separate traditions [32]. However, it may be more difficult or even impossible to prove that this is an argument against the "shortening" hypothesis. Indeed, this would imply that the second story, or the contradictory fragments, were added in a period after the one in which the LXX originated. However, the fact that the MT may have preserved two versions of the same event, does not indicate that the second version is younger than the first, nor that it was interpolated "into the primary narrative at some time subsequent to the divergence of the ancestral textual traditions that lie behind MT and LXX" [33].

J. Wellhausen adduced another argument against the shortening hypothesis [34]. It runs as follows : The contents of both 16,14ff and 17 are presupposed by 18,6ff. For this reason, in their original form, 16,14ff and 17 must have been in harmony with each other. In the short version they are in harmony. The conclusion must be that the short text is the original one and that it is not the result of a harmonisation. This argument stands on a weak footing. J. Wellhausen himself must have noticed this for in his later work he emphasised the disharmony between the story of the single combat in chapter 17 and the song of the women in 18,6ff celebrating the victory not of David in his single combat, but of David and Saul and all Israel against the Philistines. His new suggestion is that 1 Sam. 17 as a whole was a later insert [35].

We may conclude this section as follows. Not all the arguments against the shortening hypothesis are equally valid. Nevertheless, the basic ones remain sufficiently strong. Intentional shortening is unlikely. One might have to change this conclusion when it would be demonstrated that the shortening technique used in 1 Sam. 17-18 can be explained by motives typical of the translator.

2. The MT : An Expanded Text ?

If the Greek text is not shortened, must we then accept that the MT is an expanded version ? Is there no alternative ? Before we try to answer this question, we shall briefly survey some possible causes of expansion.

a. Unintentional Expansion

Since the margin was used for glosses as well as for corrections, it must have often been perplexing to a scribe to decide what to do with a marginal note. This explains how such notes were occasionally incorporated into the text. However, a series of lengthy marginal notes covering all the "pluses" of the MT in 1 Sam. 17 and 18, would be rather exceptional. An unintentional insertion of all this material would be even more unlikely.

b. Intentional Expansion

Stories like the one on David and Goliath attract complementary material. This helps to explain why in the OT we often find two parallel accounts of the same event next to each other (so the two creation accounts) or interwoven (so the flood narratives). Here, in the Greek and Hebrew texts of 1 Sam. 17-18, we probably are confronted with different stages in the formation of the text and in the use of the materials [36]. A further stage may be found in a number of manuscripts of the Targum Jonathan in which 1 Sam. 17,8 received a lengthy expansion offering more information about Goliath [37]. The insert counterbalances the additional information on David given in the Massoretic "plus" in 17,12-31.

c. Different Texttypes ?

We tend to accept the expanded character of the MT. However, this does not answer the questions concerning its relation to the shorter text provided by LXXB. We already stated that the LXXB can hardly be a shortened text. In this case two possibilities remain. First, the Hebrew was expanded after the date of composition of the LXX. Second, the expansion took place earlier, but was not taken up in all the manuscripts. The translator of the LXX worked on a shorter copy. Since the discoveries in Qumran confirm the existence alongside each other of differing Hebrew manuscripts of 1 Samuel, the latter possibility may prove to be the more plausible one.

Up to this stage we have been dealing mostly with text-critical facts and theories. In the following section we will investigate some literary critical data and see whether or not they confirm our former conclusions.

III. LITERARY CRITICAL DATA

When reading the Hebrew text, one soon finds out that verses 12-31 of chapter 17 are not needed for a full comprehension of the story preserved in 17,1-11.32-54. Verses 12-31 rather interrupt the narrative of 17,1-11.32-54. Such an interruption may be due to a later insertion. Or it may also be a literary device, causing a retarding effect. A further analysis of the text may reveal other possibilities.

1. The Composition of the Common Text

The story, as it appears in the text common to MT and LXXB, is well composed and balanced. The schema of the narrative may be outlined as follows :

a. The Setting of the Scene
   * Philistines and Israelites are encamped on opposite sides of a valley. The scene can easily be visualised. The data are simple and clear. No complicating additional background information is given (17,1-3).
   * On each side one man steps to the fore and presents himself as the champion of his army. On the Philistine side this man is Goliath : v. 4, on the Israelite side it is David : v. 40b. Their equipment is described in great detail. The contrast is obvious : vv. 5-7 and 38-40a. Goliath defies Israel : vv. 8-10 and causes terror in Israel's camp : v. 11. David brings calm and quietness taking away the terror : vv. 31-35 and answers Goliath's taunt : vv. 36-37.

```
C    ┌Goliath steps forward : v. 4
B    │  ┌Goliath's equipment : v. 5-7
A    │  │  ┌Goliath's taunt : v. 8-11
     │  │  │   vv. 12-31
A'   │  │  └David's answer : v. 32-37
B'   │  └David's equipment : v. 38-40a
C'   └David steps forward : v. 40b
```

Verses 12-31 interrupt this sequence. Verse 41 is redundant after v. 4. Both sections are missing in LXXB.

b. The Combat
   *New taunts introduce the single combat : vv. 42-47. The data of both speeches correspond : (i) Goliath mocks David who comes up armed with a stick and stones : v. 43a. In his answer, David mocks Goliath, the one who trusts in the strength of his arms whereas David puts his trust in the name of the Lord of hosts : v. 45. (ii) Goliath curses David by his gods : v. 43b. David answers : "This day the Lord will deliver you

in my hand" : v. 46. (iii) Goliath threatens David : "I will give your flesh to the birds and the beasts ..." : v. 44. David answers : "I will cut off your head and give the dead bodies of the Philistines to the birds and the beasts" : v. 46b. One element is added to David's speech which finds no counterpart in Goliath's taunt : David's victory will show to "all the earth ... that there is a God in Israel ... and that all this assembly may know..." : vv. 46c-47.

 * The single combat itself is rendered very concisely : vv. 48a-49.51a. Verse 48b is an unnecessary repetition of verse 40b. Verse 50 may be an insert offering a comment on the implications of the contest, referring to v. 47. The insert wishes to make it clear that the sword with which Goliath was killed — according to verse 51 — was not David's. However, the verse may equally well be part of an alternative story on David's combat. Both verse 40b and verse 50 are missing in LXXB.

 * The victory of Israel : vv. 51b-53. The Philistine army is routed in fear and becomes an easy prey for the pursuing men of Israel and Judah.

 * In an epilogue it is said that David took the head and the armour of Goliath : 17,54. He meets Jonathan. They enter a *berît* : 18,1b.3-4. The part of this epilogue may have been omitted by the Septuagint by mistake. It has been preserved by Hippolytus (cf. supra).
Verses 55-58 of chapter 17 and verse 2 of chapter 18 do not fit in this context. They are missing in LXXB.

 The meeting of David and Jonathan in 18,1b.3-4 may also seem to be alien to the report of the single combat. However, this is not necessarily the case. The verses in question may offer a key to the story as a whole. They probably bring Jonathan on the scene in order to refer the reader to 1 Sam. 13-14 where a deed of Jonathan is narrated, similar to David's. Both Jonathan and David, as single heroes, defeat the Philistines and leave king Saul in the shadow, deprived of a heroic deed which could have been his. In 1 Sam. 13-14, Jonathan, Saul's son and heir, seems to be pushing his father aside. In 1 Sam. 17,1-18,5 the suggestion is that David is taking over Jonathan's role. Both sections are part of a redaction focussing on Saul's fall.

 The main conclusion of this survey must be that 1 Sam. 17,1-11.32-54; 18,1b.(3).4 are a well balanced composition, interrupted by 17,12-31.55-58; 18,2 and by some shorter passages [38].

2. The "Pluses" of the Massoretic Text

 a. The schema of the "pluses" is less clear, especially in vv. 12-31. Some of the confusion may be due to redactional interventions trying to connect the section with its context [39]. Notwithstanding these editorial transitions, the "pluses" do not stand in harmony with the common text. In vv. 15ff. David is presented as an occasional visitor to the army-camp. He is not supposed to have his own tent. Nevertheless in v. 54, he puts Goliath's armour in his own tent [40]. One does not expect panic-stricken Israel : v. 11, to draw up for battle : v. 21. According to the setting of the scene in vv. 1-11, Goliath may come out of his camp (v. 4), down the hill, he cannot come up as is said in v. 23. Verse 24 further reports that it was the sight of the champion that frightened the soldiers, whereas in v. 11, it was his word (compare with David in v. 23 who "heard" the champion). The tensions increase when one takes vv. 55-58 into the picture. These verses are most often considered a late addition. However, the section, together with 18,2, forms a good epilogue to the story related in the "pluses" [41].

The most reasonable explanation for the tensions referred to, is that the editor used an existing story, or parts of it, as an insert. He adapted it so as to avoid major contradictions. But he did not succeed in avoiding all of them.

b. The structure of the "pluses" can be clarified through a comparison with 1 Sam. 1,1ff. and 9,1ff. The three anecdotic stories explain how the child who is to become the main character and hero of the following chapters, arrived at "the court". They open with a presentation of the child's father. There was a man from X, his name was Y... The opening line of 17,12 might be obscured through the insert of בֶּן־דָּוִד and הַזֶּה, serving as editorial links with the context. Nevertheless, the pattern which it has in common with the parallel opening lines (1,1 and 9,1) can still be recognised [42].

3. Two Versions and their Literary Genre

a. One cannot but think that verses 17,12-31.55-58; 18,2 contain the relics of a narrative that once was the opening story of the history of David. Indeed, the histories of Samuel and Saul were introduced in a similar way. One may assume with J. Wellhausen [43] that the story of Samuel and Saul ended in 14,52 : "There was hard fighting against the Philistines all the days of Saul; and when Saul saw any strong man or any valiant man he attached him to himself". The opening of the new section of the book in 17,12 follows very well upon this. It shows Saul at war against the Philistines. David passes along and gets involved in the battle. Saul sees him and attaches him to himself.

Especially are 1 Sam. 9,1ff. and 1 Sam. 17,12ff. closely related. The schema of both sections is as follows. A man has a son : 17,12 and 9,1. He sets a task to this son : 17,17-18 and 9,3. The task is a rather minor one but the quest for its fulfilment brings the hero into contact with the leader of his country : Saul meets Samuel : 9,17ff.; and David meets Saul : 17,55-58. Both stories end with "On that day" : 18,2 and 9,24 [44] and with the remark that the hero stays with the leader. In the following scene it becomes clear that he will become his successor. The schema of 1 Sam. 1 is very similar, but it is combined with an other tradition : the account of the birth of a son to sterile parents.

b. The narrative in 1 Sam. 17,12ff. has some of the characteristics of a "fairy tale" or of a "romantic epic" [45], with political overtones [46]. It implicitly compares David with Joseph, and thus presents David as the king of all the tribes of Israel and Judah.

Other versions of David's victory may have circulated. One of them is preserved in 1 Sam. 17,1-11.32-54; [18,1b.3-4]. Its literary genre is different [47]. It may be called a "heroic epic". More than the other story, it focusses the attention upon the single combat and on David as a hero of war. An editor of 1 Samuel may have preferred this version since he wished to present David as a hero. He probably added a didactic note, preserved in verses 46-47, and used it instead of the "romantic epic". The Greek translator must have worked on this version.

The same, or a later editor of the Hebrew text must have provided a combination of both stories. This caused some disturbance in the well balanced "heroic epic". Moreover, although the redactor reworked the "romantic epic" in order to adapt it to its new context, he could not avoid some contradictions and tensions. Through his intervention he even created new incongruities. He gave Jesse eight sons (17,12) in order to harmonise the story with 16,1ff. However, 17,28 strongly suggests that there were only four. The redactor further let Goliath speak "the same words as before" (17,23), obviously referring to 17,8ff. He let David hear the giant (17,23). However, the "romantic epic" emphasises the terrifying aspect of Goliath's appearance, and not of his words. Also, David is not supposed to have heard him, since a soldier has to explain to him the meaning of the Philistine's appearance : 17,25. These and similar data clearly confirm our opinion concerning the growth of the text. The "tale" of 1 Sam. 17,12ff., which at some stage of the growth of the book, formed the introduction to the story of David's rise to power must have been replaced by the "heroic epic" of 17,1-11.32-54; [18,1b.3-4]. This was probably done by an editor who systematically emphasised David's election and Saul' condemnation. At this stage, the text was translated into Greek. At the same time, or later, the "romantic epic" concerning David's victory was reinserted and combined with the "heroic epic" [48]. The result was the Vorlage of the MT.

TENTATIVE CONCLUSIONS

1. The results of the literary data which we investigated can be schematized as follows :

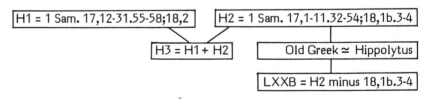

These results to a large extent conformed to the text-critical data. *"Parablepsis"* explained the absence of 18,1.3-4 in LXXB.

2. A further section should answer some remaining questions on the level of literary criticism : How do the vocabulary, style and theology of both the heroic epic and the romantic epic relate to the different levels of redaction of 1 Samuel ? Is it possible to put a date on these compositions and can one be more specific about the "Sitz im Leben" ?

NOTES

1   H.B. Swete, Introduction to the OT in Greek, Cambridge, 1902, p. 245-246.

2   I was rather puzzled by DB's statement in a letter of October 6, 1980. He thinks that I would spontaneously have preferred the Septuagint.

3   P. Kyle McCarter Jr., 1 Samuel, (Anchor Bible), New York, 1980, p. 306-307.

4   H.J. Stoebe, Das Erste Buch Samuel, (KAT), Gütersloh, 1973, p. 312. H.J. Stoebe, Die Goliathperikope 1 Sam. 17,1-18,5 und die Textform der Septuagint, VT6 (1956) 397.

5   See e.g. H.B. Swete, Introduction to the Old Testament in Greek, Cambridge, 1902, p. 245-246.

6   The same is true for H.B. Swete, op. cit., p. 245.

7   J. Wellhausen, Der Text der Bücher Samuelis, Göttingen, 1872, p. 104s.

8   J. Wellhausen, Die Composition..., zweiter Druck, Berlin, 1889, p. 250 : "Wenn die Sept. diese Verse auslässt, so scheint das harmonistische Kritik zu sein, ...". The first edition of the last chapter of "Die Composition" was printed in F. BLEEK, Einleitung in das AT, Vierte Auflage, bearbeitet von J. Wellhausen, Berlin, 1878.

9   H.P. Smith, The Books of Samuel, (ICC), Edinburgh, 1904, p. 150. See more recently J. Grønback, Die Geschichte vom Aufstieg Davids, (Acta theologica Danica, 10), Copenhagen, 1971, p. 82 n. 17.

10 The footnotes in the 3rd edition of "Die Composition" added to the ones in the foregoing edition, are put in square brackets. The one concerning our topic, p. 247, is an exception. One wonders why. The note reads as follows : "Vgl. Text der Bücher Samuelis (1S71) p. 104s". The (1S71) is of course a misprint for 1S17. The introductory Vgl. (vergleich = compare) is often used in Wellhausen's footnotes and usually implies that the author basically agrees with the text referred to. When he does not agree he puts : vgl. dagegen (p. 102, n. 1) or vgl. aber (p. 148, n. 1; p. 275, n. 2; p. 59, n. 1) or vgl. indes (p. 101, n. 1).

11 For the sigla see : The Old Testament in Greek ... edited by Brooke-McLean-Thackeray, Vol. I, Cambridge, 1906; and Bo Johnson, Die Hexaplarische Rezension des 1 Samuelbuches der Septuaginta, Lund, 1963, p. 16-18.

12 Codices cx fms wc change ειπεν into ην. See further : Bo Johnson, op. cit., p. 119; compare with Bo Johnson, Die Armenische Bibelübersetzung, Con. Bibl., OT Series 2, Lund, 1968, p. 128.

13 See J. Wellhausen, Der Text der Bücher Samuelis, p. 104; S.R. Driver, Notes on the Hebrew Text and the Topography of the Books of Samuel, Oxford, 1912(2), p. 140; N. Peters, Beiträge zur Text und Literarkritik sowie zur Erklärung der Bücher Samuel, Freiburg im Breisgau, 1899, p. 36-38. The argumentation could be elaborated further. A comparison with the B-Text in the βγ sections would be relevant, but not directly for our topic.

14 See P. Brock, Lucian *redivivus*. Some Reflections on Barthélemy's *Les Devanciers d'Aquila,* in : Texte und Unters. 103, Berlin, 1968, p. 177. The "pluses" are probably due to hexaplaric influence.

15 Antiq. Jud. VI, 175ff. Josephus probably used both the Hebrew text of the Bible and the Greek translation.

16 Traités d'Hippolyte sur David et Goliath sur le Cantique des cantiques et sur l'Antéchrist, Version Georgienne éditée par G. Garitte, CSCO vol. 263, Script. Iberici tomus 15, Leuven, 1965; Version Georgienne traduite par G. Garitte, CSCO vol. 264, Script. Iberici tomus 16, Leuven, 1965.

17 Compare with J. Ziegler, Der Bibeltext im Daniel-Kommentar des Hippolyt von Rom, Nachr. d. Akad. d. Wissensch. zu Göttingen, Phil. Hist. Klasse, 1952, 163-199 = Sylloge, MSU 10, Göttingen, p. 357-393 : "Die angeführten Stellen (im ganzen 89) zeigen deutlich das Zusammengehen von Hippol. mit dem B-Text". (p. 176 resp. 370)

18 Discoveries in the Judaean Desert, I, ed. D. Barthélemy, Oxford, 1956(2), p. 64-65.

19 The photography (plate XI) is rather vague and does not allow an untrained eye to verify the identification.

20 HSM 19, Harvard, 1978, p. 79, 177, 271.

21 We may suggest that perhaps the Lucianic codices have preserved here a trace of the early Greek text. It may also be noted here that quite a few mss. give Goliath "five" cubits. Among them are representatives of the short text : Vanyb2 as well as representatives of the middle form and longer text : msj and we. A d+ and cx have "six" cubits.

22 See, e.g., F.M. Cross, A New Qumran Biblical Fragment related to the Original Hebrew Underlying the Septuagint, BASOR 132 (1953) 23; E. Ulrich, op. cit., p. 257.

23 D.W. Gooding, Jeroboam's Rise to Power. A Rejoinder, JBL 91 (1972) 530.

24 D.W. Gooding, ibid.

25 See N. Peters, Beiträge zur Text- und Literarkritik sowie zur Erklärung der Bücher Samuel, Freiburg im Breisgau, 1899, p. 102ff.

26 C. Vercellone, Variae lectiones, II, Romae, 1864, p. 263.

27 A. Kuenen, Historisch-kritisch onderzoek, vol. I, Leiden, 1861, p. 61.

28 Compare with N. Peters, op. cit., p. 42, who answers Kuenen's thesis in a different way. According to N. Peters, the author of 1 Sam. did not have to mention explicitly the *making* of the *berît* referred to in 20,8.

29 P. Kyle Mc Carter, 1 Samuel, (Anchor Bible), New York, 1980, p. 307.

30 The latter part of the objection refers especially to 18,1-4. If one accepts our proposal concerning the "unintentional" omission of 18,1-4, then this part of the objection loses its sharpest tooth. One might plead in favour of MT saying that it has the *lectio difficilior*. However, see about this text-critical rule B. Albrektson, Difficilior lectio probabilior, in OTS 21, Leiden, 1981, p. 5-18.

31 P. Kyle McCarter, op. cit., p. 307; see also H.W. Hertzberg, Die Samuelbücher, ATD, Göttingen, 1968(4), p. 117.

32 H. Jason, The Story of David and Goliath : A Folk Epic ?, in Biblica 60 (1979) 36-70 defends the unity of 1 Sam. 17,1-18,5.

33 P. Kyle McCarter, op. cit., p. 307.

34 Der Text der Bücher Samuelis, p. 104-105.

35 Die Composition, 3rd edition, p. 248; Prolegomena, 3rd edition, p. 274. Note that, as far as 1 Sam. 18,10-30 are concerned, J. Wellhausen did not change his mind. He kept defending the short version of LXXB.

36 P. Ackroyd, The First Book of Samuel, Cambr. Bible Comm., Cambridge, 1971, p. 148.

37 A. Sperber, The Bible in Aramaic. Vol. II : The Former Prophets According to Targum Jonathan, Leiden, 1959, p. 127.

38 Compare with L. Krinetzki, Ein Beitrag zur Stilanalyse der Goliathperikope, Biblica 54 (1973) 187-236; especially p. 197-200.

39 See, e.g., S.J. De Vries, David's Victory over the Philistine as Saga and as Legend, JBL 92 (1973) 23-36; especially p. 29.

40 H.W. Hertzberg, Die Samuelbücher, p. 123 and : Mizpa, ZAW 47 (1929) 161ff. proposes to read באהלי with the final letter being an abbreviation for Jahweh. The proposal is ingenious but it is not supported by the text tradition.

41 S.J. De Vries, art. cit., p. 28.

42 See H.J. Stoebe, Die Goliathperikope, p. 400. The author sees the parallels. He also notices complications both in 1,2 and 17,12. As far as 17,12 is concerned, he insists on a very vague parallel in Judg 6,11-24 instead of paying full attention to the better parallels in 1 Sam.

43 Die Composition, 1899, p. 249.

44 See J. De Vries, David's Victory over the Philistine, p. 24-27.

45 H. Jason, The Story of David and Goliath : A Folk Epic ?, hesitates between "fairy tale" and "romantic epic". He tries to apply Propp's model and Skaftymov's model to the story. In doing so, he analyses the text as a complete literary unit. He concludes that, if 17,12-31.55-58;18,1-5 had been an addition, it would have been possible to treat the story as a unity. However he may have overlooked that most items of Propp's and Skaftymov's models apply to 17,12-31.55-58; 18,1-5 and not to the text which MT and LXXB have in common.

46 See especially H.J. Stoebe, Die Goliathperikope, p. 402ff.

47 The difference is dealt with explicitly by S.J. De Vries, David's Victory over the Philistine, especially p. 31ff.; see also H. Gressmann, Die älteste Geschichts- schreibung und Prophetie Israels, SAT 2,1, Göttingen, 1910, p. 77-81. On the literary genre of 1 Sam. 17,1-18,5 see further : G. Von Rad, Der heilige Krieg im Alten Israel, Zürich, 1949, p. 47-49; R. De Vaux, Les combats singuliers dans l'AT, in Biblica 40 (1959) 495-508; H.J. Stoebe, Gedanken zur Heldensage in den Samuelbüchern, in Das ferne und nahe Wort, Fs. L. Rost, BZAW 105, Berlin, 1967, p. 208-218.

48 1 Sam. 17,12 still shows the seam. According to S.R. Driver, op. cit., p. 140, it is possible that הַזֶּה in v. 12 is a late and unskilful insertion made with the view to connect the inserted material with the foregoing chapter. He prefers Ehrlich's suggestion that הַזֶּה is a corruption of הוּא and that "he was from Beth- lehem" was a gloss, intended to show that אֶפְרָתִי did not mean Ephraimite but Bethlehemite. We already suggested that the construction of 1 Sam. 17,12 must have been similar to the one of 1 Sam. 9,1. If this is true, the original sentence may have read as follows : "There was a man of Bethlehem, his name was Jesse". When the editor changed the text, bringing David to the fore, he called him the son of an Ephratite. This note reminds one of the glosses in Gen. 35.20;48,7 and of Micah 5,1 and Ruth 4,11. The type of sentence at the beginning of 17,55, uncommon to early Hebrew (S. Driver, op. cit., p. 148), may also be due to the redactor who reinserted the material.

THE NATURE OF THE DIFFERENCES BETWEEN MT AND THE LXX
IN 1 SAM. 17-18 [1]

In the summer of 1980 it was suggested that four scholars should address exactly the same issue, viz., the nature of the differences between MT and the LXX in 1 Sam. 17-18, or, as DB phrased the topic in a more limited way, "Comment faut-il juger les grands 'moins' de la LXX en 1 Sam 17,12-31 et 17,55-18,5 ?". DB then wisely suggested that these papers should be written without prior knowledge of the other papers. Each of us is to formulate arguments in favor of his own views, and cannot merely react on the argumentation of others.

I. THE ORIGIN OF THE DIFFERENCES BETWEEN MT AND THE LXX

The OG (Old Greek) version of the LXX and the MT differ greatly in 1 Sam. 17 (the encounter of David and Goliath) and 1 Sam. 18 (the events after that fight). These two chapters must be treated together because typologically similar differences between the OG and MT occur in both chapters [2].

The following verses are lacking in the OG of ch. 17,12-31.41.48b.50.55-58, altogether 26 verses or 45 o/o of the chapter. In ch. 18,1-16, the following verses are lacking : 1-6a.10-11.12b, altogether 8 verses or 50 o/o. In the remainder of ch. 18 (vv. 17-30), the following verses are lacking : 17-19. 21b. 29b-30, altogether 5 verses or 36 o/o. In total, some 44 o/o of chapters 17-18 in MT lacks in the OG.

We should add in parenthesis that the OG version contained in MSS B... omits the aforementioned verses, but that MSS A... do provide a Greek translation of these verses. However, the vocabulary of that translation has been recognized as Hexaplaric [3] (MSS Acx... reflect also elsewhere in 1 Samuel a Hexaplaric text [4]). The origin of the Hexaplaric pluses in 1 Sam. 17-18 is probably *kaige*-Theodotion [5].

The background of the minuses of the OG has often been treated in scholarship. The most extensive discussions are found in the works of Wellhausen, Peters, Stoebe and McCarter [6]. These analyses focus on the large minuses of the OG, thus neglecting two other aspects of the translation of 1 Sam. 17-18 without which that translation cannot be evaluated well :

1. In addition to the large minuses mentioned above, the OG lacks other elements in ch. 17-18, ranging from one to five words :

!   !

17,5	וכובע (נחשת)	18,6	(לשיר והמחלות לקראת שאול המלך)
17,9	ואם אני אוכל (לו) *	18,7	הנשים (המשחקות)
17,33	הפלשתי (הזה)	18,7	(ויחר לשאול מאד)
17,36	הפלשתי הערל (הזה)	18,11	(ועוד לו אך המלוכה)
17,37	(ויאמר דוד)	18,20	וישר (הדבר) בעיניו
17,38	(וילבש אתו שריון)	18,24	ויגדו עבדי שאול לו (לאמר)
17,39	ויסירם (דוד) מעליו *	18,26	(ולא מלאו הימים)
17,42	(ויבט הפלשתי)	18,27	ויבא (דוד)
17,45	היום (הזה)	18,27	ויתן לו (שאול)
17,48	וילך (ויקרב)	18,27	(וימלאום) למלך
17,51	ויקח את חרבו (וישלפה מתערה)	18,28	וירא שאול (וידע)
17,51	ויכרת (בה)	18,29	ויאסף (שאול)

2. The LXX reflects several variant readings (recognition of these variants is necessarily subjective). In the following list some tentatively retroverted variants are added in square brackets :

!

17,2	*εν τη κοιλαδι. αυτοι παρατασσονται	בעמק האלה ויערכו	[בעמק. אלה..]
17,4	εκ της παραταξεως	ממחנות	[ממערכות]
17,4	(υψος αυτου) τεσσαρων (πηχεων)	(גבהו) שש (אמות)	[ארבע]
17,7	και ο κοντος	וחץ	[ועץ]
17,8	Εβραιοι	עבדים	[עברים]
17,9	και εαν	אם	[ואם]
17,10	ιδου εγω	אני	
17,32	του κυριου μου	אדם	[אדני]
17,34	και η αρκος	ואת הדוב	[ואף הדוב]
17,35	του φαρυγγος αυτου	בזקנו	[בגרנו]
17,36	και τον αρχον (ετυπτεν ο δουλος σου)	גם את הארי	
	και τον λεοντα	גם הדוב (הכה עבדך)	
17,37	Δαυειδ	[דוד] המלך	[ויהיה ה']
17,37	και εσται κυριος	וה' יהיה	[וקרבע]
17,38	και (περικεφαλαιαν)	ונתן הקובע	[וילא]
17,39	και εκοπιασεν	ויאל	
17,39	απαξ και δις	כי לא נסה	
17,39	*και αφαιρουσιν αυτα	ויסירם	
17,41	εις συλλογην	ובילקוט	[בילקוט]
17,42	καλλους οφθαλμων	יפה מראה	[יפה עינים]
17,43	εν ραβδω	במקלות	[במקל]
17,46	και αποκλεισει σε	יסגרך	[ויסגרך]
17,46	τα κωλα σου και τα κωλα	פגר	[פגרך ופגרי]
17,46	*(εστιν θεος) εν Ισραηλ	(יש אלהים) לישראל	[בישראל]
17,47	*και γνωσεται	וידעו (כל הקהל הזה)	[וידע]

!

17,48	και ανεστη	והיה כי קם	[ויקם]
17,51	επ αυτον	אל הפלשתי	[עליו/אליו]
17,51	Γεθ	גיא	[גת]
17,52	οπισω αυτων	(וירדפו) את הפלשתים	[אחריהם]
17,52	Ασχαλωνος	עקרון	[אשקלון]
17,53	ανδρες Ισραηλ	בני ישראל	[איש ישראל cf. v.2]
17,54	αι χορευουσαι	הנשים	
18,8	εν οφθαλμοις Σαουλ	בעיניו	[בעיני שאול]
18,8	περι του λογου	הדבר	
18,14	*εν πασαις ταις οδοις αυτου	לכל דרכיו	[בכל דרכיו]
18,16	προ προσωπου του κυριου	לפניהם	[לפני העם]
18,21	επι Σαουλ	בו	[בשאול]
18,22	και συ	ועתה	[ואתה]
18,25	αλλ η	כי	[כי אם]
18,25	αυτον εμβαλειν	להפיל את דוד	
18,27	εκατον	מאתים	[מאה]
18,27	και επιγαμβρευεται	להתחתן	
18,28	και πας	ומיכל	[וכל]
18,28	Ισραηλ	בת שאול	[ישראל]
18,28	ηγαπα αυτον	אהבתהו	[אהבו]

3. More importantly, the LXX reflects several pluses, ranging from single words to complete sentences. With due caution, the majority of these pluses can be retroverted into Hebrew :

!

17,5	χαλχου + και σιδηρου	נחשת + וברזל
17,8	πολεμω + εξ εναντιας ημων	מלחמה + לקראתנו
17,32	μη + δη + συμπεσετω	אל + נא + יפל

17,36 +ουχι πορευσομαι και παταξω αυτον και αφελω σημερον ονειδος εξ Ισραηλ διοτι τις ο απεριτμητος ουτος +

+ הלוא אלך והכתיו והסרותי היום חרפה מעל ישראל כי מי הערל הזה +

17,37	του αλλοφυλου + του απεριτμητου + τουτου	הפלשתי + הערל + הזה
17,40	προς + τον ανδρα + τον αλλοφυλον	אל + האיש + הפלשתי
17,42	και ειδεν + Γολιαθ	וירא + גלית
17,43	+ και λιθοις και ειπεν Δαυειδ ουχι αλλ η χειρω χυνος	+ ואבנים ויאמר דוד לא כי אם ... +
17,46	και αποχλεισει σε χυριος + σημερον	יסגרך ה' + היום
17,47	και παραδωσει + χυριος	ונתן + ה'
17,49	λιθον + ενα	אבן + אחת
17,49	και διεδυ ο λιθος + δια της περιχεφαλαιας + εις το μετωπον αυτου	ותטבע האבן + בעד הכובע + במצחו
18,6	+ εις συναντησιν Δαυειδ +	+ לקראת דוד +

21

!

18,22	+ λεγων +	+ לאמר +
18,22	λαλησατε + υμεις	דברו + אתם
18,24	χατα τα ρηματα ταυτα + α + ελαλησεν	כדברים האלה + אשר + דבר
18,27	την Μελχολ θυγατερα αυτου + αυτω +	את מיכל בתו + לו +

In view of these data is it simplistic to limit the discussion to the large minuses. Any solution suggested must take into consideration *all* aspects of the relation between MT and the OG.

The opinions which have been expressed about the nature of 1 Sam. 17-18 in the LXX can be divided into two groups : Some scholars ascribed the divergencies between the two texts to the translator who was said to have omitted some 44 o/o of the text because of exegetical motives. To this view adhered Kuenen, Budde, Schmid and recently DB [7]. These scholars focused on the large minuses, usually disregarding the pluses in the translation, and if they did discuss the pluses (thus, e.g., DB), these, too, were regarded as exegetical. The exegetical motivation which was ascribed to the translator in omitting large sections of the text was "harmonization", that is, creation of a more smooth story by omitting conflicting details.

According to the other, diametrically opposed, view, the translator knew a short Hebrew text. In the nineteenth century this view was suggested by Houbigant, Dathe, Kennicott, Eichhorn, Gesenius, de Wette, Thenius, Peters, Wellhausen and Woods, and in the twentieth century by Steuernagel, Smith, Stoebe, Habel, Johnson and McCarter [8]. Peters even reconstructed the original Hebrew text of the story on the basis of the LXX. The short Hebrew text which was reconstructed on the basis of the LXX was usually considered to reflect a stage of the literary development of the story which preceded that of MT, but even if that text is regarded as an *abridged* form of MT [8a], that theory would be a mere variation of this view.

We now turn to a discussion of the merits of these two views. It seems to us that no further views need to be discussed. For one thing, we cannot think of any compromise between these two views, for it is not realistic to assume that some of the large minuses were created by the translator, while others were already found in his parent text. On the basis of what type of arguments, then, have scholars decided in favor of one of the two views ? With all due respect to the scholarship of the past, it seems that no solid arguments for anyone view have been presented sofar. Those scholars who suggested that the translator "harmonized" were probably influenced much by the negative evidence relating to the alternative explanation, since they were not aware of Hebrew texts which departed as much from MT as the reconstructed short Vorlage of the OG would depart. They therefore turned soon to the alternative view that the translator shortened his Vorlage. This view is probably based more on this negative evidence and the scholar's intuition than on a positive conviction that the translator indeed omitted large sections of ch. 17-18 because they contained conflicting data. The alternative view, too, is based mainly on intuition and a negative judgment concerning the harmonizing view. Sometimes one also meets remarks stressing that the translator was not likely to omit such large sections, and that he therefore probably found a short text in front of him.

Since in the past scholars have mainly accepted a certain view by ruling out the alternative one, we should now investigate the possibility whether there exists any positive evidence in favor of anyone view. The point of departure for a new analysis should be the recognition that the translation of 1 Sam. 17-18 has to be taken as one entity, and that any solution suggested should take all the characteristics of that translation into consideration. Not only minuses, but also pluses should be taken into account.

In short, only a study of *translation technique* in the broad sense of the word may bring us closer to a solution. Not any more an investigation of the minuses only, for their content does not provide any clue for a solution. Such a solution can come only from an examination of the complete body of details which constitute the translation and of which the minuses form a part. The idea behind this view is the conviction that each translation is internally consistent at least with regard to its general approach to the source text, to which it is either faithful or not. If indeed the translator omitted some 45 o/o of the text, he must have approached that text freely, and this free approach should be visible also in other details. If, on the other hand, there are indications that the translator approached the source text with care and introduced but little exegesis of his own, it is not likely that he would have omitted large sections because of exegetical motivations, so that in that case the short text of the LXX probably reflects a short Hebrew text. This description reflects a logical inference from the act of translating, but it can also be supported by some evidence from the translations themselves. The known translators who took care to represent the Hebrew source text exactly, showed their careful approach in all details, that is, they introduced as little exegesis as possible in the translation equivalents and produced a literal translation which was quantitatively equal with the Hebrew source text (that is without additions and omissions). This applies to the so-called revisers of the LXX (except for "Lucian") and within the canon of the LXX, to the sections which are ascribed to *kaige*-Theodotion (2 Kings, the second part of 2 Sam.), Eccl., Ps. and into a smaller degree to many other units as well. By the same token, free translators show their approach to the text in all details of their translation, that is in their word-choices, in free additions and omissions, as well as in exegetical alterations of various types. This applies to the translations of Is. and Dan. and to a greater extent to the one of Job, where large sections have been omitted from MT.

Against the background of the facts about the translation technique of the other books of the LXX, that of 1 Sam. 17-18 will now be examined. This is no easy task since the two chapters are part of much larger unit [9] whose translation technique can be examined much more easily than that of two chapters only. However, since these chapters contain unusually large minuses and some scholars may therefore claim that they reflect a separate translation unit, they must be singled out for this analysis.

As a basis for this analysis, we now list all the elements of MT according to *BHS* as well as their Greek counterparts according to the edition of Rahlfs and codex B (the text of Rahlfs is almost identical with that of B; whenever the two differ, the text of Rahlfs is printed in parenthesis) :

LXX (Rahlfs) codex B	BHS	LXX (Rahlfs) codex B	BHS
ονομα αυτω	שמו	χαι συναγουσιν	ויאספו 17,1
εχ Γεθ	מגת	αλλοφυλοι	פלשתים
υψος αυτου	גבהו	τας παρεμβολας αυτων	את מחניהם
τεσσαρων !	שש	εις πολεμον	למלחמה
πηχεων	אמות	χαι συναγονται	ויאספו
χαι σπιθαμης	וזרת	εις Coχχωθ	שכה
χαι περιχεφαλαια	וכובע 5	της (Ιουδαιας) Ιδουμαιας	אשר ליהודה
! —	נחשת	χαι παρεμβαλλουσιν	ויחנו
επι της χεφαλης αυτου	על ראשו	ανα μεσον	בין
χαι θωραχα	ושריון	Coχχωθ	שוכה
αλυσιδωτον	קשקשים	χαι ανα μεσον	ובין
αυτος	הוא	Αζηχα	עזקה
ενδεδυχως	לבוש	(εν Εφερμεμ) Εφερμεμ	באפס דמים
χαι ο σταθμος	ומשקל	χαι Caουλ	ושאול 2
του θωραχος αυτου *	השריון	χαι οι ανδρες *	ואיש
πεντε	חמשת	Ισραηλ	ישראל
χιλιαδες	אלפים	συναγονται	נאספו
σιχλων	שקלים	χαι παρεμβαλλουσιν	ויחנו
χαλχου	נחשת	εν τη χοιλαδι	בעמק
χαι σιδηρου ! +		αυτοι ! *	האלה
χαι χνημιδες	ומצחת 6	παρατασσονται ! *	ויערכו
χαλχαι	נחשת	εις πολεμον *	מלחמה
επανω	על	εξ εναντιας	לקראת
των σχελων αυτου	רגליו	αλλοφυλων	פלשתים
χαι ασπις	וכידון	χαι αλλοφυλοι	ופלשתים 3
χαλχη	נחשת	ιστανται	עמדים
ανα μεσον	בין	επι του ορους	אל ההר
των ωμων αυτου	כתפיו	ενταυθα	מזה
χαι ο χοντος	וחץ 7	χαι Ισραηλ	וישראל
του δορατος αυτου	חניתו	ισταται *	עמדים
ωσει μεσαχλον'	כמנור	επι του ορους	אל ההר
υφαινοντων	ארגים	ενταυθα	מזה
χαι η λογχη	ולהבת	(χαι ο αυλων) χυχλω	והגיא
αυτου *	חניתו	ανα μεσον αυτων	ביניהם
εξαχοσιων	שש מאות	χαι εξηλθεν	ויצא 4
σιχλων	שקלים	ανηρ	איש
σιδηρου	ברזל	δυνατος	הבנים
χαι ο αιρων	ונשא	εχ της παραταξεως !	ממחנות
τα οπλα αυτου *	הצנה	των αλλοφυλων	פלשתים
προεπορευετο αυτου *	הלך לפניו	Γολιαθ	גלית

LXX (Rahlfs) codex B		BHS		LXX (Rahlfs) codex B		BHS	
και ειπεν		ויאמר	10	και ανεστη		ויעמד	8
ο αλλοφυλοs		הפלשתי		και ανεβοησεν		ויקרא	
ιδου εγω	!	אני		εις την παραταξιν		אל מערכת	
ωνειδισα		חרפתי		Ισραηλ		ישראל	
την παραταξιν		את מערכות		και ειπεν		ויאמר	
Ισραηλ		ישראל		αυτοις		להם	
σημερον		היום הזה		τι		למה	
εν τη ημερα ταυτη				εχπορευεσθε		תצאו	
δοτε		תנו		παραταξασθαι		לערך	
μοι		לי		πολεμω	*	מלחמה	
ανδρα		איש		εξ εναντιας ημων	!+		
και μονομαχησομεν		ונלחמה		ουχ		הלוא	
αμφοτεροι		יחד		εγω ειμι		אנכי	
και ηκουσεν		וישמע	11	αλλοφυλοs	*	הפלשתי	
Σαουλ		שאול		και υμεις		ואתם	
και πας		וכל		Εβραιοι	!	עבדים	
Ισραηλ		ישראל		(του Σαουλ) και Σαουλ		לשאול	
τα ρηματα		את דברי		εχλεξασθε		ברו	
του αλλοφυλου		הפלשתי		εαυτοις		לכם	
ταυτα		האלה		ανδρα		איש	
και εξεστησαν		ויחתו		και χαταβητω		וירד	
και εφοβηθησαν		ויראו		προς με		אלי	
σφοδρα		מאד		και εαν	!	אם	9
				δυνηθη		יוכל	
om 12-31				προς εμε ~	*	להלחם	
				~ πολεμησαι	*	אתי	
και ειπεν		ויאמר	32	και εαν παταξη με	*	והכני	
Δαυειδ		דוד		και εσομεθα		והיינו	
προς		אל		υμιν		לכם	
Σαουλ		שאול		εις δουλους		לעבדים	
μη		אל		εαν δε		ואם	
δη	+!			εγω		אני	
(συνπεσετω) συμπεσετω		יפל		δυνηθω		אוכל	
(η χαρδια) χαρδια		לב			!*	לו	
του χυριου μου	!	אדם		χαι παταξω αυτον		והכיתיו	
επ αυτον		עליו		εσεσθε	*	והייתם	
ο δουλος σου		עבדך		ημιν		לנו	
πορευεται		ילך		εις δουλους		לעבדים	
και πολεμησει		ונלחם		και δουλευσετε		ועבדתם	
μετα		עם		ημιν		אתנו	

LXX (Rahlfs) codex B	BHS	LXX (Rahlfs) codex B	BHS
εχ του στοματος αυτου	מפיו	του αλλοφυλου	הפלשתי
χαι ει επανιστατο　*	ויקם	τουτου	הזה
επ εμε	עלי	χαι ειπεν	ויאמר 33
χαι εχρατησα	והחזקתי	Cαουλ	שאול
του φαρυγγος αυτου !	בזקנו	προς	אל
χαι επαταξα　*	והכתיו	Δαυειδ	דוד
χαι εθανατωσα αυτον	והמיתיו	ου μη	לא
! ~	גם את הארי 36	(δυνηση) δυνη	תוכל
χαι την αρχον	גם הדוב	πορευθηναι	ללכת
ετυπτεν ο δουλος σου	הכה עבדך	προς	אל
~ χαι τον λεοντα !		τον αλλοφυλον	הפלשתי
χαι εσται	והיה	! −	הזה
ο αλλοφυλος	הפלשתי	του πολεμειν	להלחם
ο απεριτμητος	הערל	μετ αυτου	עמו
! −	הזה	οτι	כי
ως εν	כאחד	παιδαριον	נער
τουτων	מהם	ει συ	אתה
ουχι !+		χαι αυτος .	והוא
πορευσομαι !+		ανηρ	איש
χαι παταξω αυτον !+		πολεμιστης	מלחמה
χαι αφελω !+		εχ νεοτητος αυτου	מנעריו
σημερον !+		χαι ειπεν	ויאמר 34
ονειδος !+		Δαυειδ	דוד
εξ Ισραηλ !+		προς	אל
διοτι τις !+		Cαουλ	שאול
ο απεριτμητος !+		ποιμαινων	רעה
ουτος !+		ην	היה
ος ωνειδισεν	כי חרף	ο δουλος σου	עבדך
παραταξιν	מערכת	τω πατρι αυτου	לאביו
θεου	אלהים	εν τω ποιμνιω	בצאן
ζωντος	חיים	χαι οταν ηρχετο　*	ובא
! −	ויאמר 37	ο λεων	הארי
! −	דוד	χαι η αρχος !	ואת הדוב
χυριος	ה'	χαι ελαμβανεν	ונשא
ος εξειλατο με	אשר הצלני	προβατον	שה
εχ χειρος	מיד	εχ της αγελης	מהעדר 35
του λεοντος	הארי	χαι εξεπορευομην	ויצאתי
χαι εχ χειρος	ומיד	οπισω αυτου	אחריו
της αρχου	הדב	χαι επαταξα αυτον	והכתיו
αυτος	הוא	χαι εξεσπασα	והצלתי

E. Tov

LXX (Rahlfs) codex B	BHS	LXX (Rahlfs) codex B	BHS
οτι	כי	εξελειται με	יצלני
ου	לא	εκ χειρος	מיד
πεπειραμαι	ניסתי	του αλλοφυλου	הפלשתי
και αφαιρουσιν αυτα ! *	ויסירם	του απεριτμητου ! +	
! −	דוד	τουτου	הזה
απ αυτου	מעליו	και ειπεν	ויאמר
και ελαβεν	40 ויקח	Σαουλ	שאול
την βακτηριαν αυτου	מקלו	προς	אל
εν τη χειρι αυτου	בידו	Δαυειδ !	המלך
και εξελεξατο	ויבחר	πορευου	לך
εαυτω	לו	και εσται !	וה'
πεντε	חמשה	κυριος !	יהיה
λιθους	חלקי	μετα σου	עמך
(τελειους) λειους	אבנים	και ενεδυσεν	38 וילבש
εκ	מן	Σαουλ	שאול
του χειμαρρου	הנחל	τον Δαυειδ	את דוד
και εθετο	וישם	μανδυαν	מדיו
αυτους	אתם	και !	ונתן
εν τω καδιω	בכלי	περικεφαλαιαν	קובע
τω ποιμενικω	הרעים	χαλκην	נחשת
τω οντι αυτω	אשר לו	περι *	על
εις συλλογην !	ובילקוט	την κεφαλην αυτου	ראשו
και σφενδονην αυτου	וקלעו	! −	וילבש
εν τη χειρι αυτου	בידו	! −	אתו
και προσηλθεν	ויגש	! −	שריון
προς	אל	και εζωσεν	39 ויחגר
τον ανδρα ! +		τον Δαυειδ	דוד
τον αλλοφυλον	הפלשתי	την ρομφαιαν αυτου	את חרבו
	om 41	επανω	מעל
! −	42 ויבט	του μανδυου αυτου	למדיו
! −	הפלשתי	και εκοπιασεν !	ויאל
και ειδεν	ויראה	περιπατησας	ללכת
Γολιαθ ! +		απαξ και δις !	כי לא נסה
τον Δαυειδ	את דוד	και ειπεν	ויאמר
και ητιμασεν αυτον	ויבזהו	Δαυειδ	דוד
οτι	כי	προς	אל
αυτος ην	היה	Σαουλ	שאול
παιδαριον	נער	ου μη δυναμαι	לא אוכל
και αυτος πυρρακης ! *	ואדמני	πορευθηναι	ללכת
μετα	עם	εν τουτοις	באלה

LXX (Rahlfs) codex B	BHS		LXX (Rahlfs) codex B	BHS	
ερχη	בא		χαλλους	יפה	
προς με	אלי		οφθαλμων	מראה	
εν ρομφαια	בחרב		και ειπεν	ויאמר	43
και εν δορατι	ובחנית		ο αλλοφυλος	הפלשתי	
και εν ασπιδι	ובכידון		προς Δαυειδ	אל דוד	
καγω	ואנכי		ωσει κυων	הכלב	
πορευομαι	בא		εγω ειμι	אנכי	
προς σε	אליך		οτι	כי	
εν ονοματι	בשם		συ	אתה	
κυριου	ה'		ερχη	בא	
(Σαβαωθ) θεου	צבאות		επ εμε	אלי	
(θεου) Σαβαωθ	אלהי		εν ραβδω !	במקלת	
παραταξεως	מערכות		και λιθοις ! +		
Ισραηλ	ישראל		και ειπεν ! +		
ην	אשר		Δαυειδ ! +		
ωνειδισας	חרפת		ουχι ! +		
σημερον	היום		αλλ η ! +		
!	הזה		χειρω ! +		
και αποκλεισει σε !	יסגרך	46	κυνος ! +		
κυριος	ה'		και κατηρασατο	ויקלל	
σημερον ! +			ο αλλοφυλος	הפלשתי	
εις την χειρα μου	בידי		τον Δαυειδ	את דוד	
και αποκτενω σε	והכיתך		εν τοις θεοις εαυτου	באלהיו	
και αφελω	והסרתי		και ειπεν	ויאמר	44
την κεφαλην σου	את ראשך		ο αλλοφυλος	הפלשתי	
απο σου	מעליך		προς	אל	
και δωσω	ונתתי		Δαυειδ	דוד	
τα κωλα σου !			δευρο	לכה	
και τα κωλα	פגר		προς με	אלי	
παρεμβολης	מחנה		και δωσω	ואתנה	
αλλοφυλων	פלשתים		τας σαρχας σου	את בשרך	
εν ταυτη τη ημερα	היום הזה		τοις πετεινοις	לעוף	
τοις πετεινοις	לעוף		του ουρανου	השמים	
του ουρανου	השמים		και τοις κτηνεσιν	ולבהמת	
και τοις θηριοις	ולחית		της γης	השדה	
της γης	הארץ		και ειπεν	ויאמר	45
και γνωσεται ! *	וידעו		Δαυειδ	דוד	
πασα η γη	כל הארץ		προς	אל	
οτι	כי		τον αλλοφυλον	הפלשתי	
εστιν	יש		συ	אתה	

LXX (Rahlfs) codex B	BHS		LXX (Rahlfs) codex B	BHS	
επι	אל		θεος	אלהים	
το μετωπον αυτου	מצחו		εν Ισραηλ ! *	לישראל	
και διεδυ	ותטבע		και γνωσεται ! *	וידעו	47
ο λιθος	האבן		πασα η εκκλησια αυτη	כל הקהל הזה	
δια της περικεφαλαιας ! +			οτι	כי	
εις το μετωπον αυτου	במצחו		ουκ	לא	
και επεσεν	ויפל		εν ρομφαια	בחרב	
επι	על		και δορατι	ובחנית	
προσωπον αυτου	פניו		σωζει	יהושיע	
επι την γην	ארצה		κυριος	ה'	
	om 50		οτι	כי	
και εδραμεν	וירץ	51	του κυριου	לה'	
Δαυειδ	דוד		ο πολεμος	המלחמה	
και επεστη	ויעמד		και παραδωσει	ונתן	
επ	אל		κυριος ! +		
αυτον !	הפלשתי		υμας	אתכם	
και ελαβεν	ויקח		εις χειρας ημων	בידנו	
την ρομφαιαν αυτου	את חרבו		και !	והיה	48
! −	וישלפה		ανεστη !	כי קם	
! −	מתערה		ο αλλοφυλος	הפלשתי	
και εθανατωσεν αυτον	וימתתהו		και επορευθη	וילך	
και αφειλεν	ויכרת		! −	ויקרב	
! −	בה		εις συναντησιν Δαυειδ	לקראת דוד	
την κεφαλην αυτου	את ראשו		! −	וימהר דוד	
και ειδον	ויראו		! −	וירץ	
οι αλλοφυλοι	הפלשתים		! −	המערכה	
οτι	כי		! −	לקראת	
τεθνηκεν	מת		! −	הפלשתי	
ο δυνατος αυτων	גבורם		και εξετεινεν	וישלח	49
και εφυγον	וינסו		Δαυειδ	דוד	
και ανιστανται	ויקמו	52	την χειρα αυτου	את ידו	
ανδρες Ισραηλ	אנשי ישראל		εις	אל	
και Ιουδα	ויהודה		το χαδιον	הכלי	
και ηλαλαξαν	ויריעו		και ελαβεν	ויקח	
και κατεδιωξαν	וירדפו		εκειθεν	משם	
οπισω αυτων !	את הפלשתים		λιθον	אבן	
εως	עד		ενα ! +		
εισοδου	בואך		και εσφενδονησεν	ויקלע	
Γεθ !	גיא		και επαταξεν	ויך	
και εως	ועד		τον αλλοφυλον	את הפלשתי	

LXX (Rahlfs) codex B	BHS		LXX (Rahlfs) codex B	BHS	
πολεων	ערי		της πυλης	שערי	
Ισραηλ	ישראל		Ασχαλωνος !	עקרון	
	! − לשיר		και επεσαν	ויפלו	
	! − והמחלות		τραυματιαι	חללי	
	! − לקראת		των αλλοφυλων	פלשתים	
	! − שאול		εν τη οδω	בדרך	
	! − המלך		των πυλων	שערים	
εν τυμπανοις	בתפים		και εως	עד	
και εν χαρμοσυνη	בשמחה		Γεθ	גת	
και εν κυμβαλοις	ובשלשים		και εως	עד	
και εξηρχον	ותענינה	7	Αχχαρων	עקרון	
αι γυναικες	הנשים		και ανεστρεφαν	וישבו	53
	! − המשחקות		ανδρες !	בני	
και ελεγον	ותאמרן		Ισραηλ	ישראל	
επαταξεν	הכה		εκκλινοντες	מדלק	
Σαουλ	שאול		οπισω	אחרי	
εν χιλιασιν αυτου	באלפיו		των αλλοφυλων	פלשתים	
και Δαυειδ	ודוד		και κατεπατουν	וישסו	
εν μυριασιν αυτου	ברבבתיו		τας παρεμβολας αυτων	את מחניהם	
	! − ויחר	8	και ελαβεν	ויקח	54
	! − לשאול		Δαυειδ	דוד	
	! − מאד		την κεφαλην	את ראש	
και πονηρον εφανη	וירע		του αλλοφυλου	הפלשתי	
το ρημα ! +			και ηνεγκεν αυτην	ויבאהו	
εν οφθαλμοις Σαουλ !	בעיניו		εις Ιερουσαλημ	ירושלם	
περι του λογου !	הדבר		και τα σκευη αυτου	ואת כליו	
τουτου	הזה		εθηκεν	שם	
και ειπεν	ויאמר		εν τω σκηνωματι αυτου	באהלו	
τω Δαυειδ				om 55-58;18,1-5	
εδωκαν	נתנו		!−	18,6 ויהי	
	לדוד		!−	בבואם	
τας μυριαδας	רבבות		!−	בשוב	
και εμοι	ולי		!−	דוד	
εδωκαν	נתנו		!−	מהכות	
τας χιλιαδας	האלפים		!−	את הפלשתי	
	! − ועוד			ותצאנה	
	! − לו			הנשים	
	! − אך		και εξηλθον		
	! − המלוכה		αι χορευουσαι !		
			εις συναντησιν ! +		
			Δαυειδ ! +		
και ην	ויהי	9	εκ πασων	מכל	

30

LXX (Rahlfs) codex B		BHS		LXX (Rahlfs) codex B		BHS	
και ευλαβειτο		ויגר		Σαουλ		שאול	
απο προσωπου αυτου		מפניו		υποβλεπομενος		עוין	
και πας		וכל	16	τον Δαυειδ		את דוד	
Ισραηλ		ישראל		απο της ημερας εχεινης		מהיום ההוא	
και Ιουδας		ויהודה		επεχεινα		והלאה	
ηγαπα		אהב		om 10-11			
τον Δαυειδ		את דוד		και εφοβηθη		וירא	12
οτι		כי		Σαουλ		שאול	
αυτος		הוא		απο προσωπου		מלפני	
εξεπορευετο		יצא		Δαυειδ		דוד	
και εισεπορευετο		ובא		! −		כי	
προ προσωπου του λαου !		לפניהם		! −		היה	
om 17-19				! −		ה'	
και ηγαπησεν		ותאהב	20	! −		עמו	
Μελχολ		מיכל		! −		ומעם	
η θυγατηρ Σαουλ		בת שאול		! −		שאול	
τον Δαυειδ		את דוד		! −		סר	
και απηγγελη	! *	ויגדו		και απεστησεν αυτον		ויסרהו	13
Σαουλ		לשאול		Σαουλ		שאול	
και ηυθυνθη		וישר		απ αυτου		מעמו	
	! −	הדבר		και κατεστησεν αυτον		וישמהו	
εν τοις (-) οφθαλμοις αυτου		בעיניו		εαυτω		לו	
και ειπεν		ויאמר	21	χιλιαρχον		שר אלף	
Σαουλ		שאול		και εξεπορευετο		ויצא	
δωσω αυτην		אתננה		και εισεπορευετο		ויבא	
αυτω		לו		εμπροσθεν		לפני	
και εσται		ותהי		του λαου		העם	
αυτω		לו		και ην		ויהי	14
εις σκανδαλον		למוקש		Δαυειδ		דוד	
και ην	!	ותהי		εν πασαις	! *	לכל	
επι Σαουλ		בו		ταις οδοις αυτου		דרכיו	
χειρ		יד		συνιων		משכיל	
αλλοφυλων		פלשתים		και χυριος		וה'	
	! −	ויאמר		μετ αυτου		עמו	
	! −	שאול		και ειδεν		וירא	15
	! −	אל		Σαουλ		שאול	
	! −	דוד		ος		אשר	
	! −	בשתים		αυτος		הוא	
	! −	תתחתן		συνιει		משכיל	
	! −	בי		σφοδρα		מאד	

LXX (Rahlfs) codex B	BHS	LXX (Rahlfs) codex B	BHS
! —	לאמר	! —	היום
κατα τα ρηματα	כדברים	και ενετειλατο	ויצו 22
ταυτα	האלה	Σαουλ	שאול
α ! +		τοις παισιν αυτου	את עבדיו
ελαλησεν	דבר	λεγων ! +	
Δαυειδ	דוד	λαλησατε	דברו
και ειπεν	ויאמר 25	υμεις ! +	
Σαουλ	שאול	λαθρα ~	אל דוד
ταδε	כה	~ τω Δαυειδ	בלט
ερειτε	תאמרו	λεγοντες	לאמר
τω Δαυειδ	לדוד	ιδου	הנה
ου	אין	ο βασιλευς ~	חפץ בך
βουλεται *	חפץ	~ θελει εν σοι	המלך
ο βασιλευς *	למלך	και παντες	וכל
εν δοματι	במהר	οι παιδες αυτου	עבדיו
αλλ η !	כי	αγαπωσιν σε	אהבוך
εν εκατον	במאה	και συ !	ועתה
ακροβυστιαις	ערלות	επιγαμβρευσον	התחתן
αλλοφυλων	פלשתים	τω βασιλει	במלך
εκδικησαι	להנקם	και ελαλησαν	וידברו 23
(εις) εχθρους	באיבי	οι παιδες	עבדי
του βασιλεως	המלך	Σαουλ	שאול
και Σαουλ	ושאול	εις τα ωτα	באזני
ελογισατο	חשב	Δαυειδ	דוד
αυτον εμβαλειν !	להפיל את דוד	τα ρηματα	את הדברים
εις χειρας	ביד	ταυτα	האלה
των αλλοφυλων	פלשתים	και ειπεν	ויאמר
και απαγγελλουσιν	ויגדו 26	Δαυειδ	דוד
οι παιδες Σαουλ	עבדיו	ει κουφον	הנקלה
τω Δαυειδ	לדוד	εν οφθαλμοις υμων	בעיניכם
τα ρηματα	את הדברים	επιγαμβρευσαι	התחתן
ταυτα	האלה	βασιλει	במלך
και ευθυνθη	וישר	καγω	ואנכי
ο λογος	הדבר	ανηρ	איש
εν οφθαλμοις	בעיני	ταπεινος	רש
Δαυειδ	דוד	και ουχι ενδοξος *	ונקלה
επιγαμβρευσαι	להתחתן	και απηγγειλαν	ויגדו 24
τω βασιλει	במלך	οι παιδες	עבדי
! —	ולא	Σαουλ	שאול
! —	מלאו	αυτω	לו

32

LXX (Rahlfs) codex B	BHS	LXX (Rahlfs) codex B	BHS
θυγατερα αυτου	בתו	! −	הימים
αυτω ! +		και ανεστη	ויקם 27
εις γυναικα	לאשה	Δαυειδ	דוד
και ειδεν	וירא 28	και επορευθη	וילך
Caουλ	שאול	αυτος	הוא
! −	וידע	και οι ανδρες αυτου	ואנשיו
οτι	כי	και επαταξεν	ויך
χυριος	ה'	εν τοις αλλοφυλοις	בפלשתים
μετα	עם	εχατον !	מאתים
Δαυειδ	דוד	ανδρας	איש
και πας !	ומיכל	και ανηνεγκεν	ויבא
Ιοραηλ !	בת שאול	! −	דוד
ηγαπα αυτον !	אהבתהו	τας ακροβυστιας αυτων	את ערלתיהם
και προσεθετο	ויאסף 29	!−	וימלאום
! −	שאול	τω βασιλει	למלך
ευλαβεισθαι	לרא	και επιγαμβρευεται !	להתחתן
απο	מפני	τω βασιλει	במלך
Δαυειδ	דוד	και διδωσιν	ויתן
ετι	עוד	αυτω	לו
om 29b-30		! −	שאול
		την Μελχολ	את מיכל

In the above lists, differences between MT and the LXX are denoted with either an asterisk signifying exegetical elements or an exclamation point signifying possible differences in the Hebrew Vorlage. In dubious cases both notations are used. We now proceed to an analysis of the exponents of the translator's exegesis.

1. Exegetical renderings [10]

The choice of translation equivalents is necessarily based on linguistic and semantic exegesis needed for the semantic interpretation of the words and their linguistic identification. This type of exegesis is excluded from our analysis because it forms a necessary constituent of all translations. For example, when the translator decided to render כידון (17,6) with ἀσπίς (shield) [11], his translation reflects a certain lexical-exegetical tradition with regard to the meaning of this word, but no specific content exegesis which would have been denoted with an asterisk in our list. Likewise, the rendering of הבנים (איש) (17,4) as δυνατος probably derives the Hebrew word from בנה (to build), that is, 'a well-built person', as in the midrash [12]. For the translation equivalent, cf. 2 Chr. 35,3 מבינים — τοις δυνατοις.

As much as possible, linguistic exegesis is thus disregarded in our list of exe-getical elements. Sometimes, however, it cannot be determined easily where linguistic exegesis ends and content exegesis starts.

A second problem in this regard is created by the nature of the Greek language which requires certain deviations from Hebrew syntax and thus makes a stereotyped rendering of the Hebrew seemingly impossible. However, literal translators represented as much as possible each element of the Hebrew with its stereotyped Greek equiva-lent, also when such a rendering would create a Hebraism in the Greek language. Since renderings of this type do exist within the LXX, we may legitimately search for non-stereotyped renderings, even when a stereotyped rendering would have created a Hebraism. For example, the translation of 1 Sam. 17,9 has been adapted to the rules of the Greek language : אם יוכל להלחם אתי וֹהכני והיינו και εαν δυνηθη προς εμε πολεμησαι και εαν παταξη με. Likewise, in the continuation of that verse : ואם—εαν δε ... εσεσθε. In both cases the translator preferred not to employ stereotyped renderings.

The following list contains examples of exegetical renderings (in some cases the possibility of a variant reading [!] is not excluded) :

17,2		και οι ανδρες Ισραηλ	ואיש ישראל
17,2	!	εν τη κοιλαδι. αυτοι παρατασσονται	בעמק האלה ויערכו
17,2		(παρατασσονται) εις πολεμον	(ויערכו) מלחמה
17,3		ιστατια	עמדים
17,5		(και ο σταθμος) του θωρακος αυτου	(ומשקל) השריון
17,7		και η λογχη αυτου	ולהבת חניתו
17,7		τα οπλα αυτου	הצנה
17,8		παραταξασθαι πολεμω	לערך מלחמה
17,8		αλλοφυλος	הפלשתי
17,9		(και εαν δυνηθη) προς εμε πολεμησαι	(אם יוכל) להלחם אתי
17,9		και εαν παταξη με	והכני
17,9	!	εαν δε εγω δυνηθω	ואם אני אוכל לו
17,9		εσεσθε	והייתם
17,34		και οταν ηρχετο	ובא
17,35		και ει επανιστατο	ויקם
17,35		και επαταξα και εθανατωσα αυτον	והכתיו והמיתיו
17,38		περι την κεφαλην αυτου	על ראשו
17,39		και αφαιρουσιν αυτου	ויסירם
17,42	!	και αυτος πυρρακης	ואדמני
17,46	!	και γνωσεται	וידעו
17,46	!	εστιν θεος εν Ισραηλ	יש אלהים לישראל
17,47	!	και γνωσεται	וידעו (כל הקהל הזה)
18,14	!	εν πασαις ταις οδοις αυτου	לכל דרכיו
18,20	!	και απηγγελη	ויגדו
18,23		και ουχι ενδοξος	ונקלה
18,25		βουλεται ο βασιλευς	חפץ למלך

In our analysis of ch. 17-18 we are interested to form a judgment on the exegetical renderings extant in the translation. From the above list it is apparent that the translation contains only a very limited amount of such exegesis, certainly if one takes into consideration that some of the listed deviations may reflect variant readings. Unfortunately we must content ourselves with this generalized statement, for ideally the amount of exegesis is measured statistically and then compared with other translation units, but no absolute figures are available for these units.

2. Word-order

With the exception of 17,9 יוכל להלחם אתי — δυνηθῇ πρὸς ἐμὲ πολεμῆσαι, the translator kept the exact word-order of MT. The differences in word-order in 17,38 and 18,7.22.22 probably derived from a different Hebrew text.

3. Quantitative representation

Partly as a result of the tendency towards stereotyping, literal translators did their utmost to represent each individual element in MT by one equivalent element in the translation. Others felt free to add clarifying elements or not to represent elements which, in their view, were expressed by other words in the translation.

The translation of 1 Sam. 17-18 usually follows a system of a precise quantitative adherence to the Hebrew, as can be seen easily from the above lists. Some exceptions, which partially overlap with the list of exegetical elements, are listed here :

17,7 הצנה — τα οπλα αυτου
17,9 והכני — χαι εαν παταξη με
17,7 ולהבת חניתו — χαι η λογχη αυτου
17,9 והייתם — εσεσθε
17,34 ובא — χαι οταν ηρχετο
17,35 ויקם — χαι ει επανιστατο
18,23 ונקלה — χαι ουχι ενδοξος

4. Consistency in translation equivalents

Many translators rendered all occurrences of a given Hebrew word, element (e. g., preposition), root or construction as far as possible by the same Greek equivalent, often disregarding the effect of this type of translation upon its quality. This consistency can be examined in two ways : (a) *internal* consistency in the choice of translation equivalents within a certain unit; (b) the translator's adherence to the *general vocabulary of the LXX.* No firm data for the comparison of 1 Sam. 17-18 with other translation units are available, so that we must content ourselves with mere impressions. It seems that in the matter of consistency 1 Sam 17-18 reflects a type of translation which holds the middle between literal and free translations.

a) Internal consistency

Most translation equivalents are internally consistent, that is, the translator used the same equivalent for words which occur more than once. For examples, see sub b. and further :

אסף	– συνάγω	17,1.1.2	מערכ(ו)ת –	παράταξις	17,8.10.36.45 (also 17,4)
מחנה	– παρεμβολή	17,2.46	חרף	– ὠνειδίζω	17,10.33.45
חנה	– παρεμβάλλω	17,1.2	ירא	– φοβέομαι	17,11 18,9.12
ערך	– παρατάσσω	17,2.8	כלי	– χάδιον	17,44.49
ק/כובע	– περιχεφαλαία	17,5.38	ישר	– εὐθύνω	18,20.26

Lack of consistency is visible in the following equivalents :

עבד	– δοῦλος	17,9.9.32.34
	παῖς	18,22.22.23.23.24
הציל	– ἐχσπάω	17,35
	ἐξαιρέω	17,36
מקל	– βαχτηρία	17,40
	ῥάβδος	17,43
		(the differentiation may be intentional as Goliath calls David's βαχτηρία a mere ῥάβδος)
הכה	– πατάσσω	17,9.35.35.49 18,6.27
	τύπτω	17,36 ἀποκτείνω 17,46

b. Adherence to the general vocabulary of the LXX

The basis for the vocabulary of the LXX has been laid by the translators of the Pentateuch. The later translators often adhered to this vocabulary, certainly the more literal ones. The examples mentioned in the preceding paragraph as well as the next ones reflect this approach :

בין	– ἀνὰ μέσον	passim	הריע	– ἀλαλάζω	17,52
עמק	– χοιλάς	17,2	בוא	– εἴσοδος	17,52
שריון	– θώραξ	17,5.5	מוקש	– σχάνδαλον	18,21
צנה	– ὅπλα	17,7	התחתן	– ἐπιγαμβρεύω	18,22.22.23.26.27
איש מלחמה – ἀνὴρ πολεμιστής 17,33			צוה	– ἐντέλλομαι	18,22
ערל	– ἀπερίτμητος	17,36	ערלה	– ἀκροβυστία	18,25.27
לכה	– δεῦρο	17,44	אהב	– ἀγαπάω	18,16.20.22.26.28
קהל	– ἐχχλησία	17,47	הגיד	– ἀπαγγέλλω	18,20.24

Unusual word choices are found in :

רגלים	– σχέλη	17,6
הלך לפני	– προπορεύομαι	17,7
לחם	– μονομαχέομαι (contrast πολεμέω in 17,32.33) 17,10
יחד	– ἀμφότεροι	17,10

On the basis of the above data, the translation technique of 1 Sam. 17-18 may be described as relatively literal. A similar conclusion was reached by others with regard to 1 Sam. as a whole [13]. Special mention should be made of Sollamo's thorough investigation of one aspect of the translation technique of the LXX which yielded a conclusion that 1 Sam. belongs to the most literal units of the whole LXX [14]. On the basis of a similar study by Soisalon-Soininen, 1 Sam. may be characterized as relatively literal [15].

The following data support this characterization :

1. Hebraisms in the translation of 1 Sam. 17-18

17,1   ויחנו בין שוכה ובין עזקה
     και παρεμβαλλουσιν <u>ανα μεσον</u> Σουχωθ και <u>ανα μεσον</u> Αζηκα

17,4   ויצא איש הבנים ... גלית שמו
     και εξηλθεν ανηρ δυνατος ... Γολιαθ <u>ονομα αυτου</u>

17,5   ושריון קשקשים הוא לבוש
     και θωρακα αλυσιδωτον <u>αυτος ενδεδυκως</u>
     (note the word-order)

17,9   אם יוכל ... והיינו
     και εαν δυνηθη ... <u>και</u> εσομεθα
     (contrast 9b)

17,32   אל נא יפל לב אדני עליו
     MT :   אל   יפל לב אדם <u>עליו</u>
     μη δη συμπεσετω καρδια του κυριου μου <u>επ'αυτον</u>

17,33   ללכת ... להלחם
     πορευθηναι ... <u>του</u> πολεμειν

17,40   וישם אתם בכלי הרעים <u>אשר לו</u>
     και εθετο αυτους εν τω χαδιω τω ποιμενικω <u>τω οντι αυτω</u>

17,42   נער ואדמני <u>עם יפה עינים</u> (מראה : MT)
     αυτος ην παιδαριον και αυτος πυρρακης <u>μετα καλλους οφθαλμων</u>

17,43   אתה בא אלי במקל (במקלות : MT)
     συ ερχη επ εμε <u>εν</u> ραβδω
     For similar use of εν, see vv. 43b.45.47;18,6.

18,8   וירע <u>בעיניו הדבר הזה</u>
     και πονηρον εφανη <u>το ρημα εν οφθαλμοις</u> Σαουλ περι του λογου τουτου
     For similar constructions, see 18,20.23.26.

18,12   וירא שאול <u>מלפני</u> דוד
     και εφοβηθη Σαουλ απο προσωπου Δαυειδ

18,22   חפץ בך המלך — ο βασιλευς θελει <u>εν</u> σοι (cf. also v. 25)

18,27   וילך <u>הוא ואנשיו</u> — και επορευθη αυτος και οι ανδρες αυτου

18,27   ויך <u>בפלשתים</u> — και επαταξεν <u>εν</u> τοις αλλοφυλοις

2. Hebraisms in pluses in the translation

Hebraisms in the pluses (that is, in the material which is not found in MT) underscore the translator's adherence to his parent text :

17,8   εξ εναντιας ημων = לקראתנו

17,36   ουχι πορευσομαι και παταξω αυτον και αφελω σημερον ονειδος...

        ... הלוא אלך והכתיו והסרותי היום חרפה

17,54   εις συναντησιν Δαυειδ = לקראת דוד

Note further the use of λεγων (= לאמר) in a plus in 18,22.

In our view, the above-mentioned data show that the translator remained, as a rule, loyal to his parent text, and it is therefore not conceivable that he would have omitted some 45 o/o of the text. As all arguments, this is a subjective reasoning, but under the circumstances we consider this the most feasible argument since it is based on the internal consistency of the translator's approach to his text. We therefore assume that the translator knew a text which was much shorter than MT. This working hypothesis is supported by three further arguments :

1. The reliability of the LXX has been enhanced in recent years by the finds of Hebrew scrolls of Sam. in cave 4 in Qumran. These scrolls contain many readings which are identical with the reconstructed parent text of the LXX (either the main stream or the Lucianic group of mss.) [16]. This situation gives the LXX more credibility also in those chapters of which no Hebrew fragments have been found in cave 4. At the same time it must be admitted that the differences between MT and the reconstructed parent text of the LXX in 1 Sam. 17-18 are larger than in any other section of the book in the LXX or a Qumran scroll. The only parallels which come to mind are the large plus of 4QSam-a before the beginning of 1 Sam. 11 (5 lines) [17], and the beginning of the second column of the same scroll (1 Sam. 2,13ff.) which differs considerably from MT.

2. Our working hypothesis is more acceptable if the alternative view cannot be sustained. We should therefore point out that in our view there are no cogent reasons for assuming a large scale shortening of the original text. The reason which is usually given for this shortening is that the translator recognized difficulties in certain passages which he therefore omitted. This type of abridging may be illustrated by two examples :
    a. In 16,17-23 David is introduced to Saul as a skilful harper and is made his armor-bearer. The story even tells us that Saul "loved" David (16,21). This section clearly contradicts 17,55-58 where Saul confesses ignorance of David who had just defeated Goliath. It is often claimed that the translator omitted 17,55-58 because of this reason.
    b. In 18,17-19 Saul offers David his eldest daughter Merab, while vv. 20-26 tell about David's marriage to Michal, *"the* daughter" (vv. 20.27) of Saul. The contradiction in MT is apparent, and this may have instigated the translator to omit the first section (vv. 17-19) which is now lacking in the LXX.
    To assume that a translator omitted from his parent text complete sections is a legitimate assumption, albeit a very difficult one. It presupposes not only that the translator allowed himself much liberty in his translation, but also that he was a sophisticated reader, almost a critical scholar. I wonder whether there are any parallels

for such a presumed action within the realm of the Greek translations. For not only the mere fact of the omission is surprising, but also the assumed reason for that omission, which ascribes to the translator the critical mind of an attentive exegete.

More importantly, in the aforementioned two sections a harmonizing omission by the translator is possible from the point of view of their contents, but in the other sections such an assumption is much more difficult, if not impossible. 18,1-4 informs us of the covenant of friendship between David and Jonathan, and why should that section be omitted ? And why should vv. 5-6a, which introduce the next section, be omitted ? True, also in these verses a contradiction can be recognized (in 18,2 Saul introduces David to his court, even though he had already been introduced there in 16,22), but should we expect the translator to be alert to such details ? Moreover, why would the translator omit a complete section because of one detail (18,2) ? Would it not be easier and more responsible to merely change a detail or to omit a smaller section ? Did the translator omit 18,10-11 because it repeats 19,9-10 ? Or did he consider this section conflicting with Saul's feelings of love for David ? The latter possibility is unlikely, because the translator "omitted" also 18,2a which mentions Saul's love for David.

The same type of questions may be asked regarding the translator's supposed omission of 17,12-31, the largest of the minuses of the LXX in 1 Sam. 17-18. This section contains several elements which contradict the preceding or following account (see below, p. 42), but all these contradictions are minor, and we do not think that the translator would have sensed them. But even if he did — it is likely that ancient sources may be quoted which were aware of some of the difficulties —, would a translator omit a complete section because of difficulties regarding *some* of the verses in that section ?

In again other cases, no reason for a harmonizing omission can be detected : 17, 41.48b.50; 18,12b.29b-30.

Finally, if the minuses of the LXX indeed reflect the translator's harmonizing omissions, it should be remarked that not all "difficulties" have been removed : cf. 16,18 with 17,33 (see below, n. 21).

3. The translator may have wished to omit a substantial part of 1 Sam. 17-18 in order to shorten the lengthy stories. The main argument against this assumption is again the argument from translation technique. Furthermore, also the pluses in the translation militate against such an assumption.

II. THE NATURE OF THE LXX's SHORT VERSION

In the first part of this paper we have attempted to demonstrate that the translator did not create the short version of 1 Sam. 17-18, but that he found such a short text. The nature of that text is analyzed here. When turning to this subject, we leave the realm of textual criticism for that of literary criticism and exegesis.

The short text of the LXX may reflect an earlier stage of the development of 1 Sam. 17-18 as opposed to the expanded text of MT or it may reflect an abridged version of that text. The latter possibility, however, may be abandoned, for we cannot think of any motive behind such a supposed abridgment. In a few cases only can one point to possible reasons for a stylistic or exegetical abridgment of the text, and these have been discussed above in connection with the possibility of harmonizing omissions by the translators. As this suggestion is not acceptable for a possible abridgment by the translator, it is not acceptable either for the scribe of the manuscript from which the translation was made. Besides, with regard to the possible abbreviation of a Hebrew source an argument should be used which has been avoided above with regard to the translation : it is rather inconceivable that the Hebrew text should be revised only in ch. 17-18, and not in other chapters in 1 Sam. which contain obvious contradictions and doublets of stories.

We are therefore left with the assumption that the short text of the LXX reflects an early stage of ch. 17-18 and MT a later, expanded, stage. Since the long text of MT contains additional information (traditions) about the encounter of David and Goliath, and since this information is in a way parallel to the short text of the LXX, it would be appropriate to call the short text of the LXX version 1 and the additions of MT version 2. MT thus contains both versions 1 and 2. This terminology is appropriate for the two versions of the encounter of David and Goliath and for the two versions of David's marriage, but not for other details in version 2 which do not provide alternative material to version 1, but rather simple expansions. Since, however, the majority of the pluses of MT do add parallel material, it is best to use the aforementioned terminology. The data in 1 Sam. 17-18 resemble the situation in Jer. where a short edition of the book is contained in the LXX and 4QJer-b and a long one in MT [18].

For a more detailed analysis, we now present the content of the two versions [19], disregarding small pluses and minuses.

version 1 (LXX and MT)	version 2 (MT only)
16,17-23 David is introduced to Saul as a skilful harper and he is made his armor-bearer.	
17,1-11 Attack by the Philistines. Goliath suggests a duel with one of the Israelites.	
17,12-31	David is sent by his father to bring food to his brothers in the battle field. He hears Goliath and desires to meet him in a duel.
17,32-39 David volunteers to fight with Goliath.	

17,40-54 The duel. After Goliath's miraculous fall, the Philistines flee.	
[17,41.48b.50	Short account of the duel.]
17,55-58	Saul confesses ignorance of David. David is introduced to Saul by Abner.
18,1-4	David and Jonathan tie a covenant of friendship.
18,5-6a	David is appointed as an officer in Saul's army.
18,6b-9 Saul's jealousy of David.	
18,10-11	Saul attempts in vain to kill David.
18,12-16 David's successes.	
18,17-19	Saul offers David his eldest daughter, Merab.
18,20-27 Saul offers David his daughter Michal	
18,29b-30	Saul's love for David. David's successes.

The parallels between the two versions of David and Goliath's encounter are that in both versions David is introduced to Saul and that in both David is made an officer in Saul's army (18,5.13). Furthermore, in both versions Saul offers David one of his daughters without any "cross-reference". At the same time, the two versions of the encounter between David and Goliath are not fully parallel, for version 2 lacks an account of the duel itself. Accordingly, version 2 could not have existed in its own right in its present form. Version 1, on the other hand, provides a sufficiently full picture, so that it could have existed as an independent version of the fight. In fact, version 1 presents a continuous [20] and internally consistent story [21], and if version 2 would not have been known, we would not have lacked any crucial information in chapters 17 and 18 [22].

Both versions of the encounter between David and Goliath are internally consistent, but they contain conflicting details. Whether or not version 2 existed once in a fuller form from which the present form has been excerpted will not be known. It is also not known why the two versions were juxtaposed, but it stands to reason that the final redactor of the story wanted to preserve certain traditions and details which were not included in version 1 which formed the framework of his story. More precisely, the final editor derived 17,12-31.55-58 and 18,1-6a.10-11.17-19.29b-30 from a written source, but he also added a few minor details as his own expansions. It is hard to determine why the editor wanted to add 17,12-31.55-58 (these verses comprise the major body of the addition). Possibly the editor simply liked the story; possibly he wanted to convey a certain idea, viz., that God can bring victory to his people also through initially unimportant people. Also other additions may reflect the editor's ideas. In v. 50, for example, he stressed that David did not need a sword in order to defeat the Philistine.

The short and long versions of ch. 17-18 contain only partial parallels, and because the nature of these stories (not their contents) cannot be contrasted well, it is not clear whether the duplication should be connected with other duplications in the book of Samuel. Even though in various places parallel traditions of the same events have been detected, it is hard to know whether the two versions of the encounter of David and Goliath should be connected with these strands of tradition elsewhere in the book.

From the point of view of the *literary* history we consider version 1 to be more original than version 2 which has been added to it (rather, inserted in it). However, this does not imply that the *content* of that version is more authentic than version 2. For example, we have not expressed any opinion on the type of description of David's person which is found in the different versions. It is hard to know whether "David the harper and the armor-bearer" (version 1) is more original in the history of the tradition than "David the shepherd" (version 2). The later tradition depicts David both as a musician and a shepherd (see, for example, Ps. 151 in 11QPs-a and in the LXX).

Version 1 in ch. 17 thus should not be preferred to version 2 from the point of view of its contents, but in ch. 18 it certainly is preferable because the juxtaposition of versions 1 and 2 in that chapter creates serious problems. This refers especially to the two versions of David's marriage (17-19.20-27) and to Saul's attempt to kill David (vv. 10-11). All exegetes agree that this section is not in place in this chapter (it repeats an identical section in 19,9-10). In fact, the sequence of events in the short version 1 is more logical than that in the combined text of versions 1 and 2. In version 1, Saul is at first envious of David (vv. 8-9), then suspicious (v. 12) and frightened because of David's successes (vv. 13-15); subsequently he wants to have David killed through the Philistines, and when this stratagem does not succeed, he attempts to kill him himself (19,9-10).

As noted, the juxtaposition of the two version created several conflicts. The fact that the editor created these conflicts, sometimes in important details, should not cause much surprise, because also elsewhere in the OT did expansions or interpolations create similar problems. The following difficulties may be observed :

1. David is depicted in different ways in the two versions. In version 1 he is Saul's armor-bearer (16,21) and in that capacity he fights Goliath. In version 2 he is an unknown shepherd who happens to be on the spot when Goliath calls the Israelites to a duel.

2. The most conspicuous difficulty is, as explained on p. 38, that after David has been introduced to Saul and has been in his court (16,17-23, version 1), in version 2 (17,55-58) he is still unknown to Saul who asks Abner about David after the latter had defeated Goliath.

3. According to version 1, David marries Michal, *"the* daughter"* of Saul (18,20-26) but in version 2 Saul offers David his eldest daughter Merab, in accordance with another section of version 2 (17,25).

4. In the first sentence of version 2(17,12),David and Jesse are introduced to the reader, but David was already known from version 1 (ch. 16) and his father had been introduced as well (16,1.10).

5. The detail in version 2 that Goliath paid a daily visit to the camp for forty days (17,16) is apparently not known to the author of 17,11 (version 1).

6. According to version 2 (17,25ff.), he who defeats Goliath will be given the king's daughter. Apparently this promise is not known to version 1 (18,20ff.), since Saul looks for pretexts that would convince David to marry his daughter.

7. If indeed Eliab was present at the time of David's anointing (16,13 = version 1), it is hard to understand why he should utter such harsh words to David (17,28 = version 2).

8. Twice David is made an officer in Saul's army, once in version 1 (18,13) and once in version 2 (18,5).

After the two versions were juxtaposed, an editor or a scribe made a few changes in order to smooth out some of the difficulties created by the joining of the two versions. According to McCarter's commentary (see n. 1), there were several such changes, of which the following are mentioned here :

a. "The Ephrathite" had already been introduced in ch. 16, so that the addition of הזה to his name in 17,12 ודוד בן איש אפרתי הזה מבית לחם יהודה refers to this earlier introductory statement [23]. The best translation of this — ungrammatical — הזה would be "the aforementioned" (thus V : de quo supra dictum est).

b. The juxtaposition of the verbs in 17,13 is awkward : וילכו שלשת בני ישי הגדלים הלכו. It has therefore been suggested that הלכו has been added by someone who wanted to stress that the brothers had already gone in the past. On the other hand, the same verb occurs also in 13b and 14, so that we may be confronted here with a textual rather than an editorial problem.

c. ודוד הלך ושב מעל שאול (17,15) may have been added to the text of version 2 in order to stress that David had already been in the court (ch. 16, version 1).

A comparison of the shorter text of the LXX with the expanded text of MT gives us insights in the literary development of many sections of the OT books, also when there exists no textual evidence of an earlier stage of the text.

NOTES

1   The following abbreviations are used :
Thenius   O. Thenius, Die Bücher Samuels (Leipzig 1842)
Woods   F.H. Woods, "The Light Shown by the Septuagint Version
                 on the Books of Samuel", Studia Biblica, Essays in Biblical
                 Archaeology and Criticism and Kindred Subjects, I, (Oxford
                 1885) 21-38
Wellhausen   J Wellhausen, Der Text der Bücher Samuelis untersucht
                 (Göttingen 1871)
Driver   S.R. Driver, Notes on the Hebrew Text of the Books of Sa-
                 muel (Oxford 1890)
Peters   R. Peters, Beiträge zur Text- und Literarkritik sowie zur Er-
                 klärung der Bücher Samuel (Freiburg i. Breisgau 1899)
de Boer   P.A.H. de Boer, "I Samuel XVII. Notes on the Text and the
                 Ancient Versions", OTS 1 (1942) 79-103.
Stoebe   H.J. Stoebe, "Die Goliathperikope 1 Sam. XVII 1 — XVIII
                 5 und die Textform der Septuaginta", VT 6 (1956) 397-413
McCarter   P.K. McCarter, I Samuel, Anchor Bible (New York 1980)

2   Elsewhere in 1 Sam. the LXX lacks individual phrases or clauses, but nowhere
    does it lack as much as in chapters 17-18. For some examples, see 1,9; 4,17; 6,4;
    6,11; 10,16; 12,13; 21,10; 23,23; 26,4; 29,4; 30,7b, 31,6. For a discussion, see
    J. Méritan, La version grecque des livres de Samuel (Paris 1898) 139-148.

3   For details, see Peters, 37-38; Wellhausen, 104; Driver, 140; Johnson (see next
    note), 118-123.

4   See especially B. Johnson, Die Hexaplarische Rezension des 1. Samuelbuches der
    Septuaginta, Studia Theologica Lundensia 22 (Lund 1963).

5   See Johnson, 123. The addition in codex A betrays it secondary nature also
    because of a further detail. The insertion starts off as και ειπεν Δαυειδ υιος
    ανθρωπου εφραθαιου, and since the first two words do not represent MT in v. 12
    (דוד), but in v. 32, the first verse *after* the minus of the LXX, (και ειπεν
    Δαυειδ = ויאמר דוד), it stands to reason that the person who added the large
    section in codex A erroneously repeated the first two words of the next verse
    (now 32) and then continued v. 12. As v. 12 is now phrased in codex A, και
    ειπεν makes little sense in the context.

6   For bibliographical references, see n. 1.

7   A. Kuenen, Historisch-kritische Einleitung in die Bücher des ATs, I, 2 (Leipzig
    1890) 61; K. Budde, Die Bücher Richter und Samuel Ihre Quellen und ihr Auf-
    bau (Giessen 1890) 212; J. Schmid, Septuagintageschichtliche Studien zum 1.
    Samuelbuch, unpubl. diss., Breslau 1941 (quoted from Johnson, 118); D. Bar-
    thélemy, "La qualité du Texte Massorétique de Samuel", in E. Tov (ed.), The
    Hebrew and Greek Texts of Samuel, 1980 Proceedings IOSCS — Vienna (Jeru-
    salem 1980) 1-44, esp. 17-20.

8   The views of the nineteenth century scholars are quoted from Thenius, 67; see further Peters, 30-62; Wellhausen, 105 (however, in his later work his attitude towards the short text is not clear : Die Composition des Hexateuchs und der historischen Bücher des ATs 3 [Berlin 1899] 247); H.P. Smith, The Books of Samuel, I.C.C. (Edinburgh 1899); C. Steuernagel, Lehrbuch der Einleitung in das AT (Tübingen 1912) 317; N.C. Habel, Literary Criticism of the OT (Philadelphia 1971) 10-11; for Woods and Stoebe see n. 1.

8a   Thus Kuenen (n. 7)

9   The larger unit comprises at least 1 Sam. 1-31, but probably also 2 Sam. 1,1-11,1 — thus modern scholarship in the wake of D. Barthélemy, Les Devanciers d'Aquila, SVT 10 (Leiden 1963) 36ff. According to J.D. Shenkel, Chronology and Recensional Development in the Greek Text of Kings, HSM 1 (Cambridge, MA 1968) 117-120, this unit ends at 2 Sam. 10,1, and according to Kelly it ends in 2 Sam. 5 : B.H. Kelly, The Septuagint Translators of I Samuel and II Samuel 1,1-11,1, unpubl. diss., Princeton Theol. Sem., 1948.

10   For the theoretical background of this and the following paragraphs, see the present author's The Text-Critical Use of the Septuagint in Biblical Research (Jerusalem 1981).

11   The different translation equivalents of כידון in the LXX reflect the translators' hesitations with regard to its meaning. For a discussion, see M.A. Zipor, The Ancient Versions of Samuel, Kings and Chronicles : A Comparative Study of their Translation Techniques for Terms of Realia, unpubl. diss., Bar Ilan University (Ramat Gan 1979) 196-206.

12   B.T Sotah 42b : מאי בינים, אמר רב שמבונה מכל מום . ושמואל אמר בינוני שבאחיו
     .דבי רבי שילא אמר שהוא עשוי כבנין

13   Thus Thenius, XXVff.; Woods, 21; Driver, LIX-LXII, with many examples. Likewise Kelly (n. 9) 24 ("... which aim at literalism to a greater extent than the majority of the Septuagint books."). The greater part of Kelly's dissertation, however, discusses the translator's exegetical deviations. The predominantly exegetical character of the translation is maintained by H.S. Gehman, "Exegetical Methods Employed by the Greek Translator of I Samuel", JAOS 70 (1950) 292-296. In this short article Gehman provides examples of various exegetical renderings subdivided into six groups : (1) theological changes; (2) toning down of offensive expressions; (3) maintaining of royal dignity; (4) maintaining of human dignity; (5) free approach to content; (6) contextual exegesis. In our view, however, this collection of examples is not convincing. The issue is not *whether* there are exegetical renderings in the LXX of 1 Sam. — the existence of some of these is apparent —, but *how many* exegetical renderings are found in that translation unit when compared with its literal renderings. It will then be clear, we claim, that exegetical renderings are much less frequent than literal renderings.
     A second point which must be raised against Gehman's article — as well as against the dissertation by his student Kelly — is that many — most ? — of the examples can also be explained as reflecting variant readings. The decision whether a particular deviation of the LXX from MT reflects the translator's exegesis or a variant reading can only be made on the basis of an investigation of the translation technique used in a particular unit or in the whole book.

14 R. Sollamo, Renderings of Hebrew Semiprepositions in the Septuagint, AASF, Dissertationes Humanarum Litterarum 19 (Helsinki 1979) esp. 280ff.

15 I. Soisalon-Soininen, Die Infinitive in der Septuaginta, AASF, B 132,1 (Helsinki 1965) esp. 169ff.

16 For the material, see the articles in E. Tov (ed.), The Hebrew and Greek Texts of Samuel, 1980 Proceedings IOSCS — Vienna (Jerusalem 1980).

17 See F.M. Cross, Jr., "The Ammonite Oppression of the Tribes of Gad and Reuben : Missing Verses from 1 Samuel 11 Found in 4QSamuel-a", on pp. 105-119 of the collection mentioned in the previous note.

18 For a summary of the problems, see the present writer, "Some Aspects of the Textual and Literary History of the Book of Jeremiah". in : P.M. Bogaert (ed.), Le livre de Jérémie, le prophète et son milieu, les oracles et leur transmission, BETL LIV (Leuven 1981) 145-67.

19 Most commentaries merely remark on the relation between the two versions of the story of David and Goliath, but McCarter's recent commentary (see n. 1) presents the two versions as two independent units (David and the Philistine Champion I, II) which are separately translated and commented upon.

20 17,32 links immediately with 17,11, and, in fact, not with 17,31. For עליו in 17,32 can refer only to Goliath who has not been mentioned in the verses which immediately precede v. 32 in MT, and who is mentioned in v. 11. Also in the other instances the verse in MT which immediately precedes the minus has its natural continuation in the verse after the minus.

21 A slight problem, however, is created by a comparison of 16,18 and 17,33. In the first verse David is described as a גבור חיל ואיש מלחמה, while in the second one Saul advises David not to fight because he is a mere נער. The tension between these two verses may be misleading. It is possible that the phrase in 16,18 is an exaggeration in the mouth of one of Saul's men; possibly he means to say that David has the right traits for a warrior. Likewise, also Saul's statement in 17,33 could be exaggerated.

22 One difficulty, however, is created by the covenant of friendship between David and Jonathan mentioned in 18,1-4 (version 2) and subsequently referred to in 20,8. If, however, we assume that the same editor who added 18,1-4 wrote or rewrote 20,8, the problem is solved. Besides, 20,8 may refer to 19,1.

23 Also if זה refers to David (thus Qimhi), it would still be considered an editorial or scribal addition.

TROIS NIVEAUX D'ANALYSE
(A PROPOS DE DAVID ET GOLIATH)

Il est frappant que 1 S 16-17 nous offre trois entrées en scène de David : la première dans le récit 16,1-13 que nous appellerons récit A, la deuxième dans le récit 16,14-23 (= récit B), la troisième dans le récit 17,12 et ss (= récit C).

Or, le *G ancien joint directement 17,32 à 17,11, semblant omettre le récit C. Les deux premières hypothèses qui se présentent à l'esprit sont :

1) que le *G a omis ce passage pour éviter des dissonances avec le contexte (et il aurait omis pour le même motif 17,55-18,6a),

2) que la Vorlage de *G représenterait un état rédactionnel où cette troisième entrée en scène de David n'aurait pas été intégrée encore aux deux premières.

McCarter (I Samuel, AncB, N.Y. 1980, 306 & 308) dit à propos de la matière textuelle offerte par ces 'plus' du *M dans l'histoire de Goliath : "It is easiest to conclude, moreover, that it was also absent from the Hebrew tradition behind LXX and indeed from the primitive text of Samuel itself, having been introduced into the tradition behind MT at some point after its divergence from the ancestral tradition of LXX in the fourth century B.C..." Il ajoute: "Although this account did not find its way into the text of the primary narrative until at least the fourth century B.C., it does not follow that its date of composition was late. It may have circulated for some time independently before its appropriation by a redactor to fill its present position."

Il faut reconnaître que cette interprétation des relations entre le *G et le *M est tentante. Mais il y a intérêt à distinguer ici clairement trois niveaux : celui de la constitution des récits, celui de la critique littéraire et celui de la critique textuelle. Abordons-les dans cet ordre.

I. LA CONSTITUTION DES RECITS

Si nous envisageons ces trois récits comme des essais de légitimation des prétentions de David à la royauté, le récit A est celui qui atteint ce résultat de la manière la plus efficace. Si les auteurs des récits B et C l'avaient connu, ils auraient pu renoncer à leurs essais moins convaincants. Il est donc vraisemblable que A est le dernier-né des trois récits. On a de cela un indice complémentaire dans le fait que les autres récits ignorent cette onction de David enfant.

Le récit C offre des indices de non-originalité. Il semble viser à récupérer au profit de David le haut-fait d'Elhanan tuant le géant Goliath de Gat (2 S 22,19). Il semble bien, d'autre part, que le chapitre 17 présente le duel de Goliath et de David (17,9. 11.32) en surimpression sur une victoire de l'armée d'Israël contre celle des Philistins (17,20-21.52). Ajoutons que ce récit semble influencé par l'histoire de Joseph et de ses frères.

Le récit B semble plus naturel : le jeune joueur de cithare capable d'apaiser la mélancolie du roi s'attire son affection et devient son écuyer.

On peut suggérer que B est primitif et que A, issu de milieux prophétiques, entend lui fournir une légitimation comparable à l'onction de Saül, alors que C serait une tradition populaire qui n'aurait été intégrée qu'après une certaine existence autonome dans un récit de combat entre l'armée d'Israël et celle des Philistins. Cela ne s'harmoniserait-il pas de façon assez vraisemblable avec le point de vue de McCarter ?

II. LA CRITIQUE LITTERAIRE

Malheureusement, la critique littéraire vient mettre des grains de sable dans cet engrenage.

1. Des détails caractéristiques du récit A se retrouvent dans le récit C et en son contexte. Ainsi les noms des trois fils aînés de Jessé : Eliab, Abinadab et Shamma; ou encore la description de David comme אַדְמֹנִי עִם־יְפֵה מַרְאֶה (16,12) ou אַדְמֹנִי עִם־יְפֵה עֵינִים (17,42). Mais ces données constituent en A les seuls éléments descriptifs qui viennent compléter le lieu commun présentant David comme הַקָּטָן et רֹעֶה בַּצֹּאן, alors qu'en C ces mêmes données sont intriquées dans un contexte concret où elles ont une valeur fonctionnelle : si Eliab est nommé, c'est pour préparer son altercation (17,28) avec David. Quant à la description de David, elle motive le peu de cas que le Philistin fait de cet adversaire (17,42). Il semble donc que ce soit dans le récit C que ces données aient leur contexte originel et que c'est là que le récit A a été les chercher. Ajoutons à cela une contre-épreuve : L'auteur du récit C prête à Eliab des critiques de David (17,28) qui montrent que, pour cet auteur, David n'a pas été oint par Samuel en présence de ses frères.

Le récit aurait donc pris forme avant que le récit A n'ait été constitué. Notons que cela confirme le fait que le type de légitimation offerte par le récit C aurait été inutile si son auteur avait connu la légitimation offerte par le récit A.

Cette conclusion, précisons-le, ne contredit pas l'éventualité que le récit C, constitué avant le récit A, ait vécu durant un certain temps une existence de légende transmise de façon autonome. En effet, les versets 12 et 15 du chapitre 17 portent des traces de suture rédactionnelle ayant pour but de faciliter son insertion dans un contexte en fonction duquel il n'avait pas été composé et où figuraient déjà les récits B et A : Au vs 15, les allées et venues de David entre la cour de Saül et le troupeau de son père visent à expliquer qu'on le retrouve ici jeune berger, malgré 16,21. Au vs 12, le mot הַזֶּה signale que Jessé de Bethléem a déjà été mentionné en 16,1 et 16,18. Quant à l'affirmation en ce même vs 12 que celui-ci avait 8 fils, elle semble bien, elle aussi, extérieure à la structure originelle du récit C où on nous parle seulement des trois grands frères et de leur petit frère David. En effet, s'il y avait encore quatre autres frères à la maison, on ne voit pas pourquoi David aurait dû confier le troupeau dont il avait la charge à un gardien (17,20.28). C'est donc vraisemblablement au récit A que le responsable de l'insertion du récit C a emprunté la mention des 8 fils.

2. McCarter estime que les passages que le *M possède en excédent par rapport au *G (17,12-31.41.48b.50.55-58; 18,1-5.10-11.17-19.29b-30) ont constitué d'abord un récit autonome et cohérent de l'entrée en contact de David avec Saül, récit qui aurait été ensuite fusionné avec un contexte littéraire préexistant à cette fusion, contexte littéraire qui nous est attesté par la Vorlage du *G. Pour offrir à cette hypothèse une certaine vraisemblance, il faut y ajouter deux précisions : d'abord que ce récit autonome a été complété par un certain nombre d'éléments de suture du type de ceux que nous venons de signaler; et ensuite que certaines parties de ce récit qui faisaient figure de répétition inutile par rapport au contexte préexistant ont été omises (par exemple, une bonne part de la narration du combat entre David et Goliath et les motifs
de l'hostilité de Saül envers David).

Ce qui semble le plus critiquable en cette hypothèse, ce n'est pas la préexistence traditionnelle autonome du récit C, mais c'est plutôt la préexistence littéraire du contexte en lequel il se trouve inséré dans le *M. Autrement dit, il est difficile d'admettre que l'état littéraire qu'offrait la Vorlage du *G doive s'expliquer comme un état plus primitif intégrant les récits A et B mais pas encore le récit C. Nous devrions alors nous orienter vers l'hypothèse que la Vorlage du *G est le résultat de la mutilation d'un ensemble littéraire complexe.

Si nous considérons en effet comme constitutifs principaux du récit C les deux 'plus' les plus étendus du *M (17,12-31.55-18,6a), il est difficile d'admettre que le contexte littéraire dans lequel ce récit se trouve inséré (17,1-11.32-53; 18,6b-9) ait constitué un récit autonome avant cette insertion.

Notons d'abord en faveur de cette hypothèse que les passages entre 17,11 et 17,32 et entre 17,54 et 18,6b s'opèrent assez aisément. Mais, nous le verrons, cette constatation est susceptible d'une interprétation opposée.

Voici maintenant des indices défavorables à l'hypothèse susdite :
— Le David qui est en scène en 17,32-54 est plutôt celui qui a été présenté en 17,12-31 que celui qui l'a été en 16,14-23. En effet, le David de 16,14-23 a été présenté comme גִּבּוֹר חַיִל וְאִישׁ מִלְחָמָה (16,18), et on nous dit (vs 21s) que Saül le garda avec lui, en faisant son écuyer (littéralement : son porteur d'armes). Le David de 17,32-54, par contre, n'est qu'un נַעַר, alors que le Philistin est un אִישׁ מִלְחָמָה depuis sa jeunesse. Ce David n'est pas habitué à porter les armes (vs 39), mais dispose de son équipement de berger (vs 40), de son bâton et de sa fronde (ibid.). Cela correspond mieux à l'image de celui qui vient de quitter son troupeau (17,20.28) et d'arriver au camp des Israélites.
— Le chant des femmes (18,7) attribuant les milliers à Saül et les myriades à David ne peut se comprendre comme faisant directement suite à 17,32-54, comme c'est le cas dans la Vorlage du *G. Selon cet état textuel, le jeune berger David, en effet, n'a encore vaincu que le seul Goliath. Le fait que le rédacteur ait placé là ce chant

(auquel il sera fait allusion en 21,12 et 29,5) ne s'explique bien que si cet épisode est préparé en 18,5 par le résumé des exploits militaires de David.

— En 20,8 (selon le *M et le *G), David mentionne l'alliance en laquelle Jonathan l'a fait "entrer avec lui". C'est une claire allusion à l'alliance que Jonathan a conclue avec David en 18,3 (présent dans le *M, mais absent du *G).

— Les expressions typiques dans lesquelles est employé le piél du verbe חרף unissent étroitement 17,12-31 au contexte qui l'entoure dans le *M. C'est bien en effet le même David qui a parlé en 17,26 de הַפְּלִשְׁתִּי הֶעָרֵל הַזֶּה, en qualifiant le crime qu'il a commis par : כִּי חֵרֵף מַעַרְכוֹת אֱלֹהִים חַיִּים et qui réemploiera exactement les mêmes expressions en 17,36. Il semble donc bien que nous avons là un indice littéraire confirmant que 17,32-54 a été rédigé comme la suite de 17,12-31. Nous trouvons de cela une autre confirmation dans les emprunts au récit C que nous avons relevés ci-dessus dans le récit A, l'un de ces emprunts (les noms des trois frères aînés) provenant de 17, 13, alors que l'autre (la description de David) provient de 17,42. Cela laisse entendre que pour celui qui a composé le récit A, les blocs 17,12-31 et 17,32-54 constituent déjà un même récit.

Ces indices nous pousseraient à conclure que 17,32-54 n'a été composé que comme la suite naturelle de 17,12-31 et que 18,5 n'a été rédigé que pour fournir une introduction à 18,7. Il est également fort possible que 17,1-11 ait été rédigé pour fournir une introduction à 17,12-54, puis que des allusions à cette introduction aient été insérées en 17,16.23. S'il en est ainsi, la complexité littéraire des chapitres 17-18 selon le *M ne saurait être mise en relation immédiate avec les différences textuelles existant entre le *G et le *M.

III. LA CRITIQUE TEXTUELLE

On ne peut donc considérer l'éventuelle Vorlage du *G comme constituant un état littéraire cohérent qui ne se distinguerait du *M que par le fait que celui-ci y aurait inséré (au prix de quelques retouches) des éléments littéraires complémentaires. En effet, nous l'avons dit, lorsque 17,32-54 (commun au *M et au *G) a été composé, il était déjà précédé par 17,12-31 (propre au *M). Et le chant des femmes semble bien n'avoir été inséré en 18,7 (où le *M et le *G le lisent) qu'après que le rédacteur lui ait donné pour introduction 18,5 (propre au *M). C'est donc par mutilation que le *G (ou sa Vorlage) ont séparé 17,12-31 de 17,32-54 et 18,5 de 18,6b-7.

Or, c'est en 1864 que Vercellone (Variae lectiones II, Rome 1864, 256) a suggéré que les 'moins' du *G proviennent d'omissions motivées par les difficultés que présentent les parties omises. Au point où nous sommes rendus de notre étude, cette hypothèse apparaît comme la plus probable. Aussi devons-nous étudier les objections qui ont été formulées contre elle. Celui qui a le mieux détaillé ces objections est George B. Caird (The Interpreter's Bible II, Nashville 1978, 857). Il en formule six que nous allons étudier une à une :

1e objection : "The disputed sections contain some details which are not inconsistent with the rest of the story — the covenant with Jonathan, for instance — and these cannot be said to have been omitted from the Septuagint for harmonistic reasons."

Dans l'hypothèse où le *G (ou sa Vorlage) aurait omis 17,12-31 et 17,55-18,6a pour éliminer certaines données inacceptables car non cohérentes avec d'autres déjà formulées auparavant, il faudrait admettre que l'expurgateur a travaillé de la manière suivante : il a été choqué par deux répétitions dissonantes de l'entrée en rapports de David avec Saül : en 17,12-31, David nous est présenté comme un jeune berger que son père envoie porter des provisions à ses frères mobilisés dans l'armée de Saül. Il assiste au défi du Philistin. En se renseignant sur la récompense offerte par Saül à celui qui relèverait ce défi, il montre qu'il y serait disposé, ce dont on informe Saül. En 17,55-58, il nous est dit qu'au moment où David partait combattre le Philistin, Saül s'enquit auprès d'Abner de qui était le père de ce jeune homme et qu'Abner ne le sachant pas, ce fut David lui-même qui, après sa victoire, informa Saül que son père était Jessé le Bethléemite. Toutes ces données sont inacceptables pour quelqu'un qui vient de lire les récits A et B dans le chapitre 16 et pour qui David, ayant été présenté à Saül comme le fils de Jessé le Bethléemite (16,18), a gagné par ses talents de cithariste l'affection de Saül qui se l'est attaché comme écuyer (16,21s). L'expurgateur a commencé ses omissions au début de chacune des deux péricopes qui contenaient ces données présentant David comme encore jeune berger ou comme inconnu de Saül, c'est-à-dire en 17,12 et en 17,55. Puis il a poursuivi son omission jusqu'à l'endroit où il a rencontré des données qui se liaient aisément au texte qui précédait son omission, c'est-à-dire jusqu'à 17,32 qui se lie aisément à 17,11 et jusqu'à 18,6b qui se lie aisément à 17,54.

Cette façon de procéder l'a amené à omettre des données (18,1-6a) qui n'étaient nullement inacceptables ni incohérentes avec ce qui les précédait.

2e objection : "The apparent inconsistencies are not entirely removed. For these two reasons we should have to assume that the Septuagint translators had done their job of harmonizing very clumsily".

Comme incohérence que le *G a conservée, S.R. Driver (Notes on ... the Books of Samuel, 2th ed., Oxford 1913, 150) mentionne celle qui existe entre 16,18 et 17,33. Il s'agit là en effet de deux vss que le *G a conservés. Dans le premier, il est dit que David était un גִּבּוֹר חַיִל et un אִישׁ מִלְחָמָה avant qu'il soit entré en contact avec Saül, alors que, dans le second, Saül dit à David qu'il ne pourra pas triompher du Philistin parce que lui, David, est un jeune homme alors que le Philistin est un אִישׁ מִלְחָמָה depuis sa jeunesse. Le *G qui a traduit littéralement 17,33 (καὶ αὐτὸς ἀνὴρ πολεμιστὴς ἐκ νεότητος αὐτοῦ) a évité l'incohérence en atténuant les qualificatifs guerriers de David en 16,18 où il a rendu וְגִבּוֹר חַיִל וְאִישׁ מִלְחָמָה par καὶ ὁ ἀνὴρ συνετὸς καὶ ὁ ἀνὴρ πολεμιστής, ces phrases nominales transforment l'expression toute faite "homme de guerre" qui qualifiera le Philistin en une donnée de tempérament : "et cet homme est batailleur", l'expression וְגִבּוֹר חַיִל qui la précède ayant été transformée en un tout autre trait de tempérament : "et cet homme est avisé".

Autre dissonance notée par Driver : celle qui existe entre 16,21b et 17,38ss. Dans le premier de ces endroits il est dit que David devint נֹשֵׂא כֵלִים de Saül, cette expression étant interprétée d'ordinaire à juste titre comme "écuyer" (littéralement "porteur d'armes"). Or le נֹשֵׂא כֵלִים est un combattant, ainsi que cela apparaît clairement en 1 S 14,13s ou en 2 S 23,37. C'est même un membre d'un corps d'élite de jeunes guerriers ainsi que cela apparaît en 2 S 18,15. Dans le second endroit (17,38ss), il est dit que David ne peut marcher avec l'armure dont Saül l'a équipé, car il n'en a pas l'habitude. Mais cette dissonance n'apparaît pas pour le traducteur grec qui ne rend כֵלִים par ὅπλα que dans l'expression כְּלֵי מִלְחָמָה et qui en 16,21, comme dans les autres endroits où apparaît l'expression נֹשֵׂא כֵלִים, rend celle-ci par αἴρων τὰ σκεύη, transformant l'écuyer en coolie.

3e objection : "While there are many instances of harmonistic glosses and additions, there is no known parallel to this claimed example of harmonistic omission. There are many other inconsistencies in this book, as has already been pointed out, but in no other case did the Septuagint translators attempt to remedy them, unless in the next chapter."

Caird a tort de dire qu'il n'y a pas de parallèle connu pour une omission harmonistique de la part de la LXX des Règnes. En voici quelques cas : En 1 S 13,1 le *M offre des données chronologiques évidemment inacceptables : "Saül était âgé d'un an lorsqu'il régna et il régna deux ans sur Israël." Le *G ancien omet ce vs. En 2 S 5,4-5, il est dit selon le *M que David régna 40 ans : 7 ans et 6 mois à Hébron et 33 ans à Jérusalem. Ce total est inexact, c'est pourquoi le *G ancien a omis ces deux vss, ainsi que le montrent le fait qu'ils manquent dans la Vieille Latine (palimpseste de Vienne) et le fait que le littéralisme de la tradition palestinienne en 2 S 5,4 (υἱὸς τριάκοντα ἐτῶν Δαυειδ ἐν τῷ βασιλεῦσαι αὐτόν) fait contraste avec la traduction bien plus souple qu'elle donne de la même formule lorsqu'elle représente un *G ancien, comme c'est le cas en 2 S 2,10 (τεσσαράκοντα ἐτῶν Ιεβοσθε υἱὸς Σαουλ ὅτε ἐβασίλευσεν).

Notons d'ailleurs que le 'moins' le plus étendu du *G en 1 S 18 peut s'expliquer par les mêmes motifs : en 1 S 18,17-19, il est parlé du projet de Saül de marier David à sa fille Mérab en exigeant de lui des prouesses où il risquera sa vie; cette notice s'achevant par la mention du mariage de Mérab avec Adriel le Meholatite. Mais en 2 S 21,8 on parlera des 5 fils que Mikal fille de Saül (et non Mérab) a enfantés a Adriel fils de Barzillaï le Meholatite. On comprend que, pour éviter cette discordance, le *G ait préféré omettre l'événement de 1 S 18,17-19.

Il faut souligner que dans la plupart de ces omissions harmonisantes, il s'agit d'événements ou de dates qui sont mentionnés sous cette forme ou sous une autre en d'autres parties du livre que le *G a respectées : Pour les données sur la famille de David omises en 1 S 17,12-14, on a déjà eu 16,1.6-11. Pour la prise de contact de David avec Saül omise en 17,31, on a déjà eu 16,21a. Pour l'information de Saül sur le père de David omise en 17,55-58, on a déjà eu 16,18. Pour le projet de mariage avec Mérab au prix de prouesses dangereuses, événement omis en 1 S 18,17-19, on aura juste après (en 18,20-29) le projet de mariage avec Mikal au prix de prouesses encore plus dangereuses. Pour les années de règne de David omises en 2 S 5,4-5, on a déjà eu les 7 ans et 6 mois de règne à Hébron en 2 S 2,11 et on aura les 33 ans à Jérusalem et les 40 ans de total en 1 R 2,11 où le temps de règne à Hébron est réduit à 7 ans, ce qui facilite le total; ce total n'étant inexact que dans l'amalgame de 2 S 5,4-5 que le *G a omis pour ce motif.

Quand à l'âge d'avènement de Saül et à la durée de son règne que le *G a omis en 1 S 13,1, ils ne sont pas mentionnés ailleurs formellement, mais ils sont apparus au *G absolument inadmissibles et en contradiction flagrante avec tout ce que l'on sait de l'âge de Saül pendant l'histoire de son règne ainsi que de l'âge de David lors de la mort de Saül.

D'autres épisodes ou notations non-dissonantes ont été omis par le *G en 1 S 17-18 à titre de simples répétitions inutiles : en 18,10-11 la tentative de Saül pour frapper de sa lance David tandis qu'il jouait de la cithare faisait double emploi avec 19,9-10. En 18,12b l'affirmation que le Seigneur était avec David et s'était détourné de Saül a été omise comme faisant double emploi avec 16,13-14. En 17,41 la description de l'approche du Philistin précédé de son porte-bouclier faisait double emploi avec 17,48 et 17,7b. En 17,48b la description de l'approche de David est omise comme faisant double emploi avec 17,40b. En 17,50 un résumé de l'exploit de David met en valeur la disproportion entre sa victoire et le fait qu'il n'avait pas d'épée. Le *G l'omet estimant cela connu par 17,39-40.51.

Parmi les 'moins' du *G d'importance notable, le seul qui ne corresponde à aucune reprise ailleurs et qui ne présente rien d'inacceptable est le récit de l'affection de Jonathan pour David et de l'alliance qu'il conclut avec lui (18,1-4). Comme nous l'avons noté ci-dessus, l'omission de ce récit certainement ancien a vraisemblablement été entraînée par le fait que l'expurgateur qui voulait éliminer 17,55-58 a poursuivi son omission jusqu'à 18,6b qui lui offrait une excellente soudure avec 17,54. Peut-être a-t-il considéré que l'affection de Jonathan pour David était suffisamment connue par 19,1;20,17 et que l'alliance était assez clairement mentionnée en 20,8.16.42;22,8; 23,18a.

4e objection : "In 1 Sam 18 there are Septuagint omissions which are generally agreed to give a more satisfactory text than that of the Masoretes."

Il faut préciser ce qu'on entend par un texte "plus satisfaisant". Il est évident que des omissions facilitantes ont pour but de produire un texte qui satisfasse mieux l'expurgateur. Mais prenons pour exemples les trois premières initiatives d'omission que l'on serait tenté d'attribuer au *G en ce chapitre 18 que Caird mentionne.

Nous venons de parler de l'omission de l'alliance conclue par Jonathan avec David avec le récit du don de ses vêtements et de ses armes. Personne ne prétendra que l'omission de cela améliore réellement le texte.

En 18,8, après la remarque amère de Saül ("on a donné les myriades à David et à moi on a donné les milliers") le *M lui met dans la bouche comme conclusion : וְעוֹד לוֹ אַךְ הַמְּלוּכָה. Le *G n'a pas traduit cette conclusion, ou bien parce qu'il n'en comprenait pas la syntaxe, ou bien parce qu'il estimait qu'en 20,31 Saül exprimera la même appréhension. Est-ce que l'absence de cette conclusion améliore le texte ?

En 18,10-11, le *G omet, nous l'avons vu, la première tentative de Saül pour clouer au mur avec sa lance David qui jouait de la cithare. On pourrait à première vue penser que l'omission de ce doublet permet de retrouver un état textuel plus primitif. Mais remarquons ce qui précède et suit ces deux vss dans le *M. Le vs 9 vient de dire de Saül וַיְהִי עוֹיֵן אֶת־דָּוִד en ajoutant que cela eut lieu "à partir de ce jour et dans la suite". Le *G a lu cela qu'il a traduit : "και ην Σαουλ υποβλεπομενος τον Δαυειδ απο της ημερας εκεινης και επεκεινα". Or, juste après, le *G traduit fidèlement le vs 12a du *M : "και εφοβηθη Σαουλ απο προσωπου Δαυειδ." Dans cette forme textuelle brève, rien n'explique le passage de la malveillance (qu'exprime le participe עוין : "regarder par en-dessous, guetter") à la crainte. C'est justement l'épisode omis par le *G qui explique ce passage. En effet le fait que Saül guettait David avec malveillance introduit le jet de lance, et le fait que David y ait échappé par deux fois introduit l'affirmation que "Saül se mit à craindre la présence de David", affirmation expliquée par le vs 12b (que le *G a omis) : "car le Seigneur était avec David et s'était détourné de lui", ce dont Saül venait d'avoir la preuve dans l'échec de ses tentatives et dans la chance de David qui y avait échappé. Comme on le voit, aucune de ces omissions n'améliore le texte.

5e objection : "The disputed sections form an almost continuous story by themselves. And they bear a striking resemblance to 1 S 16,1-13."
Nous avons traité de ces deux points dans l'ordre inverse dans le paragraphe que nous avons consacré à la critique littéraire.

6e objection : "The claim that the longer text is original presupposes an earlier narrative filled with those very inconsistencies which the Septuagint ostensibly sought to eliminate. This theory could therefore be upheld only on the further assumption that the original narrative was a compilation from two conflicting sources. But the analysis of those two sources would differ very little from that already provided by the Septuagint omissions, and we should still have to explain how the Septuagint text arose."
Nous avons également traité de ces différents points dans les pages qui précèdent.

———

Résumons-nous pour conclure : Les sutures apparentes que le *M offre en son chapitre 17 montrent que nous avons affaire à une compilation intégrant un récit plus ancien. Il semble bien que le 'moins' du *G commence au début de ce récit (17,12). Mais 17,1-11 constitue une mise en scène préparant ce récit et il semble bien que ce soit le même récit qui continue au-delà de 17,32 en une partie commune au *G et au *M. On ne saurait donc faire coïncider les 'moins' du *G avec le récit ancien que la compilation a intégré. L'explication la plus vraisemblable de ces 'moins' est qu'il s'agit d'omissions harmonisantes. Il n'est pas étonnant que ce soit en ce chapitre que le traducteur grec des Règnes (ou sa Vorlage) ait pratiqué de la façon la plus mutilante ce type d'omissions qu'il a pratiqué plus discrètement ailleurs aussi. C'est en effet à propos de l'entrée en contact de David avec Saül que l'hétérogénéité des récits traditionnels se trahit par les discordances les plus évidentes au niveau littéraire. Le traducteur grec (ou sa Vorlage) — dont on sait par ailleurs le souci d'améliorer la cohérence du texte — a estimé impossible de procéder seulement — comme il le fait d'ordinaire — par des retouches ou des gloses. Il a donc dû procéder à de larges omissions en veillant à garder un récit aussi coulant que possible.

AN APPROACH TO THE LITERARY AND TEXTUAL PROBLEMS
IN THE DAVID-GOLIATH STORY : 1 Sam 16-18 [1]

I. PRELIMINARIES

(i) Apology. I apologise to my three colleagues for my delay in presenting this paper, and I thank them for their patience in waiting for it.

(ii) Procedure. Since DB and ET have already published some thoughts on the problem, it would seem sensible for me to begin by responding to their expressed views and to the underlying principles on which those views are based. That I do not do the same for JL's views is simply because I am not aware of anything he may have published on the topic. I learn from DB's letter to me that JL gave a paper at Vienna in 1980 on the "short text" of Ezekiel; but unfortunately I have not seen it.

(iii) Terminology. I will adopt ET's terminology (Version 1 = LXX and MT; Version 2 = MT only : see "Text-Critical Use of the Septuagint" = *TCUS,* Jerusalem 1981, p. 298); but I do so without prejudice to the question whether there ever were two separate, independent versions, or, to put it another way, whether there ever was a time when Version 1 stood by itself before the LXX appeared.

(iv) Departure-point. Both DB (The Hebrew and Greek Texts of Samuel = *HGTS,* Jerusalem 1980, pp. 19-20) and ET (*TCUS,* p. 298-9) start by accepting the currently orthodox literary analysis of the MT according to which the MT's version of the story is a combination of two originally separate versions. They appear to regard this analysis as proved, and they cite in evidence a number of alleged discrepancies commonly cited in this connection.

Both DB and ET, then, seem to believe that there was an earlier edition of the Hebrew Books of Samuel in which Version 1 stood by itself; and that MT represents a later edition in which Version 2 was, rather clumsily, interspersed in Version 1. They disagree, however, in that :
(a) ET thinks that the LXX is translated quite faithfully from a Hebrew edition that contained Version 1 only; while
(b) DB considers that the LXX translator(s) had before them a Hebrew edition in which Version 2 had already been combined with Version 1; and that finding the discrepancies between the Versions indigestible, they tried to get rid of them by

omitting the offending passages; but that in this they were not completely thorough, but left unexpunged some elements from Version 2 which still conflict with elements from Version 1, thus betraying the fact that they must have had before them a Hebrew edition containing both versions, and that the omission of a large part of Version 2 from the LXX is the work of the translators.

Interesting and instructive, however, is the example which DB cites (p. 20) of discrepancies between Version 1 and Version 2 which still survive in the LXX : "... puisque 16,18 nous parle de David comme d'un ἀνὴρ πολεμιστής, alors qu'en 17,33, Saul lui dit : οὐ μὴ δύνῃ πορευθῆναι πρὸς τὸν ἀλλόφυλον τοῦ πολεμεῖν μετ'αὐτοῦ, ὅτι παιδάριον εἶ σύ, καὶ αὐτὸς ἀνὴρ πολεμιστὴς ἐκ νεότητος αὐτοῦ."

This apparently appeals to DB as a self-evident discrepancy, since he does not stay to point out in what the discrepancy consists. But where, in fact, is the discrepancy ? Nothing in what Saul says in 17,33 denies, or even implies, that David was not a man of war. Saul does not, for instance, say "You are only a shepherd, and he is a man of war", but "You are a youth, and he a man of war from his youth". To imagine that by calling David a youth, Saul was denying that David was a man of war, is false. Youths could be men of war [2] : indeed, in the very next breath Saul remarks that Goliath was a man of war as a youth, and has continued to be one ever since. The contrast, then, that Saul makes in 17,33 is not between David as a shepherd and Goliath as a man of war, but between David's youthful inexperience, and Goliath's long experience, of war. 2 Sam. 2,14 illustrates the point : "Let the youths (τὰ παι-δάρια) arise and play before us". These youths were, of course, soldiers, men of war (Abner's use of the term 'youths' is not meant to imply that they were not !) but junior and inexperienced compared with Abner and Joab (even Joab's younger brother Asahel, succumbed through youthful inexperience and enthusiasm to the wily trick of the more experienced Abner : 2 Sam. 2,18-23).

There is, then, no contradiction between 17,33 and 16,18; nor, it seems to me, might anyone ever have been led to think there was, if he had not been convinced on other grounds that there were two conflicting versions and so was inclined to find other instances of conflict. But the fact that there is no necessary conflict between 17,33 and 16,18 tends to reduce both ET's claim that there were originally two se-parate, conflicting versions, and DB's claim that the LXX still contains evidence of the original conflict between the two versions.

More of that later. For the moment let us turn to another, slightly different point. ET (*TCUS*, p. 298) remarks : "The contents of version 1 (LXX and MT) differ from those of version 2 (MT only). In the latter, David and Goliath are presented as the *dramatis personae* (17,12ff) as if they had not yet been introduced in version 1 (16,18ff), and in contrast with ch. 16 (version 1), David is presented as an unknown shepherd (17,15) who is sent to bring food to his brothers." This is, of course, the long-standing majority interpretation : ET is in good company ! But this criticism holds up only if we first accept that this was indeed the function of 17,12ff, namely, to introduce David and Goliath as the *dramatis personae* for the first time. It seems to me, I must say, highly unlikely that this was ever their function. Consider the situation when, according to ET's view, Version 2 stood alone, and was not preceded by Version 1. Whatever the position Version 2 filled in its larger context, if 17,12ff were its presentation of the *dramatis personae* in the Goliath story, 17,12ff must have stood at the very commencement of that story. But in that case they tell us both too much and too little to function as the presentation of the *dramatis personae*. To start with the bald statement "And David was the son of..." is not the way 1 Sam. normally introduces a new major figure at the beginning of a new major episode. The usual form is : "And there was a man of such and such a place, and his name was..."; so run the introductions to Elkanah in 1,1, to Kish in 9,1, and Nabal in 25,2-3. Grant, for sake of argument, that Version 2 did not originally belong to 1 Sam. and may have used a differently styled introduction, it still seems to me a strange way to introduce the hitherto unmentioned hero of a major episode by the bald and abrupt "And David was the son of ..." Be that as it may, worse difficulties begin in 17,13 : "And the three eldest sons of Jesse had gone after Saul to the battle". To *the* battle ? What battle ? 17,13 is hardly performing the function of introducing things and people for the first time, if we are supposed to know already which battle is being referred to. But worse. 17,16 says : "And the Philistine drew near morning and evening..." *The* Philistine ? Which Philistine ? If we had not already been told about the Philistine, an introduction would surely have said *"a* Philistine". And would it not also have told us his name ? That is what presentations of the *dramatis personae* normally do; but instead of that this one simply adds "and presented himself forty days". Whatever for ? Where ? What as ? The supposed introduction does not tell us; but in the absence of this information, it makes no sense simply to say *'The* Philistine presented himself forty days'. Of course, if the original context of Version 2 (whatever that was — and if ever there was one !) had already mentioned Saul's going to battle with the Philistines and the challenge of their champion, it would make sense for 17,16 to refer to that challenge by saying "And *the* Philistine drew near" and then to add the additional information "morning and evening and presented himself forty days". But in that case 17,12-16 would no longer be functioning as an introductory presentation of the *dramatis personae,* and it would no longer be true to say that they were introducing the *dramatis personae* "as if they had not yet been introduced".

One can only conclude, therefore, that 17,12-16 never served the function of presenting the *dramatis personae* for the first time, not even when they stood in the hypothetical context of the hypothetical Version 2; and however they got into the MT, they clearly are not intended to serve that function there. What, then, was their original function ?

This question we may leave for the moment, because at this point some remarks on basic methodology would seem to be in order. If our textual criticism of the OT in general, and of the LXX in particular, must in places presume, and be based on, the prior findings of the literary criticism of the OT, then, of course, we shall wish those findings to be as sound as possible. For that very reason we cannot afford to take over the Wellhausen-Driver-et alii-plurimi theory unexamined, and unquestioned, because both its presuppositions and its methodology are from a literary point of view highly questionable. This is borne in upon me as a classicist nowadays with ever increasing force. ET (*TCUS* p. 293) reminds us of the relevance to our problem of the state of affairs in Homeric studies. And quite rightly : there is a distinct similarity between οἱ χωρίζοντες of Homeric scholarship and their counterparts in OT scholarship (perhaps there is, as well, between the unitarians in the two fields !) both in their initial assumption of plurality of authorship and in the kind of evidence they adduce to prove that plurality. Two things, however, must be noted. The first is that the multiple authorship of the Homeric poems is not a proven fact, agreed upon by all except a few fundamentalists, the certainty of which can lend probability to the surmise of multiple authorship in 1 Sam. 16-18. Multiple authorship of the Homeric poems is a theory that in all its long history has been favoured by some and denied by others, and still to-day is hotly contested by scholars of the first rank, witness the recent attack on the theory by Hugh Lloyd-Jones of Oxford in his *"Remarks on the Homeric Question"* (in "History and Imagination" ed. by H. Lloyd-Jones, Duckworth, 1982, pp. 1-29; see also the German literature there cited).

The second point is even more germane to our immediate problem. In Homeric criticism, so unitarians like Lloyd-Jones would claim, the analysts are apt to assume that Homer would have made his narrative follow a strict undeviating chronological line, and then to convict the narrative of multiple authorship because it does not; to assume that Homer would have depicted the behaviour of his characters as following a logical rationality, and then to accuse his narrative of inconcinnity, and therefore of multiple authorship, because it depicts people behaving arbitrarily; and, above all, to claim to prove irreconcilable discrepancy, and therefore multiple authorship, by selecting a detailed feature from one context, contrasting it with a detailed feature from another context, without first carefully examining the place each feature holds and the function it performs within the thought-flow of its own particular movement. The unitarians would say that these critical methods arrive at wrong conclusions because they are inappropriate to the kind of literature that they are trying to deal with. I confess that not only do I have a great deal of sympathy with these criticisms of the analysts by the unitarians in Homeric studies, but I should wish to apply them, *mutatis mutandis*, to a great deal of the (until recently) standard literary criticism of the OT. The methods of the historian who regards it as his prime task to detect beneath a narrative the different sources from which it has been compiled, are not necessarily the best way of discovering what in fact the narrative as it stands is trying to say. And if we fail to understand what the narrative as it stands is trying to say, we may well gratuitously accuse it of inconsistency or discrepancy. Nor are the atomistic methods of the textual critic necessarily more appropriate, since he is rightly preoccupied with spotting differences, even of the smallest kind, in details taken, largely, individually. To understand a narrative from a literary point of view, we must first listen to the narrative as it stands, trying to see where and how each part fits into the thought-flow of the whole. In other words we must initially give the narrative the benefit of the doubt; for if we start out with the assumption that the narrative is likely to be composite and discrepant, we shall too easily find imaginary discrepancies that confirm our initial assumption. Only after a sustained and sympathetic attempt at making sense of the narrative as it stands should we reluctantly conclude that the narrative is an irreconcilably discrepant hotch-potch. Literary criticism of this kind is doubtless a tedious task for textual critics to have to turn their hands to; but, as I said earlier, if our textual criticism is obliged to build upon the foundation produced by literary criticism, we must not build upon an unexamined foundation. I propose, therefore, in this paper to attempt a literary criticism of cc. 16-18 myself [3].

II. A STUDY OF THREE OF THE LARGER COMPONENTS OF VERSION 2

For the sake of argument, however, let us forget some of what I have just said, and begin by supposing that at one stage there were two independent versions. Let us then begin on Version 2 by listening to what its first component has to say. It extends from 1 Sam. 17,12 to 17,31. Let us begin at its beginning. 17,12 tells us as its very first remark that David was the son of an Ephrathite of Bethlehem-judah whose name was Jesse and who had eight sons. When it adds that by Saul's time the man was old [4], we may fairly deduce that the older ones among his eight sons were by this time men in their prime. Anyhow, 17,13 next tells us that the three eldest sons *"had gone off after Saul to the battle"*; and not content with that adds the names of *"the three sons that went to the battle"*. Then 17,14 continues "And David was the youngest : *and the three eldest followed Saul"*. In view of all this repetition even the dullest reader may presumably be relied upon to grasp that this section is about Jesse's sons, David and his brothers, particularly his three eldest brothers, who, we have now been told three times in two verses, have gone after Saul to the battle. They, presumably, if none of the other brothers, were regarded fit to be soldiers and go to the battle.

As it begins, so this sections continues. 17,17-22 tell how David's father sent him to the camp with supplies of food for his brothers (17,17) and to enquire how his brothers (17,18) were doing; and how he eventually reached the camp at an exciting moment "and saluted his brothers" (17,22).

As it continues, so it climaxes, 17,28-29, with a furious scene between David and his eldest brother, Eliab. The men of Israel had asked David if he had seen the Philistine champion, and they had told him of the rewards that the king was offering to the man that should kill him, which included "making his father's house free in Israel" (17,25). David in astonishment had then asked the men to repeat what they had said about the rewards, and Eliab, overhearing the conversation, let fly an angry blast at David for ever having come down to the battle. Why this violent outburst ? It can hardly be the concern of an older brother that his younger brother was too young to see gruesome sights. At least, the other soldiers apparently did not think him too young : they eventually introduced him to the king.

Why, then, the outburst ? An analogous scene from another story may help. When Joseph's brothers saw him coming (Gen. 37,17-20) their jealousy at his dreams and at what those dreams had implied prompted their sarcastic "Behold, this dreamer comes". And if we could think that Eliab knew of David's anointing by Samuel, and what is worse, that Samuel had at first been inclined to anoint Eliab but then had passed him by in favour of David, that would account for two things : Eliab's suspicion, when he heard David enquiring about the rewards for killing the champion, that David might well be thinking of asking to be allowed to fight him; and secondly, Eliab's furiously jealous reaction, as the eldest son, to the idea that David, his youngest brother, might go and do what he himself, for all his seniority, dare not do : fight Goliath, and so win freedom for the whole family, Eliab included (17,25). But, alas, we cannot suppose that Eliab knew anything of the sort : the paragraph that tells us he did, belongs to another version, Version 1 (16,1-13). If it did not, we might of course very reasonably think that the careful mention of the fact that Jesse had eight sons, and the careful naming of the first three eldest sons in 17,12-13, were not an unintelligible repetition of what has been already told us explicitly in 16,6-9, but the storyteller's artful way of making sure we recall the details of the anointing scene among David's brothers in c. 16, so that we might then perceive the point of this story about David and those same brothers in 17,17-30. But there it is : Version 1 is Version 1; Version 2 is quite a different version.

Nevertheless, let us notice once more Eliab's bitterly sarcastic belittling of David's job with the sheep : "And with whom have you left those few sheep in the wilderness ?" (17,28). What a perfect foil this makes to David's subsequent recounting to Saul of his exploits as a shepherd against the lion and the bear (17,34-35) — or rather, would make, if only these latter verses belonged to Version 2. But they don't : they belong to Version 1.

Still, we are on indisputably firm ground when we state that the first part of Version 2, 17,12-31, is about David, his family of brothers, and his eldest brother's scornful anger at the hint that David might rival him in military prowess. With this in mind let us pass to the second major component of Version 2 (omitting for the moment the intervening smaller items 17,41 and 17,50). Here we meet the most blatant of all the alleged discrepancies between Version 2 and Version 1, so blatant indeed that there is no need to go beyond what the text says, as many do, and claim that whereas in Version 1 Saul knows perfectly well who *David* is, in Version 2 he does not know who *David* is. What Version 2 says, in its typically repetitive way, so that we should be sure to get the point, is *"Whose son* is this youth ?" (17,55); "Inquire *whose son* the stripling is" (17,56); *"Whose son* are you ?" (17,58); "I am *the son* of your servant Jesse..." (17,58). Any but the slowest of readers would surely get the point : it is David's father, not David, that Saul is wanting to inform himself about. And that is hardly surprising : Saul in Version 2 has promised, that if any man can defeat the champion, he (Saul) will make his father's house free in Israel (17,25). It is only natural, therefore, that as he sees David go out to battle, and even more as he sees him come in, he should be concerned to find out all he can about David's father and family. But, of course, if Version 1 says in 16,18-22 that Saul knew exactly who David's father was and all about him, then that is discrepant with what Version 2 says here, and there is nothing we can do about it. Never mind : we can at least enquire exactly what this second major component of Version 2 is about.

Well, to start with it is about David's father, as we have just seen (17,55-58). So, of course, was the first component of Version 2 at its beginning. But 17,55-58 labour a different point : not that David's father had eight sons of whom David was the youngest, but that David's father was an obscure man of whom neither Saul nor Abner knew anything worth knowing. And that forms the introduction to a very dramatic scene. There stands the monarch himself. There stands his son Jonathan, who by virtue of being the monarch's son might expect to succeed his father on the throne. And there with the head of the Philistine in his hand stands David, somebody else's son, who is destined to supplant Saul's son Jonathan and reign in his place. Of course, neither Saul nor Jonathan yet know that. If they did know it, what they did next would have been incredible. Of course, if we the readers knew that David had been anointed and was destined to supplant Jonathan, we should be in a position to see the tremendous irony of what Saul and Jonathan do next. But alas, we cannot know that any more than Saul and Jonathan did : the story of the anointing of David belongs to Version 1, and we are now in Version 2, whose presentation of its *dramatis personae* for the first time began only at 17,12. Nevertheless what Saul and Jonathan do next remains exceedingly dramatic. Jonathan is so filled with admiration for David and his killing of the giant, that he strips himself of his royal armour and accoutrements and with unconscious irony, makes David a present of them; and Saul, who, as 17,55-58 have laboured to tell us, has been careful to find out who David's father is (and has found, doubtless, as David later stresses, 18,18, that he is a nobody) unknowingly takes the destined supplanter of his own son into his own household, and refuses to let him go back to his own home any more (18,1-4). So much, then, for the second major component of Version 2 : it has been about two fathers, and two sons, and two households, and how David was permanently transferred from his father's household to Saul's.

With that we come to another major component of Version 2, namely 18,17-19. That, too, as it happens turns out to be about David's family. Again we hear of David's father : "Who am I", says David to Saul, "and what is my life (?) or (?) my father's family in Israel, that I should be son-in-law to the king ?" The three major components of Version 2, then, are proving to have a central theme in common : the first was concerned with David's family, in particular his elder brother's scornful, jealous derision of the idea that David could possibly fight Goliath; the second was about how David's prowess came to be so admired by Saul's son, the expert warrior, Jonathan, that David was transferred from his father's household into the king's household permanently; the third is going to tell how David, a young man from a lowly family was taken, not only into the king's household, but into the king's family by being given the king's daughter in marriage. Version 2 certainly seems to be a coherent, progressive narrative, leading to a climax. And what is more, it has the added interest that just when we think that the climax is going to be reached, we have the suspense of an unexpected *contretemps* : Saul having volunteered to give David his elder daughter, breaks his promise and gives her to some-one else. But then the *contretemps* is resolved : Saul's second daughter falls in love with David and Saul is finally obliged to let David marry her. A greater triumph for David, and therefore a greater climax.

But we have jumped ahead of ourselves. Version 2 does not have David marrying the king's daughter after all. It is Version 1 that gets him married to one of the king's daughters. Taken by itself Version 2 tells a very different, and very strange story. It tells first how Saul proposed to give his elder daughter, Merab, to David. This, of course, is not surprising in Version 2, for it is Version 2, not Version 1, that tells us that before the battle, Saul had promised to give his daughter in marriage to any man who beat the champion (17,25). But Version 2 no sooner tells us that Saul announced to David his intention of giving him his daughter, than it adds that Saul used the prospect of this marriage to stir David to valiant effort in the wars against the Philistines, in the hope that David would die in battle. Why should Saul want him to die ?

Curiously enough, Version 2 has not given us the slightest hint; it is Version 1 that tells what first provoked Saul's jealousy and made him realise that David' stunning victory (and Saul's evident cowardice) had transferred public popularity from Saul to David (18,6-9). And similarly without having told us anything that could possibly account for it, Version 2 proceeds to tell us that when the time came for Merab to be given to David she was given to someone else (18,19). So, having appeared in its three major components to be leading up to a climax, Version 2 ends in a dismal and unaccounted for anti-climax : David is *not* taken into the royal family after all.

But again we are making a mistake. We are arguing as if Version 2 originally consisted of nothing more than the various bits and pieces which in the MT have been interpolated into Version 1. That is, of course, most unlikely. Version 2, if it ever existed at all, must have been a complete story that made sense in itself, a story which would have explained, for instance, what happened to make Saul, who had so recently taken David into his household, basking in Jonathan's admiration, so turn against him as to wish him dead, and why having offered him his daughter Merab, he should suddenly give her to someone else. As the fragments stand now, one major fragment, 17,54-18,5 tells us how Saul, apparently in accord with Jonathan's love for David, took David into his household; the very next fragment (18,10-11), without explaining what provoked it, tells how the evil spirit, which David's playing normally calmed and expelled, moved Saul to attempt to assassinate David. This surely cannot have been the whole story as originally given by Version 2.

We must conclude, therefore, that what has happened is that some interpolator finding the whole story as given in Version 2, broke it up into pieces, chose out which pieces he thought he would, and interpolated them into the text of Version 1. It is to be noted what this implies. Whatever status Version 2 had, or did not have, our interpolator had no compunction in thus splitting it up and arbitrarily selecting some parts of it and rejecting others. Moreover the pieces of Version 2 that once stood in between the fragments which the interpolator selected, must have been different from the pieces of Version 1 that now stand between those fragments in their present position in the MT; for if they had been the same, or almost the same, the original Version 2 would already have been virtually the same as the MT, whereas the reigning theory supposes that MT=Version 1 plus extracts from *another* version that by definition was *not* Version 1. Faced then with two *different* versions, Version 1 and Version 2, our interpolator had no compunction in rejecting more than half of Version 2 in favour of Version 1. But this raises another difficulty. If the interpolator had such scant respect for the authority of Version 2, why did he not feel free to shape the pieces he chose from it with just a little more care so that they should fit into Version 1 without inconcinnity or discrepancy ? Take the notorious verses, 17,12-16, that give such offence by introducing the *dramatis personae* "as if they had not been already introduced" in virtually the same words as have already been used in 16,1-13. With what ease the interpolator could have re-written them so as to smooth away the inconcinnity, or else have omitted them altogether with that same freedom with which he rejected the greater part of Version 2. Alternatively, why did he not treat Version 1 with the same freedom as that with which he treated Version 2, and excise from it the pieces that would seem to conflict with the material which he wished to interpolate from Version 2 ? Perhaps Version 1 already had an authority which did not allow it itself to be changed, even if it could be added to. Or perhaps the interpolator was simply a bungler, as all OT interpolators are *ex hypothesi*, otherwise they could not be detected. Perhaps he just took the pieces which he happened to like from Version 2, and put them roughly into contexts in Version 1 where at first sight they seemed to fit more or less, without first carefully considering the detailed though-flow of Version 1 which he was thus disturbing. Perhaps. But before we so decide, we ought at least to examine exactly what he has done, both with the components which we have already considered and with the others.

III. THE POSITIONING OF THE COMPONENTS OF VERSION 2 WITHIN VERSION 1 AND THEIR RELATION TO THE WIDER CONTEXT

Let us consider first the context of the book as a whole. It is a matter that has often been remarked upon that there is a vivid similarity between the major theme of the opening chapters of 1 Sam. and that of the middle and subsequent chapters. In cc. 1-4 the *house* of Eli proves unsatisfactory (see 2,27.28.30.31.32.33.35.36 for the emphatic reference to Eli's father's house, and Eli's own house); and it is announced that it will have to be removed in favour of another (2,35). So in the middle chapters as a result of Saul's sin, his dynasty is not established; another house is destined to take its place. Within this general similarity of theme, there are also a number of smaller features which the two stories have in common. They are not necessarily exact parallels; but the similarity between the second occasion and the first is striking enough for the second, when we meet it, to recall the first.

So, for instance, it is a remarkable thing that in both instances God having decided to discipline the unsatisfactory house, immediately insinuates his new man into the very heart and vitals of that house, before he disciplines it. So not only is Samuel chosen to supplant Eli as God's mouthpiece to the people (3,1-2), but before all the people, or even Eli, realise it (3,20), Samuel is transferred from his own obscure father's house into Eli's own very temple. So also with David. He is destined to supplant Saul and Jonathan as the leading warrior in the nation, and therefore subsequently as their king; but by the time the people and Saul realise it (18,6-9.16.30), David has already been transferred into the very household of Saul (16,19-23; 18,1-4); and subsequently into his family (18,17-28). The transfer of David from his own obscure father's house into the royal house of Saul is thus shown to be not a merely incidental detail : it belongs to the very woof and warp of the book. In view of that, it is surely significant that while it is Version 1 that tells us about the beginning of the transfer (16,14-23) and about its end (18,20-29), it is, as we have seen above (p.62), Version 2 that not only fills in the middle of the process, but concentrates our attention, by its simple yet insistent repetitions of phrase, on the two houses, the two fathers, the two sons, and the permanent transfer (18,2) of David from the one house to the other. At the very least, the interpolator has managed to make his insertions mesh in well with this major theme of the book.

But now let us take another common theme. With Samuel, not only do we have a contrast between the two houses : Elkanah and Hannah's son versus Eli and his sons, but we also have a rivalry within Elkanah's house : Peninnah, his other wife, the first to give him children, scorned and mocked Hannah as being an inadequate wife, unable to give Elkanah children (1,1-8). This matter is no incidental detail : it carries great prominence as the opening scene of the book; it accounts in great part for Hannah's distress, provokes her to prayer and leads to her eventual vindication. But as with Samuel, so with David. Not only do we have a contrast between the two houses : Jesse and his son versus Saul and his son, but we also have a rivalry within Jesse's house : Eliab, David's eldest brother, eldest of the three who as the warriors in the family had followed Saul to the battle (see p. 59 above), scorns, mocks and rebukes David as being unsuitable even to see the battle (17,26-30). The parallel with Samuel is obvious : but this time we are altogether dependent on Version 2 for it, for Version 1 lacks the whole of 17,12-31 and the Eliab-David scene along with it. Now this lack is usually regarded as a pristine virtue in Version 1, and the presence of the whole paragraph in MT is regarded as a discrepant interpolation from Version 2. Well, the parallel which Version 2 thus presents, is certainly not discrepant : it so beautifully completes a major pattern in the book, that, if it is an interpolation at all, we must think that the interpolator knew exactly what he was doing and did it well. Certainly he was no bungler; and this in turn casts added doubt on the contention that verses 12-16 which commence this "interpolation" are a bungling, unnecessary repetition of what we have been given in 16,1-13.

Now let us proceed to the detailed thought-flow of the major elements in 16,1 -17,54.

The immediate juxtaposition of the two paragraphs which form c. 16 is very impressive. God wants a man to replace Saul as king, chooses David and sends Samuel to anoint him. Had Saul known what Samuel was doing, he might well have executed him (16,2). But the very next paragraph tells us that Saul, wanting a comforter to soothe his vexed spirit, himself chose — David ! We need not stay to make explicit the profound lesson on the ways of God's government which the narrative in its artfully artless way teaches by simply juxtaposing the two stories without further comment. We might expect, however, that the remaining paragraphs in this section of the book were all originally placed in order with similar care and precision, so that any interpolation will show up as disturbing the thought-flow. So let us now take the MT with its supposed mixture of two conflicting versions, and see if the thought-flow is in fact spoiled by interpolations.

Here are the first three paragraphs :

1. 16,1-13   God needs a king, and chooses David.
2. 16,14-23   Saul needs a comforter, and chooses David.
3. 17,1-11   Israel is challenged to find a champion to fight Goliath but for the moment none is forthcoming.

The function of these three paragraphs is at once obvious. Not only do they set the scene for the major event, the combat with Goliath : by their progression of thought they lead us to the question, Who will the champion turn out to be ? Of course, at the same time their progression of thought leads us to expect that it will be David; but for the moment we are left in suspense : how will it come about that David is chosen for the task ? In paragraph 1 God wanted a king, and sent Samuel to select one; but *how and by what criteria* Samuel selected him — and how Samuel at first used the wrong criteria and nearly selected the wrong man — this forms the heart and interest of the story. In paragraph 2 David, now anointed, enters Saul's service; but how he ever got into that position is of course the interest of the story. The third paragraph presents a dramatic situation : Israel are faced with enslavement unless they can find a champion to fight and defeat Goliath; and with Goliath strutting the field and taunting them, they cannot find one. Will one be found ? Who will it be ? Of course, even if we had never read the story before (and that is how we ought to read it), we would sense that a champion was going to be found and that the champion would turn out to be David. And in any case the very next word in the story is 'And David'. But once more the interest will be to see how he comes to be put forward and selected as champion.

The narrative, therefore, turns to answer this question. But as it does so it employs a very common and very ancient narrative device. Its first three paragraphs have led us along one road of thought to a point of unbearable suspense : Israel is in dire straits : the giant Goliath is demanding a champion, or else — and they cannot find one. Instead of resolving this suspense at once, the narrative calmly leaves that road, and goes back to the beginning of another road to explain how under God's detailed providence David, without his intending it, came to the battlefield precisely at the right moment (N.B. 17,20); and how after his innocent enquiries, and incredulous surprise at everybody else's dismay and cowardice, and in spite of the scornful discouragement of his eldest brother, his words were reported to Saul and *Saul sent for him* (17,31). So the pattern is repeated. No sooner had God had David anointed than Saul in his personal need and at the recommendation of his courtiers *sent for* David (16, 19.22) and appointed him as harpist; now at the moment of the nation's dire peril, Saul at the suggestion of the soldiery once more *sends for* David, this time be the nation's champion. Saul would live to regret both these sendings for; but the care with which the narrative on the second occasion builds up suspense, then deliberately keeps us there asking ourselves, How will David come to be selected, and finally leads us to the answer at its climax : "Saul sent for him"; and the emphasis this answer achieves by repeating the situation and the phrasing of 16,18-22, would lead one to think that the narrative by its literary skills is making a profound theological point.

But, of course, the majority see it differently. According to them 17,12-31 is an interpolation from Version 2. Take these verses away and you get the original story. And a very different story it is : for in this story Saul does not send for David. All unasked David simply volunteers himself. And then the majority hold that 17,12-31 are not only an interpolation; their self-evident inconcinnity with their context exposes them as a very clumsy interpolation. So what I read as an easily recognisable, sophisticated — but well known and in all periods very common — literary device of suspense narrative, the majority hold to be the work of a clumsy interpolator. Perhaps it is all a matter of taste. And there's no accounting for taste.

But next consider the following series of false valuations of the hero :

1. **16,1-13**   Samuel nearly makes the mistake of anointing Eliab instead of David. The reason ? He looks on outward appearance instead of looking on the heart (16,7).

2. **17,25-30**   Eliab thinks he can read David's heart and says : "I know your pride and wickedness of heart" (17,28). But Eliab is wrong. What moves David is neither pride nor wickedness, but the fact that the giant's defiance of the armies of the living God is being left unanswered.

3. **17,32-37**   Saul thinks David unable to fight the Philistine, not because he is a shepherd (see p. 56 above) but because as a youth he lacks the necessary military experience (17,33). Saul is wrong. What is needed is not military experience : Saul himself has plenty of that and is still afraid to fight Goliath. What is needed is faith in, and experience of, God's direct help against impossible odds in situations of extreme danger. And David has had plenty of experience of that as a shepherd (17,34-37). In the confidence born of this experience he tells Saul : "Let no man's heart fail because of him" (17,32).

Let us interrupt the series for a moment at this point, in order to notice the precision of this beautifully structured sequence. Each of the three components deals with the attitude of the heart. But none either repeats or contradicts the other; and none, not even No. 2, disturbs the thought-flow of the series. The literary analysis which would require us to believe that No. 2 is part of a later discrepant interpolation inserted by a bungling interpolator is fast losing probability. Indeed, is it not already far more probable that the whole passage, 17,12-31, is not a later interpolation, but an integral part of a narrative which was constructed, out of whatever sources, by one unifying mind ?

But we must proceed with the remaining item of the series. It deals with the evaluation not of the hero himself but of his weapons. On that point David first disagrees with Saul, and then Goliath violently disagrees with David.

4 (a). 17,38-40. At first Saul, afraid to go and fight Goliath himself, gives David permission to go and fight him, and piously (or perhaps even sincerely and fervently) adds "and the Lord be with you" (17,37). Next, Saul puts his own armour on David and gives him his sword. A classicist, at this juncture will recall the similar scene in Homer's *Iliad XVI*, 65ff, where Achilles, unwilling to go and fight himself (though for a different reason from that of Saul) gives Patroclus permission to go and fight, and dresses him in his (Achilles') armour. The idea is that the enemy, seeing Patroclus in Achilles armour, shall think it is Achilles (lines 40-2), and be scared off [5]. It is different, of course, with Saul and David, but both the similarity and the contrast are instructive. David dressed up in Saul's armour might appear as an *alter* Saul; but that would strike no fear into Goliath's heart, when Saul himself was afraid to fight Goliath. Secondly, before David came on the scene, the reader has already been told (17,4-7) Goliath's height and the tremendous length and weight of his spear. The reader can see, therefore, even while he is watching David put on Saul's armour, that if he goes to fight in it, it will be fatal : before he gets anywhere near the giant, the giant with his superior reach, will run him through. But above all, the reason why Saul's nerve has failed him is, we know, because as a result of his disobedience in the war against Amalek, "the spirit of the Lord has departed from him" (16,14). It will hardly do for David to go out in front of all Israel as their representative to fight the champion as another Saul dressed in Saul's armour and virtually indistinguishable from him. Our suspense, therefore, in seeing David dress in Saul's armour and try it out, is very real; and we are relieved to see David reject it, take it off again, and go to meet Goliath with his shepherd's staff, sling and stones, highly unconventional as these weapons are in heroic single combat.

But if this arming scene recalls the ways of classical heroes, so does what follows. In a duel between two Homeric heroes, the combatants would first approach each other, until they were within earshot. At that point they would both halt and address each other. Hero A would address hero B without interruption, and then hero B would address hero A likewise without interruption. After one or two rounds of this, they would fling a javelin or two at each other, and then, (or alternatively) close in on each other and fight hand to hand. And this is what now happens in our narrative. David approaches the Philistine (17,40) and the Philistine approaches David (17,41). Then they halt and the Philistine harangues David without interruption (17,42-44). Then it is David's turn, and he harangues the Philistine, again without interruption (17,45-47). Then the Philistine rushes at David, and David rushes at him, lets fly with his sling and brings him down (17,48-50).

At least, this is what happens in Version 2; Version 1 has it differently in three respects. First, it lacks 17,41; and the effect is that when David makes his initial move in the direction of Goliath, Goliath does not advance toward him, but stays put. This lack could be original, though it is not self-evidently so. Whether in the end we think it is or not, will depend on factors to which we shall come later. The other two distinguishing features of Version 1, however, are not so innocent : they ruin either the sense, or the thought-flow of the passage, or both. We shall see this more easily if we first follow the narrative in the MT : it is, we remember, concerned with the overall theme of the evaluation of weapons.

4 (b). 17,42-49. When Goliath caught sight of David's appearance he despised him [6] (17,42); when he saw what weapons he was carrying, he was enfuriated : "Am I a dog" he protested, "that you come to me with staves ?" (17,43). The reason for his fury is clear : David's choice of weapons to fight him with is, in Goliath's estimation, an insult to Goliath's status as an hero and champion. Staves were the implements a man might take to chase a dog away : he would not need to use a sword for that humble operation. But to propose to fight an heroic champion with a staff was a dire insult to his status and professional pride : Goliath curses David for the proffered insult (17,43) and promises that he will return the insult by inflicting on David the final indignity that one hero could inflict on another, that is to refuse burial to the fallen hero's body, and allow it to become a prey to bird and beast (17,44). So far Goliath's harangue.

Now it is David's turn to speak (17,45-47), and he immediately takes up the theme of weapons which Goliath has introduced, and explains to Goliath why he does not intend to fight Goliath with the conventional heroic weapons such as Goliath is himself armed with (17,45). David is going to win (17,46); but to match Goliath's sword with another sword, his spear with another spear, would obscure both what the real issue at stake is and the power by which victory is achieved. The issue at stake is not which of the two is the better fighter, or has the better weapons, but rather whether Israel's God whom Goliath has defied is real or not (17,45). God will therefore bring about Goliath's ignominious defeat (17,46). But God will do it in such a way as to make it evident that the battle is won not by David's superior use of sword or spear, but by direct divine intervention : "the battle is the Lord's and he will give you into our hand" (17,47). Thus David answers Goliath's protest at David's humble weapons. David is not using these weapons to insult Goliath; but the very inadequacy of the weapons in and of themselves will make it clear that the "Lord saves not with sword and spear" (17,47). With this the haranguing is over, the battle begun, and Goliath slain.

All this makes excellent sense, but it is Version 2; and we must now consider Version 1's two further special features. Unlike its normal self, Version 1 has two plusses in this paragraph [7]. And they are both ruinous !

In the first place, instead of Version 2's "Am I a dog that you come to me with staves ?" Version 1 has "... with a staff *and stones* ?" The addition is an imperceptive blunder. *Before* David set off to meet Goliath (17,40) he took his staff in his hand, put five stones in his shepherd's scrip, and his sling in his hand. When he came close enough for Goliath to see what weapons he had, Goliath would see the staff : *that* could not be hidden. But he would not see the stones, for they were in David's scrip; and David would certainly not wave the sling in front of Goliath's nose to advertise the fact that he had a sling, and was going to use the sling and not his staff ! The reader knows, of course, that David had sling-stones hidden away in his scrip and intended to use them. But Goliath did not know that; all he could see was the staff; all he expected David to use was the staff; he makes no mention of the sling. It was pedantic enough of Version 1 to change the plural "staves" into the singular "staff" : certainly David had only one staff, but Goliath was thinking of the class of weapon, "staves", not just the individual and particular staff which David was carrying. But it was nothing other than imperceptiveness, and failure to understand the detailed thought-flow of the narrative, that led Version 1 to add "and stones" and so make Goliath complain about stones which he could not see, and did not know were there. It is of the essence of the original story, as it is of David's tactics, that Goliath should concentrate on the staff, and think David is going to use it, and so be utterly taken by surprise when David uses a sling.

Worse is to come. To Version 2's protest by Goliath "Am I a dog that you come to me with staves ?", Version 1 adds a reply by David : "No, but worse than a dog."

The first bad thing to notice about this reply is that it looks uncomfortably like an attempt at a joke. At least, it has the form of a type of joke that is quite frequent in the ancient comedians, particularly in Aristophanes. In this type of joke, the first speaker negatives an idea as being too strong; the second speaker confirms the negative, as if agreeing with the first speaker, but then, to everyone's surprise, it turns out that he is negativing the idea, not as being too strong, but as being too weak. So, for instance, in *Peace* 6-7, Aristophanes has the following sequence :

Slave 1.   (enquiring about the large cake that has just been given to the dung-beetle) Did he eat it up ? (κατέφαγεν — implying, Surely he has not eaten it all up already).

Slave 2   No, by Zeus, he grabbed it out of my hands and gulped it down whole (οὐ μὰ τὸν Δί᾽ ἀλλ᾽ ἐξαρπάσας ὅλην ἐνέχαψε).

So Goliath's indignant question, "Am I a dog ?", implies the negative : I am not a dog, am I ? David appears to agree : "No," and then adds unexpectedly "but worse than a dog".

We cannot, of course, be sure that this was intended as a joke, or even as a smart remark; though if it was, the humour is hardly suited to this tense, heroic occasion. Joke, or no joke, however, it exposes its author as having failed completely to perceive the thought-flow of the context. And this is true whichever of the two possible meanings is given to χείρων. When Goliath protests "Am I a dog ?", he does not mean "Am I an evil, unclean man ?" but "Am I such a petty nuisance that you think a mere staff is enough to beat me with and send me packing ?" Interpret, then, David's reply as meaning "No, but inferior in status to a dog", and all David's subsequent argument is ruined. For now the implication is that Goliath is such an insignificant foe that he could be despatched more easily than a dog.

On the other hand, we can give the author the benefit of the doubt and suppose he meant χείρων in a moral sense. Then we should have to suppose that when Goliath says "Am I a dog = petty nuisance ?", the author has David deliberately play on the double meaning of the word dog and reply "No, (not a dog = an evil, unclean man) but worse than a dog (*scilicet*, a blasphemer against God)". Yet even so we cannot rescue the reply from the charge of being a self-evident interpolation; for it has David interrupting Goliath in the middle of Goliath's harangue, before his own turn to speak has come, and doing so briefly, without explaining the meaning of his remark; and when his own turn to speak does come, he still does not explain what he meant by "worse than a dog". Thus did not heroes !

The conclusion is inevitable : Version 1 has an irredeemably inept addition to the original story.

But we have still not quite completed our survey of the sequence dealing with the evaluation of the weapons. We must come to

4 (c).   17,50-51. For this we return first to Version 2. Having told us in 17,49 that David felled the giant with his sling-stone, Version 2 is going to tell us in 17,51 that David then ran and decapitated Goliath with a sword. But before it tells us this new piece of information it interposes 17,50 : "So David prevailed over the Philistine with a sling and with a stone, and smote the Philistine, and slew him; and there was no sword in his hand". The function, or rather, functions of this verse in the thought-flow are obvious. The theme of David's deliberate choice of weapons and the reason for his refusing to use a sword against Goliath are so important to the thought-flow of the narrative, that Version 2 will not allow the necessity of continuing the story to its end to risk misleading us as to where the true climax lies, and what the theological message of the story is. David has not only felled the giant, but mortally wounded him : the stone has pierced his skull and Goliath will never rise again, not at least to fight. But the story cannot now cease, for the two armies standing at a distance are waiting to see what the outcome of the duel will be. From where they stand they cannot, of course, see whether Goliath has simply stumbled, or has been momentarily stunned, or is in fact mortally wounded. The story must go on to its conclusion. David runs, therefore, cuts off Goliath's head; and the Philistines seeing it (17,51), run for their lives, and the Israelites seeing it chase after them, wounding and killing as many as they can until the Philistines reach the safety of their nearest cities.

But the decapitation of Goliath and the rout of the Philistines are neither the climax, nor the main message, of the story, which is *how and by what means* the giant was overcome; and that was not by the sword which finally cut off Goliath's head, but by the sling and stone. Accordingly, as soon as the thought-flow reaches it climax and the stone mortally wounds Goliath and brings him down, Version 2 marks the climax with its verse 50, and makes explicit the whole point of the evaluation-of-weapons section, 17,38-50. Then the final phrase of 17,50, "and there was no sword in David's hand" neatly serves a double purpose : it sums up the main message of 17,38-50, and at the same time it leads on to the next operation [8], the decapitation of Goliath, by explaining why it was that David had to use Goliath's sword to perform the operation. Once more, then, Version 2 makes excellent sense, which detailed analysis reveals as fitting into the thought-flow perfectly.

It is different with Version 1. It lacks verse 50 entirely. The effect is that without the summary comment of verse 50, the narrative sweeps on unchecked and the decapitation of Goliath and the rout of the Philistines instead of being merely the consequence of the great victory, become the climax of that victory. The effect is unfortunate : for now the thought-flow, which has through many verses been building up the idea that David is not going to defeat Goliath with a sword, climaxes in the observation that, while indeed he brought the giant down with a stone, he actually slew him (17,51 is now the only verse to mention slaying) with a sword.

Of course, in lacking verse 50 Version 1 obviates an apparent difficulty that Version 2 has. In the latter David seems to slay Goliath twice, once in verse 50 and again in verse 51; and every schoolboy knows a man cannot be killed twice. On the other hand schoolboys do not necessarily understand carefully constructed epics with sophisticated thought-flows. The absence of verse 50 from Version 1 looks all too much like a pedantic and ruinous attempt to get rid of an apparent difficulty. But more of that later.

Meanwhile we must consider the final stretch of our narrative. It extends from 17,55 to 18,30; and we will start with the combined edition of this part of the narrative. The section is composed of a series of three paragraphs, all of which end with a similar refrain, commenting on three things : (1) that David constantly went out to do battle for Saul and Israel; (2) that he behaved himself wisely; (3) that he thereby gained great popularity with the people. Thus :

Para. 1. **17,55-18,5.** As we have earlier seen, this paragraph is concerned with the transfer of David from his father, Jesse's household to Saul's household. Jonathan loves David, and Saul sends him on various military forays and appoints him as commander over the men of war. The refrain reads (18,5) "And David went out wherever

Saul sent him; he behaved himself wisely, and Saul set him over the men of war, and it was good in the sight of all the people, and also in the sight of Saul's servants".

Para. 2. **18,5-16.** This paragraph deals with Saul's spasms of suspicion and jealousy. The suspicion was aroused by the song composed and sung by the women who welcomed Saul and David back from the battle (18,6-9). It led to another violent attack on Saul by "the evil spirit from God", and a double attempt by Saul to transfix David to the wall with his spear. David's double escape impressed Saul even more with the fact that God was with David and had departed from Saul. He feared him all the more; but instead of continuing with futile attempts at murdering him, Saul removed him from personal attendance on him both as harpist and commander, relegating him to the position of a captain over a thousand. The refrain reads (18, 14-16) : "And he (David) went out and came in before the people. And David behaved himself wisely in all his ways; and the Lord was with him. And when Saul saw that he behaved himself very wisely, he stood in awe of him. But all Israel and Judah loved David; for he went out and came in before them".

Para. 3. **18,17-30.** This paragraph, as we have earlier seen, deals with the introduction of David into Saul's family through marriage to his daughter, and with Saul's frustrated hope that love for his daughter would induce David to rash attacks on the Philistines and so to his death. The refrain reads (18,30) : "Then the princes of the Philistines went forth : and it came to pass, as often as they went forth, that David behaved himself more wisely than all the servants of Saul; so that his name was much set by".

Obviously, then, here three paragraphs form a series with a common theme : David's ever increasing popularity in spite of all that Saul could do to the contrary. But let us next notice that none of these paragraphs, and none of these refrains, needlessly repeats the other. In Para. 1 Saul with Jonathan's approval and in recognition of David's victory, sets David over the men of war (18,5), i.e. presumably, as commander over the elite troops; and the refrain comments that this met with the approval of two, rather different, groups : "all the people", i.e. the nation at large, and "Saul's servants". The approval of the former group is understandable : the nation at large doubtless idolised David for his victory. That Saul's officers, both civil and military, approved of the appointment of young David to this exalted position, is, however, more noteworthy since they might have been expected to resent it out of jealousy.

The refrain in Para. 2 (18,16) makes a different and additional point. In order to get David out of the court, Saul appoints him (18,13) a captain over a thousand. Compared with what he had been hitherto, "over the men of war" i.e. presumably, captain of the elite corps of troops, this new post may have been a demotion. But whether it was so thought of or not, it obviously brought him much more in contact with the general soldiery as the very next phrase observes : "and he went out and came in before the people". The result was the opposite of what Saul intended. To have him as their own commander widened David's popularity with the army in general and the army's devotion to him increased : "all Israel and Judah loved David, for he went out and came in before them" (18,16).

The third refrain (18,30) makes yet another and distinct point : in the numerous battles in the ongoing war against the Philistines David gained the reputation of being the cleverest commander in all Saul's army : "David behaved himself more wisely than all the servants of Saul, so that his name was much set by". In Para. 1 David owes his appointment as captain of the elite corps to his prowess as a fighter in single combat : now in Para. 3 he excels in the very different role of a regimental commander.

We find, therefore, that the three paragraphs present a picture to the completeness of which all three are necessary. There is no hint of unnecessary repetitiousness that might suggest that an originally shorter account has been filled out by an expansionist addition. And the same is true of the two marriage stories (18,17-29). At first sight it might seem odd that having made two attempts to murder David (18,10-12) Saul should then take the initiative [9] and suggest to David that he marry his daughter Merab. But closer inspection removes this apparent inconcinnity. First, both the assassination attempts and the offer of marriage to Merab come from Version 2. If there is any inconcinnity, it existed already in Version 2 : it is not the accidental result of a clumsy merger of Version 2 with Version 1. Indeed there is no inconcinnity in the combined version *as it now stands* [10]; inconcinnity only arises when one divides the narrative into two separate versions and then takes each version's story separately, since in that case, as we have already noticed (p. 62), the double assassination attempt (18,10-12 = Version 2) would lack adequate explanation (the women's praise of David, 18,6-9, = Version 1) and the promise that whoever killed Goliath would get the king's daughter in marriage (17,25 = Version 2) would remain unfulfilled, since the offer of Merab (18,17-19 = Version 2) is withdrawn and the marriage to Michal comes only in Version 1. But in the combined narrative, the narrative-sequence is perfectly intelligible. Saul, in the hearing of all the army promises his daughter in marriage to any man who kills Goliath. The intervention of the women's song and of Saul's suspicions accounts for the delay in the fulfilment of the promise and for the private attempt to assassinate David. But that attempt having failed, Saul cannot postpone fulfilment of the promise indefinitely without losing face with the people, with whom David's popularity continues to increase. So presently it occurs to him that he could turn the obligation to his own advantage and get rid of David by a much more sophisticated way than murder. He would fulfil the promise, hold out to David the prospect of the marriage, laying down the apparently reasonable requirement "only be valiant for me and fight the Lord's battles (it even sounded pious)" and hoping that David's excess of zeal, sharpened by prospect of royal marriage, might betray him to death at the hands of the Philistines (18,17). The scheme does not, however, work. David not only responds in a self-depreciating way (18,18) − he does that on the second occasion too (18,23) − but he shows no enthusiasm for Merab such as he subsequently shows for Michal (18,26). Saul is therefore once more frustrated, until the rise of Michal's love for David (18,20) allows Saul to withdraw Merab, substitute Michal and thus still fulfil his promise, yet, because of the ardour of the young romance which is now involved, to substitute a much more vigorous and particular, in fact a seemingly suicidal, condition (18,25). In this connection, it is important to notice this difference between the generality and reasonableness of

Saul's request in 18,17, and the particularity, unreasonableness and patently murderous intention of his demand in 18,25. The narrative is progressive, not repetitious. The thought-flow is describing Saul's ever mounting frustration both in his attempt to stop David's ever increasing reputation with the army and the nation at large as we have already seen, and now in his efforts to avoid the necessity of fulfilling his promise and giving David one of his daughters to wife. And when David against all Saul's expectations and calculations succeeds in paying the impossible dowry twice over, the theme of Saul's mounting frustration in these two respects is brought neatly to its climax by two general statements : the first, summing up the marriage concerns of Paragraph 3, comments appropriately on the embarrassment to Saul of Michal's continuing and increased (by the dowry incident) love for David, and of the further evidence provided by the dowry exploit that the Lord was with David (18,28-29); and the second, as we have already seen (p. 71), sums up the message of all three paragraphs (18,30). And so Saul's mounting frustration at his failure to get rid of David by private and devious means leads on naturally to 19,1 where he issues an explicit, official, public command to all his officers that David must be executed.

The combined version, then, shows that it knows how to build up a story of mounting tension and frustration, and to develop a theme by repetition with variation, without falling into repetitiousness. What, then, of Version 1, taken by itself ?

To start with, it lacks the whole of Paragraph 1, 17,55-18,5. The effect is that it has no initial welcome and acceptance of David by Saul after the battle, to act as a foil to the subsequent jealousy and growing hostility. Instead, it proceeds at once from David's success in the battle (17,54) to Saul's suspicion of him (18,6-9) and then, as a consequence of the further lack of 17,10-11, to the immediate removal of David from attendance upon Saul to become a captain of a thousand (18,12-13). The story is unlikely in itself. However jealous of David's success Saul was, initially he must, outwardly at least, have made some display, however insincere, of welcome and acceptance of the great new hero. Moreover, Version 1's lack is textually suspicious. It has at 18,9, καὶ ἦν Σαοὺλ ὑποβλεπόμενος τὸν Δαυειδ ἀπὸ τῆς ἡμέρας ἐκείνης καὶ ἐπέκεινα which is a very apt description of the result of the women' song, viz. angry suspicion. But then it immediately adds (18,12) καὶ ἐφοβήθη Σαοὺλ ἀπὸ προσώπου Δαυείδ, (18,13) καὶ ἀπέστησεν αὐτὸν ἀπ' αὐτοῦ. This gives us two results, suspicion and fear together, which goes against the normal practice both of Version 2 and of Version 1 itself elsewhere : 18,9 suspicion; 18,12 (Version 2) fear; 18,15 awe; 18,29 increase of fear leading to permanent enmity (Version 2), or increase of awe (Version 1). The reason why Version 1 has two results, jealousy and fear, coming one directly after the other at 18,9/12 becomes clear when one looks to see what Version 2 has in this position : between 18,9 and 18,12 Version 2 has Saul's double attempt at murdering David, and it is David's double escape from what Saul thought would have been certain death, that makes Saul aware that the Lord is with David and has deserted Saul, and that, therefore, makes him not only suspicious of David but now in addition afraid of him. It looks very much, therefore, as if Version 1's lack at this point has telescoped its narrative.

At any rate, the absence of Para. 1 from Version 1 means of course the absence of the first refrain (18,5). Version 1 nevertheless has the second refrain (18,14-16) but lacks the third refrain completely (18,30). The progression, therefore, that we found in Version 2 (first refrain : David's appointment as a result of his victory over Goliath, popular with the nation and with Saul's officers; second refrain : all Israel and Judah love David as their own military commander; third refrain : David gains reputation as the cleverest commander in the army) is ruined (or simply non-existent) in Version 1. Version 1's summary of the dowry exploit in Para. 3 (17,28-29) is both shorter and less satisfactory than Version 2's summary. They both begin "And Saul saw and knew (Version 1 omits 'and knew') that the Lord was with David"; but while Version 2 continues "and Michal Saul's daughter loved him", Version 1 continues "and all Israel loved him". But this is inept. Para. 3 has been talking of Michal's love for David, not Israel's, and how Saul tried to use it to get David to undertake a suicide mission, and how David to Saul's embarrassment succeeded, and thus obliged Saul to give him Michal. And now the crowning embarrassment for Saul is that Michal loves David all the more for the courageous exploit he has performed in order to get her; and this love of Michal for David will later (19,11-17) prove ruinous to another of Saul's murderous schemes. To introduce Israel's love for David as the summary of Para. 3 shows Version 1 again as imperceptive of the thought-flow. Similarly, the conclusion of the summary in Version 2 : "And Saul was yet the more afraid of David, and Saul was David's enemy continually" : presents a logical progression. Saul's dowry-ruse has had the opposite result from what he intended, having led to a spectacular feat of arms on David's part, and having made Michal more in love with him than ever. Saul is understandably yet more afraid of David; and the increased fear leads to permanent hostility. Version 1's conclusion of the summary has simply "And Saul was still more wary of David". Its brevity is a mark of poverty more than of grace.

Moreover, in lacking two out of the three refrains not only does Version 1 show itself imperceptive of the narrative progression, but, lacking the initial acceptance — scene (17,55-18,5), the two mad but unsuccessful murder attempts (18,10-11) and the abortive offer of marriage to Merab (18,17-19), Version 1 scarce has any narrative-progression worth talking of.

Now let us sum up our findings so far :

In Section I we observed that certain features which, superficially understood, are commonly cited as evidence that Version 2 is discrepant with Version 1, do not in fact evince discrepancy at all. In themselves they give no ground for thinking that there were originally two versions, let alone that those versions were mutually discrepant.

In Section II we studied the major components of Version 2. We found that these portions of narrative dealt with a common theme, and showed evidence of forming a narrative-progression; but that to bring out their full significance they needed to be placed in the context of a story strangely like the story as found in Version 1. Indeed, without the context of that story, Version 2's story would in the end be inexplicable.

In Section III we have been looking at the combined (Version 1 plus Version 2) story, i.e. the story as it now stands in the MT, and trying to trace its thought-flow. Our idea was that if Version 1's original thought-flow had been infiltrated by later, ill-adapted, elements from another version, those elements would show up as disturbances within an otherwise smooth-flowing narrative-sequence. We have discovered no such disturbances. On the contrary, we have found that the combined version as it stands is a highly-wrought, sophisticated, narrative-sequence, that everywhere makes excellent sense. The only unsatisfactory features we have found have been features peculiar to Version 1.

IV.

We must now make some attempt to interpret these observations. In this section we shall do so from the point of view of literary history. In a final section we must briefly attempt the same thing from the point of view of textual history.

The question of literary history is : How have these two versions, the shorter and the longer, come to be ? Having so much in common they cannot be unrelated. Is then Version 1 an earlier version of the David-Goliath story, into which some later interpolator has inserted elements from some other version, so producing the MT ? Is the brevity and thinness of Version 1 a mark of primitiveness, even perhaps of classical restraint and good taste — compared with which the insertions from Version 2 stand out as a later and better stage in the evolution of the story, or alternatively as expansionism and bad taste ? Is the consistency of Version 1 a sign of the unifying mind of the original author, and the apparent inconsistencies introduced by Version 2 the tell-tale mark of an inept interpolator ? Or does the brevity of Version 1 show it to be a truncated version of the original story ? Is its consistency the result of a pedantic correction of the apparent inconsistencies of the combined version ? Is its thinness an impoverishment of the original story ?

If the observations of III above are at all, or for the most part, sound, they must already have inclined us towards the second alternative. In so saying, I am basing myself on the same axiom as that adopted by the (completely opposite) majority view, namely the assumption that the original version of a story makes sense, and thus later alterations can be detected because they disturb the original thought-flow and mar the sense. Time and time again we have found that the combined version presents a thought-flow that makes excellent, detailed, well-constructed, sustained sense, in comparison with which Version 1 is inferior; while its two additions are ruinous to the thought-flow. It is not likely that the combined version's richer and beautifully constructed narrative is the result of interpolations.

But if the combined version is to be regarded as the original form of the narrative, we are faced with the question why Version 1 has so many "omissions". Two observations are relevant to the question : (1) there is in our three chapters and their immediate context a whole series of apparent doublets in the combined version of which Version 1 consistently lacks one member; (2) in some instances the lack of one member of the doublet obviates an apparent difficulty.

1. *17,41*   *And the Philistine came on and drew near to David; and the man*
             that bare the shield went before him.

   17,48   *And it came to pass, when the Philistine arose, and came and drew near*
             to meet David, that David hastened and ran toward the army to meet
             the Philistine.

Version 1 lacks 17,41, and so avoids an apparent doublet. But, as we have seen above
(p. 67), these two verses are not in fact doublets at all, for 17,41 does not duplicate
the information given in 17,48. Along with 17,40 ("... and he (David) drew near to
the Philistine") 17,41 describes the initial approach of the two heroes towards each
other before they halt to interchange harangues; 17,48 describes the closing in on each
other for the actual combat. Even if 17,41 is an addition in Version 2, it is not a
doublet. But to be fair to Version 1, we must at this point notice a feature which we
have so far neglected : Version 1 lacks not only 17,41 but part of 17,48 as well, and
has the rest of 17,48 differently phrased into the bargain. Its actual description of the
heroes's approach to each other is :

   17,40   "And he (David) drew near to the Philistine"
   17,48   "And the Philistine arose and went to meet David".

This implies that when David initially advanced towards Goliath, Goliath stayed put
[11], and that similarly when Goliath eventually closed in on David, David stayed
put, and simply used his sling from a standing position against the oncoming giant.
In itself this neater version makes sense. Perhaps it is original. But against it so being
stands the fact that by its simpler phrasing and its twin omissions it obviates an apparent difficulty. When Version 2 says in 17,48 "And it came to pass that when the Philistine arose and came and drew near to meet David...", it might at the first reading
seem to be referring back to the giant's approach in 17,41 — at least, it might so seem
to someone who did not perceive the flow of the narrative too well; and in that case
Version 2 would appear to contradict itself. Its verses 41ff. would say that on the Philistine's approach he harangued David and David harangued him, whereas its verse 48
would say that on the Philistine's approach David hastened, ran and felled him with a
sling-stone. The solution of this difficulty would be simple : remove from 17,41 the
approach of the giant altogether and simplify the statement of his approach in 17,48;
then 17,48 will not appear to refer to 17,41; and remove David's approach to the
giant from 17,48, and it will not then be confused with his approach in 17,40. If this
then were a true account of the genesis of Version 1 here, Version 1 would be secondary. Version 1 has in fact elsewhere already (p. 69) given evidence of not perceiving
the true narrative-flow; but let us on this occasion reserve our decision for the time
being.

2. *17,50*   *"So David prevailed over the Philistine with a sling and with a stone,*
             and smote the Philistine, and slew him; and there was no sword in
             David's hand."

   17,51   *"And David ran and stood over the Philistine and took his sword, and*
             drew it out of its sheath, and slew him and cut off his head." (Version
             1 omits "and drew it out of its sheath")

Again Version 1 lacks the first member of the pair, and we have already considered (p. 70) what a disastrous shifting of the climax of the story this lack produces. But here let us consider the nature of the difficulty that is obviated by this lack in Version 1. Version 2 has David apparently slay Goliath twice; once in verse 50 with a stone, and once in verse 51 with a sword. Now a man certainly cannot be killed, and then when dead, be killed all over again; and if Version 2 implies Goliath was so treated, Version 2 must stand convicted of the most incompetent bungling, while Version 1's lack is nothing but virgin innocence. But Version 2 does not necessarily imply anything of the sort. A man may deliver his foe a mortal wound from which he would never recover even if he received no further wound : and in that sense the man may rightly be said to have killed his foe. But then if as the foe lies dying the man despatches him with a second mortal wound, this second act could also rightly be described as killing the foe. And this is all Version 2 means; there is no real discrepancy between its verses 50 and 51. On the other hand a pedantic interpretation might well assume a discrepancy and attempt to remove it. And that is what Version 1 seems to have done — at what cost we have already seen.

3. *18,10-11 Saul twice tries to transfix David to the wall with his spear and David twice escapes.*

   19,8-10 Saul attempts to transfix David to the wall with his spear and David escapes.

Yet again Version 1 lacks the first member of the pair, and we have already seen (p. 72) the unsatisfactory state in which it leaves the narrative by this lack. Nor is Version 1 self-evidently better as a story or truer to life in having only one attempt. In fact by this criterion Version 2 is much more true to life. It is a very common thing with mentally disturbed people of homicidal or suicidal tendencies, that after the first incident they will repent and promise improvement, and then when circumstances repeat themselves they will attempt to commit the same violent deed again. So here. The circumstances on both occasions were very similar : David had just won a resounding victory over the Philistines (18,6-9 and 19,8) : Saul, in consequence, had just had one of his "attacks" (18,10 and 19,9); and David was trying to soothe him by playing (18,10 and 19,9). After the first occasion, according to Version 2, Saul had removed David from him (18,13), that is David ceased to be a courtier in personal attendance upon Saul. Obviously, when the official order went out for his execution (19,1) David was not at court. But when Jonathan reasoned with his father, Saul relented and professed he would not kill David. And so "Jonathan brought David to Saul and he was in his presence as beforetime" (19,7), and David had resumed his office as harpist which had been interrupted so rudely on the first occasion. And then it happened all over again. This is not only a true to life feature; it was apparently a recurring feature in Saul's illness : chapter 24 records Saul's attempt to find and destroy David, and then his professed repentance; but there presently follows in chapter 26 another almost identical attempt on David's life.

Version 1's lack, then, can scarcely claim to present a self-evidently better narrative; but it could easily be the result of a dislike of apparent doublets.

4.   *18,17-19 Saul offers his daughter Merab to David to wife, then gives her to
     someone else.*
     18,20-29 Saul gives his daughter Michal to David to wife.

Once more Version 1 omits the first member of the pair; but we have already shown
(see above p. 72f) that these two incidents are not doublets : they differ significantly,
and fit superbly well into a very carefully constructed narrative-sequence in Version 2.
There is no obvious reason for preferring Version 1's paler and thinner story. Its lack
is much more likely to result from its typical dislike of apparent doublets.

5.   *18,1-4   Jonathan loves David as his own soul and expresses it by gifts and a
     covenant.*
     20,16-17 Jonathan loves David as his own soul and expresses it in an oath.

Yet once again Version 1 lacks the first member of the pair. Its lack seems to be bound
up with its lack of the immediately preceding verses, 17,55-58, and is part of its complete lack of any favourable "reception-scene" after David's victory over Goliath.
On the general unsatisfactoriness of the absence of such a scene from Version 1
we have already spoken (p. 73) and must presently speak again. For the moment we
should notice that in Version 2, Jonathan's love for David expressed in 18,1-4, is the
first member of a progression (see next 19,1-7; 20,1-42) which climaxes in Jonathan's
championing of David before Saul and in Saul's declaration : "... do I not know that
you have chosen the son of Jesse to your own shame ... as long as the son of Jesse
lives ... you will not be established, nor your kingdom (20,30-31)". This matter is, of
course, supremely important to the major theme of 1 Samuel : the eclipse of the
house of Saul by the house of Jesse. Jonathan the crown-prince's love for, and preser-
vation of, David, would, as Saul shrewdly saw, spell the eventual demise of the dynasty
of Saul. Therefore the point at which the narrative will place the rise of this love for
David on the part of Jonathan is exceedingly significant in the development of the
book as a whole.

According to Version 2, the very moment David returned from the field with
the head of Goliath in his hand (17,58), Jonathan was there, along with Saul, to welcome him (18,1-3); and so filled was Jonathan with admiration for David as a single-
combat warrior that he gave him his own royal warrior's weapons in recognition of
his excellence, and made a covenant with him. And this is very natural. [A classicist
will think of the exchange of armour and the making of a pledge by the warriors
Diomedes and Glaucus in Homer, *Iliad VI* 212-236 and of the gifts of armour
between Ajax and Hector in *Iliad VII* 303-305.] The earlier chapter, 14, has shown
that Jonathan, as a single-handed warrior, was far superior to his father. By the time
Goliath challenged Israel, Jonathan was Israel's chief hero; and when David did, what
even Jonathan was afraid to do, it is only to be expected that Jonathan would be the
very first, after the king, to welcome him, and to acknowledge his prowess by giving
him a set of hero's armour, his own in fact. This gesture eventually proved more significant than Jonathan realised at the time; but Version 2 is surely right in beginning
the progression of the Jonathan-David theme at this point.

Compared with this Version 1 is incredible. According to it Jonathan, Israel's
leading single-combat warrior, might as well not have existed. When David returns

from killing Goliath, Jonathan is not there to meet him; nor is any reaction from Jonathan heard of throughout the whole of chapter 18. All Israel and Judah love David (18,16), but what Jonathan felt we are not told. Saul was suspicious of David, and removed him to be a captain over a thousand; but still nothing about Jonathan. Even Saul's daughter Michal is reported as falling in love with David, and marrying him, before anything is heard of Jonathan's reaction (18,20). And when at last Jonathan's delight in David is mentioned (19,2), it is mentioned almost casually, by way of explaining why Jonathan warned David of the execution order. One can only repeat that after the build-up of Jonathan as Israel's finest hero in chapter 14, Version 1's complete lack in the immediate post-combat scene in chapter 18 of any reaction on Jonathan's part to David's stunning victory is, if original, incomprehensible both as history and as epic. But it surely is not original. Version 1's typical dislike of doublets has doubtless been at work here too; but perhaps other factors have been involved, and to their consideration we must now turn.

In the first place we notice that the "welcome-scene" (18,1-5) is introduced by the famous (or notorious) verses, 17,55-58 in which Saul enquires who David's father is, so apparently contradicting 16,18-22 which represent Saul as knowing full well who David's father is. 17,55-58 moreover are inseparably connected with the "welcome-scene", because 18,1 explicitly makes the point that it was while David stood there with the head of the giant in his hand, answering Saul's questions about his father, that "the soul of Jonathan was knit with the soul of David". If, therefore, 17,55-58 were felt to be discrepant with 16,18-22 by some ancient editor (as they are by most modern commentators) and on that score removed, they would be almost bound to take 18,1-5 with them.

For that reason we must turn aside here to consider this alleged discrepancy which has convinced so many scholars that 17,55-58 are a secondary interpolation. This discrepancy depends on the insistence that 16,18-22 must mean nothing less than that Saul informed himself fully on everything to do with David's father, and on a similar insistence that 17,55-58 must not mean anything more than that Saul was interested to know the *name* of David's father. Neither insistence is necessary, nor, in the light of the narrative thought-flow, reasonable. Having been supplied by his servants with an acceptable harpist, it was natural for Saul to "request" (i.e. command) his father to let the young man stay at the royal house. It is not true to life to imagine that that means that Saul sent the message directly himself — he would have left that to one of the officers who had found and suggested David. It is not even true to life to imagine that Saul thereafter necessarily remembered the name of David's father, or cared twopence about him, let alone investigated his background, family and all about him. Similarly, it is not true to life to imagine that in 17,55-58 Saul is simply concerned to know the name of David's father. Saul has just promised to give his daughter in marriage to the man who kills Goliath, and to make his father's house free in Israel (17,25). Naturally, when Saul sees David actually going out to meet Goliath, and even more so when he sees him returning triumphant, Saul will be concerned to know not just the name of, but everything about, David's father and the family which, if he keeps his promise, is now to be allied by marriage to the royal family. And we as readers must at this point be made aware that David is of the house of Jesse, for it is the house of Jesse that has at this moment eclipsed the house of Saul in military prowess, and is destined eventually to supplant it as the reigning house.

The discrepancy then is far from irreconcilable, and when we consider the last-mentioned literary considerations that made necessary at 17,55-18,6 a heavy emphasis on the fact that David was the son of Jesse (see also p. 60), we cannot allow that the apparent discrepancy proves 17,55-58 a secondary interpolation. But if modern scholars hold 17,55-58 to be an irreconcilable discrepancy, so may an ancient editor, and he may have removed the whole section 17,55-18,5 in consequence.

But there are more pressing reasons why an ancient editor may have removed this section. To understand them we start with another apparent doublet :

17,57 And as David returned from the slaughter of the Philistine...

18,6 And it came to pass as they came, when David returned from the slaughter of the Philistine...

The point here is that these almost (but not completely) identical time notes introduce very different, and at first sight incompatible, incidents. The first time-note says that on David's return from the slaughter of the Philistine Jonathan fell into deep admiration for David, Saul would not let him go home any more but took him into the royal house, Jonathan gave him his armour and made a pledge with him, and Saul set him over the elite corps of soldiers. The second time-note says that when David returned from the slaughter of the Philistine, the women sang a song that enfuriated Saul (18,8) and made Saul suspicious of David from that day onwards.

Version 1 has apparently felt that these two reactions on Saul's part to David's victory are so incompatible that they could not possibly have both happened at the same time. It has, therefore, removed the whole of 17,55-18,5, and since this excision brought the dancing-women episode to stand immediately after David's victory (17, 54) there was no need for the introductory time-note in 18,6; it excised that as well. But it excised more, for the same reason. Version 2 says that the day after (18,10) the women sang the song that caused Saul such anger and suspicion, David was playing to Saul in the palace when Saul tried to murder him (18,10-11) and having failed, removed him from him. Version 1 will have none of that, and its sequence shows why : "And Saul was suspicious of David from that day onwards, and Saul was afraid of David and removed him from him", that is to say, Version 1 feels that if Saul was suspicious of David, he could not have taken David into the palace, let alone have him play to him; he must remove him from his presence at once.

Now this results in the most unlikely story as we have already remarked, that David should not only get no welcome from Saul and Jonathan after the battle, but should instead be almost at once removed from the royal presence; and it springs from a pedantic attitude to the two time-notes, a false sense of psychology, and a failure to understand the narrative technique of 1 Samuel.

The fact that both incidents are described as taking place "as David returned from the slaughter of the Philistine" does not imply that they happened at the same hour. The first happened immediately after the victory, on the battlefield, just outside the royal tent. David still had the giant's head in his hand, and Jonathan being still armed, naturally strips himself of his armour and gives it to David. The second incident, though still happening as David returned from the slaughter of the Philistine, would not have happened until hours, or maybe days, afterwards.

Secondly, it would be simplistic psychology to imagine that when the women's song provoked Saul's resentment and suspicion, Saul could not have proceeded with his earlier decision to keep David at the palace, but must have immediately removed him from the royal presence. Version 2 is much truer to life in relating that though suspicion was sown in Saul's mind by the song, it did not break out into open hostility until later [12].

Thirdly, there is another apparent time-table difficulty. Version 2's apparent succession of events is : at the return from the victory Saul appoints David to the command of the men of war, and David fulfils all the commissions Saul gives him wisely (18,5); at the return the women sing and Saul grows suspicious of David : next day he tries to murder him (18,11); failing, he grows afraid of David (18,12) and removes him from him, and appoints him captain over a thousand (18,13).

Now, if this succession is intended in strict chronological order, with each item happening immediately after the other, then certainly Version 2 has blundered appallingly. To see how appallingly, let us be pedantic ourselves for a moment. On his return from the slaughter of the giant David is appointed commander of the men of war and goes on several successful errands; at the same time, on his return from the slaughter, the women sing and Saul becomes suspicious. The very next day Saul tries to murder David, fails, and becoming afraid immediately sends him away to become a captain of a thousand. How then would David have gone on errands as commander of the men of war, and gained great popularity thereby, as 18,6 says, if the very next day after being appointed commander he was in fact exiled from the palace and given a different post as captain of a thousand as 18,10-13 says ?

But to suppose that Version 2 has constructed its narrative after such a pedantic sense of time-table is to miss an important feature of its narrative technique. To illustrate that technique let us cite an analogous case from a much later author. In chapter 3 of his Gospel Luke the Evangelist describes the ministry of John the Baptist, beginning with its inception in verses 1-2 and ending with its close when John is imprisoned in verse 20. And then in verse 21 Luke proceeds to tell of the baptism of Jesus. Now we know from the other Evangelists (1) that John in fact baptised Jesus *before* John was imprisoned, and (2) that John was not imprisoned until some considerable time *after* the baptism of Jesus. It would be absurdly pedantic to demand that, because Luke has John imprisoned in verse 20, and only begins to mention Jesus' baptism in verse 21, Luke means to tell us that Jesus' baptism happened after John's imprisonment and that John did not baptise Jesus. The fact is that Luke's narrative is not strictly chronological, and was not intended to be. By a narrative device, very common in all ages, Luke has decided first to deal with John's ministry from beginning to end in one sweep, concentrating attention on the manner and content of John's preaching, the people's reaction to it and finally Herod's reaction to it. That done, Luke with his next verse goes back in time, without saying so, to describe an incident, Jesus' baptism, which in fact took place before John's imprisonment; and he does it this way because in his train of thought the baptism of Jesus is linked not so much with John the Baptist as with other things.

And so with Version 2's account of what happened "as David came from the slaughter of the giant". The first narrative-succession says he was immediately welcomed by Saul and Jonathan on the battlefield. And then it carries on that theme and relates how he was subsequently appointed commander of the men of war and went out on sundry successful errands for Saul and became very popular as a result. And so this narrative-succession follows its theme to its proper climax which it marks with the first "refrain" (18,5).

Then the narrative back-tracks, not all the way to the point of Saul and Jonathan's welcome on the battlefield, but to a somewhat later point when Saul and David were returning home and were welcomed by the singing women. Though Saul at once becomes angry and suspicious, he carries on with his intention of taking David into the palace. But the next day he tries to murder him. Failing, he becomes afraid of David; and then he removes him and makes him a captain of a thousand. But again, the fact that verse 11 reports the failed murder attempt, verse 12 Saul's fear, and verse 13 the removal of David to the different post, is not necessarily meant to imply that the removal happened the very next hour, day, week or month after the murder attempt. Version 2 is simply continuing with the anger-suspicion-succession in the narrative and describing what it eventually led to. In strict chronology there may well have been a considerable time between the failed murder attempt and Saul's eventual decision to remove David from the palace, during which interval David would have gone on his forays as commander of the elite men of war. But this narrative-succession is no longer interested in that interval; rather it pursues its own interest (see p. 71 above) until it too arrives at its own climax which it marks with a "refrain" (18,16).

That done, it turns itself to another narrative-succession, concerned with the reward of David after his victory over the giant, namely the marriage-to-the-king's-daughter-succession (18,17). At what exact chronological point after David's return from the slaughter of the giant, these marriage proposals began to be made, we are not told, nor is any attempt made to relate them chronologically to the detailed events of the first two narrative-successions. Version 2 is not interested in such matters of time-table. This is its third picture of the different reactions to David's victory : like the other two it is told as a self-contained unit, leading up to its own conclusion (18,28-29) and then followed by a general refrain (18,30) which indicates that it too belongs to, and now completes, the series of three sketches which describe the results and repercussions of David's victory.

Now Version 1's narrative sequence is far more simple and chronologically straightforward than this; but the simplicity is not a sign of originality; rather is it an indication that Version 1 has failed to appreciate the more sophisticated narrative-technique of Version 2, and, seeking to correct Version 2, has reduced it to its own simplistic and impoverished story.

In general, therefore, we conclude that Version 1 is not some earlier independent version which has subsequently been interpolated by an inept reviser. The combined version is the original version, which someone with a very literalistic, unimaginative mind has truncated, thinking thereby to improve it by removing doublets and discrepancies. It may not be without significance that a pedantic sense of time-tabling has contributed to the truncation.

V.

The final question is one of textual criticism : at what point in the transmission of the original story did the truncation take place ? On this question I do not feel at all certain, and I would in fact like more time than I have recently had at my disposal, in order to investigate the textual question in its wider contexts. For the moment I reserve my opinion.

Nevertheless I feel it important that we should recognise all the theoretical possibilities. The truncation could have happened :

(i)   at the level of the transmission of the Hebrew text;

(ii)   at the level of the translators into Greek;

(iii)   at the level of some reviser of the Greek.

As for (i), ps.-Aristeas (Section 30) is witness, if we need one, that in his day there were carelessly edited Hebrew texts in circulation. And we should not forget what Zuntz pointed out long ago, namely that the verb σημαίνω which ps.-Aristeas uses is also used by Aristobulus to describe his re-writing of Aratus' poem in which he deliberately changes what Aratus originally wrote in order to make the poem say what Aristobulus thought Aratus meant — or ought to have meant.

As for (ii) I take ET's point (*TCUS* p. 52) that if a book is in general translated literally, it makes it less likely that the translator omitted large sections which were found in his Vorlage. But I do not think that this should be exalted into an absolute rule. Just as you cannot say that a translator who 95 o/o of the time translates faithfully will never indulge in a Targumic paraphrase which completely changes the sense of a passage which he finds unacceptable — the translator of, say, Exodus, does precisely that; so you cannot, it seems to me argue, that a translator who translates fully all he finds acceptable will never omit passages that he finds unacceptable or unintelligible.

There is, of course, evidence that the translator did not perceive some of the finer details of the story. At 17,6 he took כידון to be a shield, perhaps because it is said to be between Goliath's shoulders, and because Goliath's spear is mentioned in the next verse. כידון is, of course, a dart, and this detail, that a single-combat hero would have both a spear and a dart, is true to the mode of ancient warfare. But having mistaken כידון for a shield in verse 6, when he comes to the real shield (the big full length צנה, which, again true to life, the Hebrew says the hero's squire carried for him) in verse 7, he simply paraphrases it vaguely as τὰ ὅπλα. Repeating the mistake in 17,45 he spoils the sense, though doubtless unwittingly : mention of a defensive weapon is out of place in a list of offensive weapons by means of which Goliath hopes to kill David.

This shows the translator ignorant of the exact meaning of technical terms, and imperceptive of the finer details of the thought-flow : but this is not the same thing as showing that he would have deliberately omitted passages. Certainly, as we have shown above, the person who made the additions in 17,43 was disastrously imperceptive of the narrative thought-flow; but again that does not prove that he was the same person as the translator.

As for (iii) ps-Aristeas says that when the translation of the Law was finished, curses were pronounced on any who should revise the text by adding or transposing, or excising anything (Section 311). This certainly shows that ps-Aristeas regarded it as all too possible that people might revise the *Greek* by addition, omission and change of order. He may even have known of editions that had in fact suffered these things. Not all revisions of the Greek were aimed at bringing the Greek closer into line with the Hebrew of the proto-MT. The person responsible for the editorial remarks at 1 Kings 2,35e and 2,35k knew of the order which we now have in the MT and disapproved of it. At any rate, believing, as I do, that a pedantic sense of time-tabling lies behind some of the peculiarities of order in the Greek of 1 Kings, I am naturally suspicious that a similar pedantic sense of time-tabling, which seems to have contributed to the truncation evident in Version 1, may have arisen in the same quarter. But, as I say, for the moment I reserve my opinion.

————————————

And now I apologise for the length of this paper and for its discursiveness. But the time necessary to make it more concise would have delayed it even further; and I have already delayed it for an unconscionably long time. I thank you all for your great patience.

NOTES

1   In the course of producing this working paper I have profited greatly from lengthy discussions with my colleagues, Dr. M.J. Alden of the Greek Department and Mr. D.F. Payne of the Semitics Department, of The Queen's University of Belfast. I thank them both.

2   The famous Irish single-combat hero, Cúchulainn, was a beardless youth; on first encountering him older heroes felt it an insult to their skill and status to be asked to fight him. See T. Kinsella, The Tain, Oxford University Press, 1970, pp. 119, 127. I owe this reference to Dr. Alden.

3   My readers at this stage will be conversant with the scholarly literature on the literary criticism of these chapters and will readily perceive where I differ from the majority view. I shall, therefore, refrain, at this stage, from burdening this working paper with detailed references to the scholarly literature.

4   There are, of course, translational and, possibly, textual difficulties in this verse; but they do not materially affect the argument at this point.

5   I owe this observation to Dr. Alden.

6   As Etarcomol does Cúchulainn, The Tain, p. 119. Similarly, "Cúr went forth, but he drew back when he saw a beardless boy opposing him. 'This is unfitting' he said. 'You pay my skill a great compliment ! If I knew this was the one I had to meet, I would never have come. I'll send him a boy of his own age from among my people.'" ibid. p. 127.

7   Strictly speaking according to ET's definition of Version 1 (Version 1 = LXX & MT, Version 2 = MT alone) these two plusses are not Version 1, since they are not shared by the MT. What then are they ? They are deliberate enough, the second particularly so. Are we to regard them as deliberate alterations of Version 1 ? Or must we speak of a Version 3 ? Actually ET's definition does not mean to imply that the LXX got Version 1 from the MT; it got it from some other Hebrew text. That other text might well have had these plusses — indeed, if ET is correct in claiming that the LXX translators were faithful to their Vorlage, that other text which was the LXX's source of Version 1 did have these plusses. For that reason, therefore, I attribute these plusses to Version 1.

8   I owe this second observation to Mr. Payne.

9   It is to be noted that Michal fell in love with David, and that only when Saul had been told of it (18,20) did he grasp the opportunity with which this budding romance presented him, and suggest her marriage to David. There is no suggestion that Merab fell in love with David. In her case Saul took the initiative, prompted solely by the promise made before the battle (17,25).

10   I refer here simply to the marriage stories and their immediate context.

11 Subsequent rabbis had their own reasons for maintaining that Goliath was in fact unable to advance towards David. A propos of 17,44, "R. Abba b. Kahana said : The earth held him fast. R. Tanhuma remarked : I will state the reason. It does not say, 'And I will come to thee', but 'Come to me', teaching you that the earth held him fast" (Midrash Rabbah, Leviticus, XXI.2. transl. by J.J. Slotki, Soncino Press, 1951).

12 Classicists will recall how differences between Alexander and his foster brother Clitus which had been rankling in the latter's mind for some time, eventually erupted at a dinner-party when both men were drunk and led to Alexander's running through Clitus with his spear.

SECOND THOUGHTS ON DAVID AND GOLIATH

A comparison of the four papers on the differences between the LXX and the MT in 1 Sam 17-18, written respectively by DB, DG, ET and myself, is most challenging. Our approaches to the problems and the proposed solutions are to a large extent divergent. It seems to me that further discussion among the four authors will not lead to an agreement in as far as the solutions are concerned. On the other hand, some additional thoughts on the methods used in the analysis of the problem might be appropriate. In this short paper, these methodological comments will be followed by a few remarks on particular details in 1 Sam 17-18.

I. METHODS

On the level of methodology, some agreement seems to exist : in the discussion of the model case concerning the differences between the LXX and the MT in 1 Sam 17-18, textual criticism should be complemented with literary criticism. Neither method in question can be strictly separated from the other. In the literary critical approach a historical investigation concerning the origins and the growth of the text should be included. Thus far, everybody appears to agree. A first point of discord can be found in the sequence in which the different methods are applied. DB and DG begin with some sort of literary criticism, whereas ET and I start with textual criticism.

A. Textual criticism

A close reading of the four papers strengthened my conviction that the data and questions of textual criticism should be handled first. To a certain extent, they present facts, providing a sound basis for further more hypothetical theories. The differences between the Hebrew and the Greek texts should be noted carefully, including both pluses and minuses (cf. ET). The witnesses should be taken seriously, not overlooking the evidence from Qumran and from patrological sources such as Hippolytus. Once these data are listed and checked, one should ask whether the difference between the Greek and the Hebrew texts are intentional or unintentional and whether they are due to a scribe, an editor or a translator. It is not to be taken for granted that all of the differences are due to one and the same cause. In order to define the responsibilities of the translator, attention should be paid to the degree of literalness of his translation. The text value of so-called Hebraisms in the pluses of the Greek text should not be overestimated, however tempting this may be. Indeed, it is not always easy to make a sharp distinction between Hebraisms on the one hand and idioms proper to the style and language of the translator on the other. Moreover, when a translator added his remarks, he often took his inspiration from the context, so that his own Greek could hardly be distinguished from his translation-Greek. An example can be found in verse 36. The longer Greek plus is stuffed with Hebraisms. However, this does not prove that the translator simply followed his Hebrew Vorlage. Theoretically at least, he might have been inspired by verse 26, where similar expressions occur.

When no priority is given to textual criticism, the hypothetical character of the discussion is likely to be too obvious from the outset. This might be the case in the paper of DB which from the beginning distinguishes between three stories in 1 Sam 16-18. The approach of DG might seem less hypothetical. He reads the final text presented by the MT as a self-contained unit. He considers it a beautiful narrative with a good plot. Though this approach may be interesting, one wonders whether it is appropriate when attempting to explore the difference between the MT and the LXX. When, for the sake of argument, he supposes that at one stage there were two independent versions, he forgets to take into consideration that the final editor may have adapted the stories. The editor's effort might explain some repetitions as well as some similarity in style and expressions.

B. Literary criticism

The textcritical study soon reveals that the differences between the Hebrew and the Greek texts can hardly be attributed solely to a copyist. If copyist it be, then this copyist must also have been acting as an editor, reworking the text and not purely transcribing it. A similar reasoning applies to the translator. When one accuses him of having shortened the text, then one considers him not merely a translator but an editor as well. In both cases we are entering the realm of literary criticism and more specifically the realm of the history of the redaction. When the editorial activity was due to the translator, then it probably should be characterized as an attempt towards harmonization with the context. When it was due to a copyist of the Hebrew text, then it most likely implied a combination of two originally independent stories, or a reworking and a framing of one older independent narrative.

Unambiguous traces of editorial activity are not always easy to be found. The editor was not necessarily pedantic, or stupid, or both. He may have done a good job and produced a hight quality final product. When the longer Hebrew text proves to be a nice piece of literature, to be preferred over the Greek text, it does not necessarily follow that it preserved the more original version. On the other hand, when one prefers the shorter Greek text over the Hebrew with its many tensions and alledged contradictions, one should not hastily conclude that the Greek version is the more original one. Contradictions, tensions and doublets are sometimes less obvious than they are thought to be often. Moreover, tensions and doublets may be part of an original, fine literary composition, and contradictions may be original ingredients of a less refined literary product. On the other hand, the occurrence of expressions or even sentences in several parts of a text does not necessarily prove the original unity of the narrative. The final editor may have used and reused these terms and turnings in order to produce a better unity between several originally independent sections.

II. PARTICULAR DETAILS

After these rather general remarks on methods and methodology, we come to some particular problems proper to the present case. We have to single out a couple of them since it is impossible here to react to all the arguments brought to the fore by the other authors. We will first deal with the passages on Merab and Michal in 1 Sam 18,17-19 and 20-27 and second, with the introductory verse in 17,12.

One of the reasons why I pay special attention to the stories of Merab and Michal here is that I neglected them in my first paper where I confined myself inasmuch as possible to the battle of David and Goliath in 1 Sam 17,1-18,5. In his paper, ET merely remarks that in both versions (18,17-19 and 18,20-27) Saul offers David one of his daughters without giving any cross reference (p. 41). According to him, this juxtaposition creates serious problems (p. 42). The views of DB and of DG are more detailed and more unusual. According to DB, the notice about Merab in 18,17-19 collides with 2 Sam 21,8 (p. 52). The LXX omitted the section in order to avoid the contradiction. DG on the other hand, insists on the perfect harmony of the MT (p. 72-73, 78). According to him, him, the narrative in 1 Sam 18,17-27 is progressive and not repetitious (p. 73). One wonders how he solves the problem brought up by DB. Does 2 Sam 21,8 fit the harmonious presentation of the MT ? Other objections and questions may disturb his views. Are the sections on Merab and Michal still part of the story (stories) on David and Goliath ? Contrary to DG's opinion, they have not connection with Saul's promises in 17,25 : "The king will enrich (him) with great riches, and will give him his daughter, and make his father's house free in Israel". When one wishes to connect the gift of Saul's daughter with the promise in question, then one should be able to show how the other aspects of the promise were kept. However, this may be difficult. Nothing is said about the riches bestowed on David nor about the freedom given to his father's house. Moreover, the story does not present the stories of Saul's daughters as a fulfillment of the promise but rather as a part of Saul's plan to remove David.

I agree with DG in saying that the two episodes on Merab and Michal respectively can be seen as successive steps in Saul's plan. However, this does not allow us to conclude that the original story had both episodes. The present MT version may be due to an editor who knew different stories about David and Saul's daughter(s). The LXX knew only the one on Michal. If his Vorlage had attested to Merab's story as well, the translator might not have omitted it in order to avoid the contradiction with 2 Sam 21,8. He might rather have changed Michal's name into Merab's in 21,8. This is indeed the solution proposed by many of the Greek manuscripts having the section on Merab in 1 Sam 18,17-19. A similar solution is found in 2 Sam 21,19 where the MT states that Elhanan slew Goliath, which obviously is in contradiction with 1 Sam 17, where David kills Goliath. The LXX simply changed Goliath into Godolias. Or was it the author of the Vorlage of the LXX ? The name Godolias (גדול) as a Hebraism pleads in favor of this supposition.

The reasons for turning once more to 17,12 are different. When one does not accept the MT of 1 Sam 17-18 as an original unit, then 17,12 most likely presents a suture in which editorial activities may be expected. As far as I could see, DG merely notes that the verse in question and the following ones, if taken as the very commencement of a story, tell us both too much and too little to function as the introductory presentation of the *dramatis personae.* He compares the verses with the usual introductory lines found in 1,1; 9,1 and 25,2-3 without however working out the comparison and without weighing the possibilities of editorial reworking of 17,12ss (p.57). DB notes that verses 12.15 betray traces of a redactional adaptation, suggesting that the MT combined several originally independent stories (p.48). ET does not seem to pay much attention to the verse.

In my opinion, 17,12 and the following verses have been reworked by an editor. Moreover, the original form of the verse and even its present one appear to show many similarities with the incipits in 1 Sam 1,1; 9,1 and Judges 13,2. The stories following upon these incipits also display striking similarities in their composition.

The grammatical structure of verse 12 is odd. With S.R. Driver we may say that הזה added to אפרתי is contrary to grammar. "The Ephratite" would be האיש האפרתי הזה. An editor may have added הזה in order to connect verse 12 and following with chapter 16 : "Now David was the son of an Ephratite, this very one (הזה) from Bethlehem in Judah, named Jesse" (cf. P. Kyle McCarter, p. 301). Further, the final part of the sentence בא באנשים does not seem to make sense. Some other details in 17,12 are most unusual and even incongruous. When David is in evidence in the beginning of the sentence one expects him to be the subject of some major feat. Sentences with a similar structure, "X, son of Y, a Z-ite", confirm this expectation : compare with 1 Kings 11,26 : "Jeroboam, the Son of Nabat, an Ephraimite of Zeredah ... lifted up his hand against the king"; 2 Sam 21,20 : "Elhanan the son of Joareoregim, a Bethlehemite, slew Goliath...". In 1 Sam 17,12, one finds nothing of the sort. Not David, but Jesse, his father, is focused upon. Moreover, hardly one of the sentences beginning with "X, son of Y, a Z-ite", show the variant given in 1 Sam 17,12 : "X, son of a *man* (a Z-ite) from W whose name was Y". The only instance coming close to it is to be found in 2 Sam 17,25 : "Amasa, son of a *man* whose name was Ithra, the Ishmaelite". However, this notice follows upon a sentence in which Amasa was brought to the fore by the narrator. The reader of this sentence expects further information about him. No similar context is given in 17,12. David enters the scene unexpectedly.

The verse appears to have been tampered with. The comparison with 1 Sam 1,1; 9,1 and Judges 13,2 invites some minor reconstructions :

Judges 13,2ff		1 Sam 1,1ff		1 Sam 9,1ff		1 Sam 17,12ss	
v.2	ויהי איש	v.1	ויהי איש		ויהי איש	v.12	[ויהי] איש
(locality)	מ	(locality)	מן	(locality)	מ	(locality)	מ
	ושמו		ושמו		ושמו		ושמו
(his wife)	ו	(2 wives)	ולו	v.2 (a son)	ולו	(8/4?sons)	ולו

The subject of all these introductory verses is the father of the hero. This entails that 17,12, like the parallel verses had ויהי at its beginning and not David. The father in question probably had four sons only and not eight. Indeed, 17,20.28 strongly suggests that David had only three brothers and they had followed Saul to the battle. When David had to leave as well, the sheep had to be left with a keeper, no brother being available to tend them. The final redactor gave the father eight sons in order to harmonize the story with 16,1ff.

Verse 12 must have been reworked in a period in which it had become customary to associate Ephrata with Bethlehem and with the house of David. Compare with Micah 5,1; Ruth 1,2; 4,11; Gen 35,19; 48,7. The insert of Ephrata suggested a link with Rachel and Jacob and their sons (cf. Gen 35,19; 48,7). Verse 12 in its reconstructed form was undoubtedly the opening line of a tale : "There was a man...". It could not have been an original part of the story beginning in 17,1. The editor who inserted the tale had to adapt it a little to its context.

Not only the opening lines but also the pattern of the narrative in 1 Sam 17,12ff have much in common with 1 Sam 1,1ff; 9,1ff. The three anecdotic stories explain how the child who was to become the main character and hero of the following episodes, arrived at the court. Especially are 1 Sam 9,1ff and 17,12ff closely related. The theme of both sections is as follows: A man has a son : 17,12 and 9,1. He sets a task to his son : 17,17-18 and 9,3. The task is a rather minor one, but the quest for its fulfillment brings the hero into contact with the leader of his country : 17,55-58 and 9,17ff. It is remarkable that both stories have been framed into another story : 1 Sam 9,1-10,16 has been taken up into the dtr composition of 1 Sam 8,1-22 and 10,17ff; and 1 Sam 17,12ff has been intertwined with a more systematic description of David's victory over Goliath.

If our reasoning concerning 17,12ff is correct, then it follows that 17,12ff can hardly be a subsection of a larger story beginning, say, in 17,1. Verse 12 must be regarded as the opening line of an independent story. It follows very well upon 14,52 with its concluding statement of the foregoing section : "There was a hard *war* against the Philistines all *the days of Saul,* and when Saul saw any strong man, or any valiant man, he attached him to himself". Our story beginning in 17,12 uses some of the same terms : it explains that in *the days of Saul* Jesse had grown old, too old to be a soldier. However, he had sons who could follow Saul to *the war* ... If one goes on thinking along these lines, 1 Sam 17,12ff must have belonged to the early layers of the book. It remains difficult to explain why exactly this story is not attested by the LXX. My views on this problem and on the convergence between the text-critical and the literary critical data have not changed and can be found in my earlier paper.

With great pleasure and interest I read the articles by my three colleagues. I think the procedure suggested by DB was correct, because all of us have independently examined the material and weighed the evidence. I find it very interesting that there is not much duplication in the four articles, and we even used different scholarly works. It would, in fact, be helpful if someone would take the effort to produce one synthesis out of our four papers. To produce such a synthesis, however, is not easy, and by the same token the four papers could be reproduced without change, or possibly only with stylistic changes, but without cross-references.

The purpose of the undertaking was that our respective papers would reach different conclusions. This has, indeed, happened, and it causes therefore no surprise that JL and I took the LXX as point of departure, accepting the short Greek text as evidence for a short Hebrew text, which preceded the MT. DB and DG on the other hand, rejected the evidence of the LXX as secondary and hence irrelevant to the literary development of the story of David and Goliath. We should, of course, react particularly on those papers and aspects with which we disagree, and this makes me almost skip the paper by JL. However, I wish to emphasize how much I learned from that paper which stressed different matters than I did myself, yet we reached similar conclusions. It is important to sketch the textual witnesses in detail as JL did on pp. 6-8. It would be ideal if indeed 4QSam-a can be explained as witnessing to the text of the LXX (JL, p. 8) but I believe that JL too much stressed one detail in that scroll which is not related directly to the issue of the shorter text of the LXX. The literary argument, which indicates the special places of vv. 12-31 in the context (p. 11), is very enlightening.

I also learned much from the papers of DB and DG, from their distinction between textual and literary issues and from the detailed literary analysis, especially in the paper by DG, which many a biblical exegete would be proud to present to his readers. I feel uneasy with regard to both papers, because I disagree with some of their basic presuppositions and this disagreement relates to matters so fondamental that I can hardly react on the detailed arguments presented in the papers which deserve a more extensive reaction than I present here. I feel also uneasy because my reactions to both papers do not go much beyond what I have already said in my own paper. I shall therefore have to repeat myself somewhat, but I shall remain as brief as possible. I might add that the arguments which I use below with regard to DB and DG refer to most of the treatments of this story, and not only to theirs.

For the story of David and Goliath we possess two main sources, MT and the LXX, and these are by implication *textual* sources, witnessing that abstract entity which we call the biblical text. In our discussion we must attempt to approach these sources as impartially as possible. This means by implication that we should *not* speak first about the literary problems of the story nor about its textual difficulties, but we should first assess the value of the LXX because the LXX is one of the *sources* which contain the story. Now, the Greek translation can only be assessed from its own background, that is, as a Greek translation of the Hebrew book, of a Hebrew original. We all know, there are different levels at which the data in the LXX should be taken into consideration; if it is likely that the Greek translator omitted the sections under consideration, the omission is of interest only for our understanding of the translator's techniques and his exegesis, and not at all for the Hebrew text. On the other hand, if it can be made likely that the translator used a short Hebrew text, not the translation technique and exegesis are the center of our interest, but all at a sudden the Hebrew text behind the translation becomes the focus of our interest, and subsequently also the relation between that Hebrew text and MT. This being the situation, the starting point of the discussion of the Greek version of David and Goliath should be the *translation technique* of the Greek translator and the question whether or not that translator would have omitted these sections. In my paper I addressed these issues and the approach presented there may be correct or not, but at least it starts off with a discussion of the evidence. As long as the value of the data in the LXX is not discussed thoroughly, these data do not yet present evidence in one way or another.

How then should we evaluate the minuses of the LXX ? I, as you know, followed the principle that the very existence of these minuses must be examined within the framework of translation technique and I appealed to logics when referring to that translation technique as one entity. As the translation technique is approached as one entity, certain conclusions can be drawn from its analysis which are relevant to the minuses. I feel that this examination is as objective as possible under the circumstances. I also sense that other types of examination may lead to a *petitio principii*, in particular the examination of the minuses themselves. The papers by DB and DG examine the logic of the minuses, the logic and feasibility of the long text and the feasibility of the short text. In my view, this examination leads to a *petitio principii.* Indeed, the probability of the existence of a short Hebrew text does not have to be investigated. That short text either existed or it did not. I regard the reconstructed short text as I regard all reconstructed variants : they can be improbable, unlikely or secondary, but such improbable variants also existed in Hebrew, both as individual variants and as complete sections. It is well-known that there are many sections in MT which are rewritten, revised, and which contain duplications, truncated stories etc. All these types of secondary literary documents exist in Hebrew, so that in our case the secondary nature of either the short or the long text is not relevant to the discussion at this level. At the initial stage of our discussion there is, in my view, only one question : does the deviating Greek text reflect a deviating Hebrew text or not ?

There is one further reason why I donot favor an investigation of the minuses themselves in order to determine whether they reflect Greek or Hebrew minuses. The type of arguments used in such an examination are highly subjective. The arguments used concerning the feasibility of the short and long text in their context are necessarily personal. Two scholars may reach directly opposed conclusions, and I believe that it is therefore better to follow a course which I consider more objective.

My point of departure, therefore, is the textual level and only the textual level. If certain conclusions are reached, we have to evaluate them later on the literary level. If the textual data are discarded because in our view the translator omitted large sections, there is no need at all to embark upon a literary analysis for these omissions do not bear on the Hebrew text. On the other hand, if the textual data are accepted as trustworthy, that is, if it has been made likely that the translator did *not* omit them, all at a sudden these textual data become evidence, which is as important as the evidence contained in MT. There is no middle course, I believe. Now, if the short Greek text is taken as evidence, it has to be taken as it is, with all its difficulties. Among other things, these difficulties refer to contradictions within version I (cf. n. 22 in my paper) and the assumption of harmonizations between version 1 and 2 after their combination (see p. 43 in my paper). These difficulties have been discussed more extensively by my colleagues, so I need not dwell on them here.

It must, however, be stressed that these difficulties are part and parcel of the text, as stressed above, and they cannot be taken as proof against the theory that the LXX knew a short text. The analysis of that theory belongs to a different level of discussion.

As stated above, my approach differs fundamentally from those of DB and DG. I therefore refrain from drawing conclusions on the very existence of versions 1 and 2 on the basis of a literary analysis of the story. I deal with these issues at a different level. Naturally, if my analysis of the translation technique is incorrect, the whole picture changes. Indeed, DG (p. 83) questions the logic behind my view, and this point should be discussed further.

J'ai trouvé un grand intérêt à lire les contributions de JL, ET et DG. Un grand nombre de leurs remarques me semblent complémentaires, plutôt qu'opposées. Lorsqu'elles paraissent se contredire, c'est souvent parce que l'un des participants, trop préoccupé par un aspect de la problématique, liquide de façon hâtive une autre question qui était justement le point qui préoccupait le plus son partenaire. Il est évident, par exemple, que DG, par les mots "out of whatever sources" (p. 66), liquide toute une préhistoire littéraire qui a préoccupé beaucoup ses trois collègues. A l'inverse, ceux qui voient dans le texte long une production complexe se sont attachés à préciser si le texte bref attesté par *G peut avoir été l'une de ses sources, mais n'ont pas attaché à l'analyse littéraire du texte long le dixième de l'attention que DG lui a consacrée.

Commençons par éviter les termes "version 1" et "version 2", mis en circulation par ET (*TCUS* 298). Dans une argumentation ad hominem, DG en fait usage (p. 55), mais il remarque (n. 7) que cela l'amène à des inconséquences. En effet, ces termes présument déjà d'une certaine option dans le domaine de la critique littéraire : à savoir, que les 'plus' de *M aient constitué autrefois un récit autonome. Parlons donc plutôt seulement de *M, de *G, ainsi que des 'plus' et des 'moins' qui les caractérisent. On peut alors résumer ainsi ce qui fait à mes yeux l'intérêt principal des contributions de ET et de DG :

ET a consacré la plus grande partie de son étude (pp. 19 à 39) à étudier la relation existant entre la traduction grecque et la Vorlage à partir de laquelle elle a été faite. La conclusion qu'il en tire est que le traducteur a eu pour base un texte qui était d'environ 45 o/o plus court que le *M. ET est arrivé à cette conclusion par une étude détaillée de la manière dont le traducteur s'est comporté à l'égard de sa source dans les passages que *G et *M possèdent en commun et où l'on peut constater en effet (p. 23) que le traducteur a traité sa source avec soin en n'introduisant que peu ou pas d'options exégétiques personnelles. ET conclut de cela à juste titre qu'il est invraisemblable qu'un traducteur, par ailleurs respectueux des données de sa Vorlage, ait pris l'initiative d'omettre en certaines péricopes près de 45 o/o du texte.

DG a consacré la plus grande partie de son étude (pp. 59 à 75) à une double étude littéraire. Il montre d'abord (pp. 59 à 63) que les 'plus' principaux de *M ont un thème central qui progresse en trois étapes et postulent un climax du type de celui qu'offre ensuite 18,27b (commun à *M et à *G). Ensuite (pp. 63 à 75), il montre que les 'plus' de *M ne peuvent être l'oeuvre d'un interpolateur maladroit, car ils s'insèrent comme des étapes requises dans la progression naturelle du récit. Une analyse littéraire patiente conduite avec sympathie montre que plusieurs éléments textuels que la critique littéraire classique a pris l'habitude de considérer comme des interpolations qui sont en dissonances avec leur contexte sont en réalité les parties intégrantes d'un récit qui a été construit à partir de quelques sources par un homme doué d'un réel esprit de synthèse. Par contre *G (ou sa Vorlage) en est un reliquat qui a été tronqué par quelqu'un qui — faisant preuve d'une tournure d'esprit très littéraliste et fort peu imaginative — a pensé améliorer le récit en supprimant ce qu'il considérait comme des doublets et des dissonances. Deux petits 'plus' de *G en 17,43 ("et de pierres" et "et David dit : 'non, mais pire qu'un chien'") montrent d'ailleurs une profonde incompréhension à l'égard de la progression du récit.

Je suis prêt à accepter le résultat de la partie la plus poussée de l'étude de ET : il ne faut pas accuser le traducteur grec d'avoir mutilé sa Vorlage en la traduisant. Il a respecté le contenu d'une forme textuelle hébraïque brève qui lui servait de base. Je suis également prêt à accepter le résultat de la partie la plus poussée de l'étude de DG : le *M n'est pas l'oeuvre d'un interpolateur stupide et maladroit. C'est l'oeuvre d'un rédacteur aux vues amples et synthétiques. Des balancements et des progressions subtiles lui donnent une remarquable unité qui a été méconnue par ceux qui voudraient y voir l'assemblage maladroit de morceaux hétérogènes.

Je reconnais volontiers que, partant de "l'analyse littéraire orthodoxe courante" et influencé par elle, j'ai d'abord été frappé par les "prétendues dissonances que l'on relève d'ordinaire" et que, les considérant comme un fait bien établi, j'ai raisonné à partir de là. Mais j'ai ensuite (pp. 49 et 50) été frappé par le fait que la forme textuelle hébraïque brève qui a servi de Vorlage à *G ne peut constituer un récit originairement indépendant, plusieurs de ses éléments ne trouvant leur vrai sens qu'en référence aux 'plus' de *M. Cela m'a amené (p. 50) à considérer la Vorlage de *G comme issue de *M par voie de mutilation. J'estime d'ailleurs que l'un des résultats les plus importans de l'analyse littéraire de DG est de montrer que cette solution s'impose. La partie la plus poussée de mon étude (pp. 50 à 54) a donc consisté à réfuter les objections (bien détaillées par George B. Caird) que certains ont élevées contre cette vue que la forme textuelle brève serait issue de la forme longue par voie de mutilation. Or je constate que JL (p. 9) et ET (p. 40) ont repris brièvement certaines de ces objections sans leur apporter de développements nouveaux. Ils insistent cependant tous deux sur le fait que l'on manque de parallèles montrant qu'en d'autres parties du premier livre de Samuel un *M senti comme dissonant ou surchargé aurait été abrégé par la Vorlage de *G. Pour ce qui est des dissonances, j'ai relevé (p. 52) des données chronologiques (en 1 S 13,1 et 2 S 5,4s) qui ont été omises par la Vorlage du *G ancien pour ce motif. 1 S 30,7b a pu également être omis par elle (ainsi que le complément au datif du verbe précédent) parce qu'il semblait anormal que l'éphod que portait le prêtre soit apporté à *David*. 1 S 4,21aβ et la plus grande partie de 2 S 23,23a ont pu être omis parce que la Vorlage de *G les considérait comme des surcharges inutiles. Il est évident que ces omissions n'ont pas la même ampleur que celles que la Vorlage de *G présente dans les chapitres 17 et 18. Mais il n'est pas surprenant que, dans le texte long de ces deux chapitres, l'abréviateur ancien ait cru déceler les mêmes dissonances et surcharges que l'analyse littéraire aujourd'hui classique a elle aussi cru déceler justement en ces mêmes chapitres. Ajoutons que l'argument du manque de parallèles peut également se retourner contre l'hypothèse inverse selon laquelle *M serait issu de larges interpolations relativement tardives.

JL a relevé (p. 7) dans le sermon d'Hippolyte sur David et Goliath qu'Hippolyte faisait usage d'un texte grec qui omettait 17,12-31 mais qui connaissait 18,1b.(3).4. Il suggère ensuite (pp. 9 et 12) que la Vorlage de *G contenait 18,1b.(3).4 qui auraient été omis ensuite dans la transmission textuelle de *G par une *parablepsis.* Cette conclusion me semble très fragile. En effet, même si nous admettons qu'ici la traduction géorgienne (et la traduction arménienne dont elle émane) reproduit fidèlement le grec du sermon d'Hippolyte, il reste que l'on est en droit de douter qu'Hippolyte témoigne exclusivement ici pour le *G ancien. En effet, J. Ziegler (Sylloge 390s) a relevé dans le commentaire de Daniel d'Hippolyte "solche Stellen, die abweichend von o'- und θ'-Text eine bisher nicht erkannte Wiedergabe der Hebr. (oder aramäischen) Vorlage darstellen". Dans ce même commentaire (conservé en grec), il a relevé (ibid. 384) une citation d'Ez 9,2 "das ... deutlich auf Aquila und Theodotion zurückgeht". Il serait donc imprudent de conclure, à partir du résumé de 18,1b.(3). 4 donné par Hippolyte, à la présence de ce passage dans le *G ancien auquel il avait accès. Hippolyte connaissait en effet encore d'autres formes textuelles bibliques. Il en va d'ailleurs de même pour Flavius Josèphe qui, un siècle plus tôt, faisait usage en ses Antiquités de certains éléments du texte qui sont attestés seulement par *G (par exemple, la réponse de David : "pire qu'un chien !" en 17,43 est citée en Ant VI §186) et d'autres éléments attestés par *M seul (par exemple, la répétition du défi du Philistin durant 40 jours, selon 17,16, est mentionnée en Ant VI §174).

Il est très intéressant de comparer la brève analyse littéraire que JL offre aux pp. 11 à 13 à l'analyse plus développée de DG que nous avons mentionnée ci-dessus. Ces deux analyses aboutissent à des conclusions opposées. Faut-il accueillir ce résultat avec résignation en se disant que le goût personnel de l'analyste est déterminant en ce domaine ? Je me demande cependant si l'on ne pourrait pas intégrer certaines des conclusions en apparence opposées de JL et de DG en les situant à deux niveaux distincts : JL, ET et DB ont relevé (à la suite de nombreux critiques) certaines hétérogénéités qui font ressortir que le rédacteur a utilisé des sources diverses (ce que DG reconnaît aussi, comme je l'ai signalé au début de cette réponse) et qu'il a respecté certaines caractéristiques de l'hétérogénéité de ses sources, si bien que l'analyste littéraire classique (comme déjà l'abréviateur qui a produit la Vorlage de *G) n'a pas tort d'en déceler des traces dans le récit actuel. Cependant DG a bien montré que le rédacteur n'a rien d'un interpolateur maladroit et stupide. A partir de sources diverses, il a construit un récit très bien balancé. Par exemple, de 16,1 à 17,54 il a ménagé un remarquable suspense sur l'identité du champion d'Israël, suspense suivi d'une mise en valeur (par le contraste entre les armes des deux champions) de la maîtrise du "Seigneur Sabaoth, Dieu des lignes d'Israël" (cf. DG, pp. 64s et 67 à 70). Ou encore, de 17,55 à 18,30, il a ménagé une progression rythmée de refrains, progression qui aboutit à un climax en surmontant un contretemps (cf. DG, pp. 59 à 61 et 70 à 74).

Ces analyses très fines de DG m'ont confirmé dans la conclusion que la Vorlage de *G ne peut avoir précédé *M, mais qu'elle doit en être issue par élimination de nombreux passages et par deux gloses inintelligentes en 17,43.

En résumé

- je suis d'accord avec ET pour penser que *G est fidèle à sa Vorlage. C'est donc à celle-ci (et non au traducteur ni à des accidents plus tardifs) qu'il faut attribuer la plupart des caractéristiques qui distinguent *G de *M.
- je suis d'accord avec DG pour reconnaître au rédacteur qui a produit *M des qualités littéraires de premier ordre.
- j'estime avoir réfuté les objections que l'on a coutume d'élever contre l'hypothèse que la forme textuelle brève serait issue de la forme longue par voie de mutilation.
- je suis d'accord avec DG pour considérer que les résultats de son analyse littéraire "non-orthodoxe" rendent cette hypothèse beaucoup plus vraisemblable que l'hypothèse contraire.
- je suis d'accord avec ET et JL pour estimer que la forme textuelle longue a été construite par son rédacteur à partir de plusieurs récits-sources préexistants. Mais je place cette diversité au niveau de la préhistoire littéraire (c'est-à-dire de l'histoire des traditions), estimant que l'analyse littéraire nous permet seulement de l'inférer mais ne peut nous y faire accéder directement, les éléments des récits-sources ayant été savamment intégrés dans l'oeuvre remarquable du rédacteur. Notons d'ailleurs combien diffèrent les préhistoires littéraires qu'ébauchent JL (p. 13s), ET (p. 41s) et DB (p. 54). Ces reconstitutions risquent de nous entraîner en des sables mouvants.

Reading my colleagues' papers has for me been very pleasurable and instructive. ET's magnificently thorough study of the LXX's translation-technique has a value which quite transcends its relevance to our present purpose. Especially valuable, too, is JL's citation of the evidence of the *Sermo Hippolyti* and of Josephus, while DB's discussion of Caird's six objections strikes me as a particularly fine piece of argumentation.

My further response to the three papers is as follows.

I. UNDUE LIMITATION OF THE THEORETICAL POSSIBILITIES

A. On the Greek side

ET seems to hold that if the Greek *translator* cannot be thought to have been responsible for the LXX's minuses, then the only alternative is that the minuses must be credited to some Hebrew ms. JL allows that some minuses could have happened accidentally in the course of the Greek scribal transmission; otherwise he seems to agree with ET. This is too narrow. We must consider at least the following possible levels of activity : 1. the original translation; 2. ordinary scribal transmission; 3. learned criticism of, and interference with, the text; 4. revisions aimed at bringing the text nearer to the Hebrew. Activity at Level 2 could lead to considerable changes, as we see at the comparable level of early NT papyri, or "wild" texts of Homer. But Level 2 activity is not to be confused with Level 3 activity. With Homer Level 3 would be represented by the learned criticism of Alexandrian scholars (marking of supposedly spurious passages, criticism and changing of Homer's vocabulary and word-order, etc.). With the LXX the counterpart would be the work of Jewish scholars like Demetrius, who tried to deal with apparent contradictions in the text and other *aporiai* [1]. It is perfectly possible that such criticism led to the edition of texts, rearranged, or shortened in order to remove difficulties and doublets, etc. In this connection JL's observation that Josephus followed a text which while it omitted much of that which LXXB omits, nevertheless contained 17,12-31, is highly suggestive. The fact that Josephus has some minuses suggests that he was not following a Greek text which had been revised to make it conform to the proto-MT; and it is far from certain that he was following a Hebrew text. It is a distinct possibility that he was following a basically OGr text which had suffered some excision, but not so much as we now find in LXXB.

ET's argument that, because the OGr translator normally translated faithfully, we cannot suppose that he introduced any minuses, seems not to be 100 o/o valid : DB, (pp. 52f), it seems to me, has cast serious doubt on that. But even if it were valid, it still leaves open the possibility that the OGr translator translated, with equal faithfulness, the passages that are now wanting in LXXB, and that they were later removed by learned scholars.

B. On the Hebrew side

Here it seems generally to have been assumed that if the major minuses/pluses must be traced to the Hebrew, they must have occurred at the level of the constitution of the texts. But the theoretically possible levels of activity are surely not less than three : 1. constitution of the texts — however long or short this process was — comparable to the composing of the *Iliad* in its present form; 2. normal scribal transmission with its accidents and minor changes; 3. learned, secondary, revision of the text from a literary, historical or exegetical point of view.

As a possible example of Level 3 activity, I cite the OGr chronology in 1 Kings. I myself think that the probability is that this chronology arose at the level of the Greek. But many, perhaps the majority, think that the OGr derived this chronological system from some Hebrew Vorlage. Let us suppose it did, and work out its implications.

Neither chronological system can be thought to have arisen from mere scribal activity (Level 2). Equally the difference between the two systems cannot be thought to have arisen at Level 1, since the OGr system presupposes the MT system. Both systems share the same characteristic, alternating pattern for recording the history of the Judaean and Israelite kings. Now if one adopts the MT's synchronism for Jehoshaphat (= 4th Ahab), then the rules of the pattern demand that when Jehoshaphat's turn comes to have his history told, that history should come after Ahab's and should receive a mere summary, the major part of it having already been told in connection with Ahab. And that is of course what happens in the MT (1 Kings 22,41-50). If one adopts the OGr's synchronism for Jehoshaphat (= 11th Omri) the same rules would demand not only that Jehoshaphat's history be told before Ahab's, but that it *be told in full*, with the details of Ahab's story being told simply as incidental to Jehoshaphat's story. But what in fact we find in the OGr is that while Jehoshaphat's history has indeed been placed before Ahab's (1 Kings 16,28a-h), all it receives is a summary, basically the same summary as the MT has in ch. 22. But this breaks the rules of the pattern. Whoever is responsible for this chronology, obviously realised that it necessitated a consequential change in the positioning of Jehoshaphat's history from ch. 22 to ch. 16, but failed to realise that the change in position also demanded, according to the rules of the pattern, a re-writing of the history itself so as to give Jehoshaphat's history the proper priority of proportion that it now required. No original composer, working at Level 1, would have committed such a mistake. Whoever was responsible was a reviser working at Level 3.

In this connection JL's observation (p. 10) that some manuscripts of the Targum Jonathan have suffered lengthy expansion at 1 Sam. 17,8 is a further reminder that not all expansions are necessarily to be traced to Level 1. If, for instance, the MT's pluses are indeed expansions they could have arisen at Level 3. And if expansions could, so could reductions.

II. PRINCIPLES OF LITERARY CRITICISM

A. The need not to confuse historical criticism with literary criticism

The use now of historical now of literary criticism is inevitable when dealing with a sophisticated narrative of historical events. I have myself made use of both types of criticism (e.g. p. 77). My point here is that we must be on guard against logically confusing them.

1. ET (p. 41) for instance, says "version 1 presents a continuous and internally consistent story, and if version 2 would not have been known, we would not have lacked any crucial information in chapters 17 and 18".

Crucial for what ? Is this a literary judgement or a historical judgement ?

Suppose historical. Then we could use the analogy that an account of the last World War that presented a coherent and self-explanatory story would not necessarily be an original story : it could be an abridged account, or, even worse, a simplified story. A full, real-life story is often more complicated and difficult to understand than abridged stories make out.

Suppose literary. What then does "crucial information" mean ? Does ET mean to imply that the story in the MT is an example of what Aristotle would have regarded as a bad plot, because it has, or is alleged to have, a number of elements which are not essential to the plot, and which can be removed without damaging the dramatic action or the 'message' it conveys ? I have argued at length that the so-called pluses are in fact necessary to the thought-flow and 'message' of the story. ET may well disagree. But to prove his claim that the pluses are not crucial to the thought-flow, he would need to demonstrate it *in detail*; his skeleton-outline (pp. 40-41) is hardly sufficient to do that.

2. On the ground that 17,4 ("Goliath steps forward") can be construed as the counterpart of 17,40b ("David steps forward") in a literary symmetry, JL (p. 11) suggests that verse 41 is undoubtedly redundant. But this literary judgement seems to ignore certain historical features and conventions of ancient single-combat, at least as far as Homer is witness to them.

(a) It was not always the case in the ancient world that, a challenge to single-combat having been offered by one side, the other side at once put up a hero and the duel took place immediately. In *Iliad* VII after Hector issues his challenge (66ff) there is a long interval of frightened debate among the Greeks before their Ajax strides forth to fight Hector (206ff). Similarly in *Iliad* III, there is a long interval of truce between Hector's formal announcement that Paris is prepared to meet Menelaos in single-combat (76) and the actual striding out of the heroes to fight each other (340ff). Whether the "40 days" of the interval in 1 Sam 17 is a round number or not, there is nothing improbable in the story that after Goliath's initial challenge there was a long interval of truce before the Israelites in their fright could put forward a champion.

(b) When a hero offered single-combat he did not necessarily stand still in the same place until the hero from the other side came out to meet him. The first hero could retire while he waited, and there could be many toings and froings before his foe emerged and he finally advanced to meet the foe to begin the duel. Witness again the duel in *Iliad* III. 16ff. So Goliath in 17,4 steps forward to deliver his challenge. Then comes an interval. 17,41 describes a different thing altogether : here after the interval (17,16) Goliath steps out to meet David as David advances to begin the fight (17,40b).

(c) When JL further says (p. 12) "Verse 48b is an unnecessary repetition of verse 40b", he is again surely confusing two different things : vv. 40b-41 are describing the heroes' advance towards each other *before* they halted to taunt each other; v. 48a and b is describing how *after* the taunting they closed in on each other.

(d) JL (p. 12), "One does not expect panic-stricken Israel : v. 11, to draw up for battle : v. 21". But why not ? What they were afraid of was not fighting the Philistines with their whole army, but single-combat with Goliath. The situation is exactly the same in *Iliad* VII : the Greek army has long been fighting the Trojan army without fear until Hector offers single-combat; *then* the Greeks are afraid (92ff), and take a long while to pluck up enough courage to put forward a single-combat fighter (175).

(e) JL (p. 12), "Goliath may come out of his camp (v. 4), down the hill, he cannot come up as is said in v. 23". Why not ? When a hero proposed single combat, he would first make his own army stop fighting and sit down, as Hector does, *Iliad* VII 55-56, or again, III. 77-78. The other side might continue shooting for a while, but then their commander would stop them too. So Agamemnon, *Iliad* III. 79-84. And then there would be a truce : there had to be, or else the ensuing duel would not be a single-combat. During the truce the challenging hero might go as near the enemy's walls as he liked, for normally there would be no danger. So, for instance, after Paris mysteriously vanished half-way through his duel with Menelaos, Menelaos went searching for him right up to the Trojan lines (III. 449-52), until a Trojan soldier broke the truce by shooting Menelaos (IV.104) which led to the armies resuming the battle (IV. 220ff). Goliath, likewise, having offered single-combat would not have been afraid to come up the hill, as far as he needed, towards the Israelite camp during the truce.

(f) JL (p. 12f) notices that in 17,24 it is the *sight* of the champion that frightens the soldiers, whereas in 17,11 it is his *word* that frightens them. JL seems to see some disharmony here, and later (p. 14) takes this as evidence not only of two different sources, but of two different genres. But if this were valid, what should we make of the duel in *Iliad* VII ? Within the space of a few lines (214-236) Ajax first rejoices the Argives and scares the Trojans with his *appearance,* and then in his *taunting* of Hector tries to scare him by assuming superiority and offering Hector the chance to shoot first. First frightening appearance, then frightening words : but no evidence whatever of different sources, let alone different genres.

3. When DB (p. 48) says that ch. 17 presents the duel between Goliath and David (17,9.11.32) "en surimpression sur une victoire de l'armée d'Israel contre celle des Philistins (17,20-21.52)", I wonder whether he would describe the duels in *Iliad* III and VII (*mutatis mutandis*) any differently.

To me it is instructive to find modern scholars, on the ground of the supposed difficulties discussed above, deciding that the MT's account contains serious discrepancies. It strengthens me in my view that in Hellenistic times similar unfamiliarity with the conventions of ancient heroic single-combat led other learned scholars to feel similar difficulties and to attempt to eliminate them by excision.

B. On conjecturing the purpose of any section of narrative

Two senses of 'purpose' should be distinguished : *Purpose 1.* Internal. Answers the question : how does this paragraph fit into its narrative-sequence ? What contribution does it make to the work as a whole ? *Purpose 2.* External. Appropriate answers to the question, "Why did the author write this paragraph (and the rest of the work) ?" would be : to further his political ideas, to make money, to flatter his friends, etc.

Now DB (pp. 47ff), having observed that "1 S 16-17 nous offre trois entrées en scène de David", (Stories A, B and C), conjectures that each of these three sections of narrative once had separate, independent existence and that the Purpose 2 for which each was written was to legitimise David's claims to royalty. DB then suggests that Story A achieves its Purpose 2 so much better than Stories B and C, that Story A must have been written last; for had the authors of Stories B and C known Story A, they could have abandoned their own less convincing efforts to achieve this purpose.

But (a). In the course of a play a character may have a number of "entrées en scène"; but that does not mean that the play was made up of a number of pre-existent passages each written by a different author for the same purpose.

(b). The Purpose 2 attributed to Story B is highly questionable. Would anyone ever have seriously attempted to base David's claim to the throne on the fact that he had been a court-musician and one of Saul's armour-bearers ? DB himself describes this alleged attempt as not very convincing (p. 47). But it is surely unfair to the author of Story B to attribute to him a Purpose 2 which he nowhere claims to have had, and then to criticise him for not achieving that purpose very convincingly. The real unconvincingness lies in the attribution to him of this conjectured purpose in the first place. And if my criticism is valid, DB's case falls.

My contention is that true criticism should start the other way round. If an author has not told us what the Purpose 2 of a passage is, and we have to deduce it ourselves from the narrative, we must start by studying the Purpose 1 of the passage. Otherwise we run the risk of not fully understanding the detail of the passage; and if we fail to understand that, how shall we rightly discern its Purpose 2, either at its present level, or at the hypothetical level of its hypothetical pre-existence ? If we accepted DB's conjectured original Purpose 2 for Story B, we should then have to assume that the eventual compiler either had no Purpose 1 or 2 of his own for incorporating the story into his narrative, or had both, but was so undiscerning that he did not realise that the original and continuing Purpose 2 of Story A ruined the effect both of Purpose 2 and of Purpose 1 of Story B. Must it be an axiom of OT literary criticism that the compilers of the OT were so incompetent ?

C. On Reading the Story of David Against its Wider Context

JL's remarks on this score (p. 12) are very helpful. All I would add here is that the emphasis on the "father/son" theme thus secured for 17,12 continues through 17,55-58 and 18,1-4, and thus binds the last two passages together (*contra* JL, middle of p. 12; but see my pp. 60-61).

On the other hand I do not see the force of DB's argument (p. 48) that Eliab's criticisms of David in Story C show that its author did not know of David's anointing by Samuel. Analogy with the story of Joseph who was criticised and maltreated by his brothers *because* they knew of his prophetic dreams, suggests the very opposite. Even Samuel's public presentation of the anointed Saul (1 Sam 10,17-27) did not stop all criticism. (See also ET p. 43.7)

D. Some Detailed Points

1. ET p. 42 "David is depicted in different ways in the two versions. In version 1 he is Saul's armour-bearer (16,21) and in that capacity he fights Goliath. In version 2 he is an unknown shepherd...". See also DB p. 49.

But 16,1-13 is Version 1 and here David is with the sheep (v. 11) when he is called and anointed. 16,14-23 is Version 1 and here David is with the sheep (v. 19) when he is called to be harpist and, subsequently, armour-bearer. 17,32-54 is Version 1 and here David, far from fighting Goliath in his capacity as Saul's armour-bearer, refuses to take Saul's armour, or even any armour at all, not even a sword, takes only a shepherd's staff and sling, and explains in detail and at length (17,32-37) that his courage to fight Goliath comes from his experience of God's protection and enabling which he experienced *as a shepherd*.

Where is the contradiction between version 1 and version 2 ? And how, after version 1's repeated statements, can anyone claim that version 1 depicts David fighting Goliath *"in his capacity as Saul's armour-bearer"* ?

Moreover, 17,15 is not an embarrassed, harmonising, addition, but a perfectly reasonable explanation. To start with, are we to suppose that 16,21 means that David, there and then, immediately became Saul's armour-bearer ? That from then on other experienced armour-bearers were all dismissed and David became Saul's only armour-bearer ? And that, if the campaign of ch. 17 took place soon after David's appointment as musician/armour-bearer, Saul would have taken the inexperienced (see 17,33) David to the battle in preference to some seasoned and experienced armour-bearer ? If David was in fact left behind as being too inexperienced, it is perfectly reasonable that in his off-duty from the court, he should go home to the farm (cf. 1 Sam 20,28).

2.   With reference to ET p. 38. 2b and 43. 3., the phrase "Michal *the* daughter of Saul" (18,20.27) does not necessarily imply that Saul had only one daughter. It may equally well be meant to explain which Michal (among the many Michals in Israel) it was that fell in love with David, i.e., Michal the daughter of Saul.

3.   ET's claim (p. 42) that "in fact, the sequence of events in the short version is more logical..." has been well dealt with by DB (p. 53f). See also my pp. 72-73.

4.   ET p. 43.5 "The detail in version 2 that Goliath paid a daily visit to the camp for forty days (17,16) is apparently not known to the author of 17,11 (version 1)". But this judgement depends on the prior judgement that 17,16 is by a different author from 17,11. There is no self-evident contradiction between the two verses.

5.   ET p. 43.6 The point is answered on my pp. 72-73.

6.   ET p. 43.8 "Twice David is made an officer in Saul's army." How is this a difficulty ? "Over-the-men-of-war" (18,3) and "captain-over-a-thousand" (18,13) were in fact two different posts as is evident from the fact that the first was held by David when he was near to Saul's person, whereas to occupy the second he had to be removed from Saul's presence (18,13).

7.   JL p. 14 claims that 17,28 strongly suggests that Jesse had only four sons (see also DB p. 48f). Surely not ! First, Eliab's remark is sarcastic. Secondly, the fact (17, 20) that David "left the sheep with a keeper" suggests, what 16,5-11 implies, that all David's older brothers were considered to be superior to the chore of looking after the sheep.

8.   The fact that 17,25 reports that some soldiers asked David if he had seen Goliath does not logically imply (*pace* JL p. 14) that David had not yet heard Goliath. If a Londoner asked a foreign visitor, "Have you seen the Queen ?", it would not imply that the visitor had not seen or heard the Queen yet.

9.   The numbers used by the women in their song (18,7) are hardly meant to be taken literally, are they ? Surely they are a poetic, hyperbolic, figure of speech, that could easily refer to David's superiority over Saul, demonstrated by his victory over Goliath, which overshadowed all Saul's other achievements : *pace* DB p. 49f.

III. MY OWN POSITION

While I do not pretend that the MT is without difficulty, I adhere to my view [2] that the MT's account represents a coherent story with an intelligible, carefully constructed, detailed, thought-flow, which has been mutilated to give the truncated story in LXXB. I do not see how, given the present state of the evidence, we can be sure at what level the truncation took place, though considering the evidence of Josephus' text and of the *Sermo Hippolyti* to which JL has called attention, I incline to the view that it took place at the Greek level, probably at some time after the OGr translation.

NOTES

1   See especially *GCS* 43 1 p. 528 and p. 538. See also my p. 84 (iii).

2   On my p. 73 'dowry' should be 'bride-price'. I owe this observation to my colleague, Dr. M.J. Alden.

RELATION DE LA SECONDE ETAPE DU TRAVAIL COMMUN

(D. Barthélemy)

En communiquant les quatre réponses aux participants, je leur écrivis, le 29 décembre 1982 :

Le 6 octobre 1980, dans une lettre à DG (dont JL et ET ont reçu copie), je proposais le planning de travail suivant :

"Chacun de nous quatre rédigerait une petite contribution sur le même sujet : 'Comment faut-il juger les grands 'moins' de la LXX en 1 Sam 17,12-31 et 17,55 à 18,5 ?' Il s'agit essentiellement de formuler et de peser des arguments ... Puis chacun d'entre nous rédigerait une prise de position sur l'ensemble des contributions, en visant à dégager une méthode pour aborder les problèmes où interfèrent la critique littéraire et la critique textuelle."

L'envoi que je vous fais aujourd'hui des quatre prises de position constitue l'achèvement de la seconde étape alors prévue.

Que faire maintenant ? En vous communiquant, le 11 mai dernier, les contributions initiales, je vous disais : "il s'agira de voir si nous estimons utile de tenir ensemble un colloque (ici par exemple) ... ou si nous publions ensemble le résultat de ces deux "étapes" d'études ... ou si chacun tire personnellement de ce parcours réalisé ensemble les conséquences qu'il estime utiles.

Pourriez-vous m'écrire sans tarder vos réactions à ces propositions."

A cette question, j'ai reçu les réponses suivantes :
de DG : "Thank you too for your letter of 11th May. I may say at once that my reaction to its propositions is that I shall be happy to agree to whatever procedure my colleagues wish to adopt. In particular, I can quite understand that in view of the delay which has occurred — and the delay is altogether my fault — JL should wish to publish his contribution independently. I certainly would have no objection to his doing so.

On the other hand, my original understanding was that our initial contributions were to be in the nature of working-papers and not polished articles ready for publications; and that these working-papers were to be the basis of a thorough-going *viva-voce* discussion when all four of us should meet; and that after that discussion we were each to produce our final viewpoints.

I am still happy to proceed on these lines; but if my colleagues feel that it would take too much time and effort, then we can adopt the suggestion that now seems to be advocated, namely that we should now simply, each one of us, write a further article containing his reactions to the working-paper submitted by his three colleagues, and that the whole (that is to say, the original working-papers and the four articles of reaction) should then be published."

de ET : "The suggested procedure is certainly desirable. If no other date is suggested, I propose that we meet in connection with the meeting in Salamanca, but let us discuss this only after we send our second series of remarks."

de JL : "J'espère qu'on n'envisage pas de discuter nos problèmes au congrès de Salamanque puisque nous avons les 'Journées bibliques' à Leuven la semaine du 15 août et puisque j'ai une communication à faire dans le grand congrès de Salamanque la semaine du 29 août."

La première question à régler me semble être de déterminer si la prochaine étape de notre travail doit être :

1) une discussion viva-voce entre nous quatre,
2) un colloque plus large où seraient invités (par exemple) ceux des membres de la IOSCS qui le souhaiteraient,
3) une nouvelle étape écrite en nous concentrant sur un (ou plusieurs) point(s) de méthode que nous choisirions,
4) une publication de nos productions dans l'état où nous nous les sommes communiquées.

La solution (4) est la plus simple. Ce serait une réalisation assez unique dans l'histoire de la recherche. Nos contributions ne font pas double emploi et nos quatre réponses révèlent des accents qu'il est important de souligner. Je crains que nous ne puissions aboutir à une position commune. En ce cas, il est utile de livrer au public le point où nous en sommes, et cela sans modifier, dans les contributions de base, les points qui ont fait réagir ensuite tel ou tel autre d'entre nous.

Cependant, même sans aboutir à une position commune, je crois qu'il nous est possible de serrer un peu plus certaines questions de méthode qui se dégagent de nos réponses. Si nous nous engageons sur cette voie, je craindrais de choisir comme prochaine étape la solution (2). En effet, lorsque nous discutons à quatre, nous risquons, certes, de nous disperser ou d'affronter des positions trop unilatérales; mais, du moins, nous avons l'oreille et l'esprit habitués à tels ou tels arguments de nos partenaires, arguments qui commencent à faire leur chemin dans notre réflexion. Si, par contre, nous nous trouvons, dès notre première rencontre, intégrés dans un groupe de discussion plus large, nous risquons de nous contenter de quelques échanges superficiels, en faisant appel, même involontairement, aux réactions d'un public qui ne se sera pas initié laborieusement à la question comme nous l'avons fait jusqu'ici. Je crains donc que l'effort que nous avons fait jusqu'ici, de manière plus ou moins réussie, pour définir les difficultés ne se trouve réduit à néant, si nous optons actuellement pour la solution (2).

Personnellement, je donnerais donc la préférence à la solution (1) ou à la solution (3). Je suggère même que nous les choisissions toutes les deux : d'abord (3), puis (1), et enfin, si nous en avons alors le courage, chacun rédigerait son point de vue final sur la question... ce qui irait dans le sens du "original understanding" de DG. Qu'en pensez-vous ?

En ce cas, je vous suggérerais déjà les point suivants qui pourraient faire l'objet de notre prochaine "étape écrite" (= 3) :

a) ET formule de façon précise, de la p. 93, l.37 à la p. 94, l.8 en sa réponse, un problème de méthode (depuis : "At the initial..." jusqu'à "... I believe.") Je suggère que chacun se prononce là-dessus, en tenant compte du §I.A de la réponse de DG (depuis la p. 99, ligne 11 : "ET seems..." jusqu'à la p. 100, ligne 6 : "... by learned scholars.") et du premier alinéa du §I.A de JL (depuis la p. 87, ligne 22 : "A close reading..." jusqu'à la p. 88, ligne 12 : "... occur.").

b) Dans nos contributions initiales, nous avons tous relevé certaines dissonances (= discrepancies) et certaines redondances à l'intérieur du texte long (= *M) ou bien nié qu'il s'agisse de dissonances ou de redondances. DG, dans le §II.A.2 de sa réponse (depuis la p. 101, ligne 30 : "On the ground..." jusqu'à la p. 103, ligne 12 : "... by excision."), discute certaines remarques de JL et de DB en se référant aux "conventions of ancient heroic single-combat", ce qui l'amène à préciser les rapprochements avec Homère qu'il avait esquissés en sa première contribution. Que pensons-nous de cette référence et de l'usage qui en est fait ici, ainsi que des conséquences que DG en tire dans la dernière phrase ?

c) JL, dans sa réponse, p. 89, depuis la ligne 15 ("one of the reasons...") jusqu'à la p. 90, ligne 8, traite des passages sur Merab et Michal en essayant d'expliciter certaines problématiques impliquées. Il s'agit là d'un exemple d'ampleur limitée, mais assez caractéristique. Que pensons-nous de la manière dont il traite cet exemple ?

d) DB, dans sa réponse, p. 96, depuis la ligne 26 ("La partie...") jusqu'à la ligne 45 ("... relativement tardives.") fait allusion aux objections formulées par ET et JL contre l'hypothèse que la forme textuelle brève serait issue d'une abréviation de la forme longue. Il mentionne aussi sa propre tentative pour réfuter les objections formulées par G.B. Caird. Que pensons-nous de ces objections et de leur réfutation ?

Ces quatre points placent chacun l'accent sur le travail de l'un des participants. Certains de ces points sont plus théoriques et d'autres plus concrets. Je propose que chacun d'entre nous prenne position sur les trois points où ses partenaires ont l'initiative. Il peut d'ailleurs ajouter une éventuelle mise au point, là où c'est lui qui a l'initiative. Je crois en effet que la "discussion viva-voce" sera plus profitable si nous avons essayé de nous faire un jugement plus précis sur chacun de ces quatre points.

Je voudrais finir en vous proposant *deux questions précises* :
I. Préférez-vous comme prochaine étape l'une des solutions (1), (2), (3) ou (4) que j'ai formulées, ou la succession (3) + (1) que j'ai suggérée, ou une autre solution ?
II. Au cas où vous opteriez pour une solution autre que (4), acceptez-vous que nous concentrions nos efforts sur l'un des quatre points que j'ai formulés ou sur les quatre, ou suggérez-vous un autre point ?
Si vous optez pour les solutions (1) ou (2), il faudra trouver une date et un lieu de rencontre qui conviennent à chacun de nous. Je crois que rien ne presse trop. Je propose cependant (au cas où vous choisissez (1)) que nous nous réunissions ici où je vous recevrai volontiers, après Salamanque, pour trois ou quatre jours. Nous aurions l'avantage de disposer d'une bibliothèque assez complète et de pouvoir entrecouper le travail de quelques excursions agréables. Cette rencontre pourrait nous permettre d'aborder une dernière étape de rédaction finale.

Dès que je recevrai vos réponses à ces questions, je vous les communiquerai. Au cas où vos réponses s'accordent, je suggérerai le mode de réalisation de la solution qui aura eu votre agrément.

Le 12 mai 1983, je leur écrivis à nouveau :

Je viens de recevoir (11.5.83) la dernière de vos trois réponses aux questions que je vous avais posées le 29.12.82.

Vous êtes tous d'accord pour envisager une certaine forme de publication commune de nos contributions et réponses. Vous êtes aussi tous d'accord pour estimer utile une discussion viva-voce auparavant. Les *solutions (1) et (4)* sont donc acceptées en principe.

La *solution (2)* n'a pas recueilli une adhésion nette :

JL : "Je n'ai pas d'objections absolues, même pas contre l'option (2)."

DG : "I do not think that Suggestion 2 is wise."

ET : "The meeting may be attended by some colleagues, but they would first have to do the homework of reading our papers."

Sur la *solution (3)* les avis divergent :

JL : "Si nous optons pour la solution (1), il serait possible de préparer d'avance des réponses à des questions dans le genre que vous proposez. Ces réponses n'impliqueraient pas nécessairement une nouvelle étape écrite. On pourrait les donner 'viva-voce' à Fribourg. Je demanderais alors d'ajouter une question à la liste. Qu'est-ce qu'on pense de la comparaison entre 1 Sam 17,12ff et 1 Sam 9,1ff; 1 Sam 1,1ff; Jud 13,2ff (JL réponse p. 90, l.20 'In my opinion' à p. 91, l.30)".

DG : "It does seem to me that this stage 3 would be very helpful, because a quick read through the responses by ET and JL suggests to me that ET at least has not quite understood my attitude towards his methodology. I agree with him more than he thinks." De fait, DG m'a envoyé (8.4.83) sa contribution écrite pour cette étape 3 où il traite des points qui le concernent (a,c,d) parmi ceux que j'avais proposés.

ET : "I am not in favor of a continued discussion through correspondence, as outlined in (3) as I don't know whether we will be able to advance the discussion much through correspondence. We have reached some basic difficulties which must be ironed out in a face-to-face discussion."

Etant donné l'accord de principe sur la *solution (1)*, quand pourrions-nous la réaliser ?

Ni DG, ni DB ne seront à Salamanque. JL et ET y seront. Mais ET écrit : "After Salamanca I must immediately return to J'lem. I am Grinfield Lecturer in Oxford, so I will be in the UK this fall, but I am afraid I cannot combine a meeting with that event. As far as I am concerned, we may have to wait until early next summer, late next summer or Oct. 1984."

Options essentielles à prendre

J'hésite entre deux options :
Option A : Une discussion face à face est nécessaire pour avancer. Puisqu'elle ne pourra avoir lieu qu'en 1984, fixons dès aujourd'hui sa date parmi celles que ET envisage comme possibles.
Option B : Avec nos quatre articles et nos quatre réponses, nous avons déjà une matière publiable. Puisque la discussion n'est pas possible cette année, envisageons de publier cela sans plus tarder et de nous mettre d'accord sur le mode de cette publication.

J'attends donc de vous trois que vous me disiez par retour du courrier si vous préférez l'option A ou l'option B. Je ne prendrai pas position personnellement. Celle de ces deux options qui aura reçu *au moins deux voix* sera considérée comme adoptée.

Deux questions annexes

1. Eventuelles publications particulières :
JL a retouché sa contribution initiale (avant d'avoir pris connaissance des trois autres) pour publication dans les E.T.L. Il en a communiqué une photocopie à ET et à moi et m'a demandé d'en communiquer une à DG, ce que je fais par ce courrier.

ET compte publier sa contribution initiale. Je copie ici ce qu'il m'écrit sur ce projet : "There is one further matter connected with the publication of our work in outside sources. I have been asked to submit my article to a book — edited by J. Tigay, of U. Penn., — "Empirical models for the development of the Hebrew Bible". The manuscript for the book, composed of individual articles, will be submitted this fall to the publisher, and we don't know when the book will be published. I have agreed to the proposal, realizing that also Lust's article will be published, and knowing that this publication will not disturb our continued discussion nor the joint publication of our work. In this book I also include a description of my work on the LXX of Jeremiah, and the two articles, together with contributions by others, help Tigay to develop his own ideas in the book. The form which will be published in this book is more or less my original article with my own stylistic improvements and with editorial intervention by J. Tigay. So far I have not added references in the footnotes to the contributions of my three colleagues, because I cannot do this without the consent of the three of you. I stress that I speak only of the footnotes, as I donot want to touch the text itself. The whole matter is not very crucial for me, and if my colleagues are not so happy about these cross-references, I will not include them. I can also limit myself to a general reference merely mentioning the existence of our discussion. I would like to have the opinion of my colleagues on this matter. JL has a similar problem in his article in ETL, of which he has kindly sent me a pre-print. He has written to me, upon my request, that he will incorporate cross-references when needed."

Je comprends que JL et ET souhaitent ajouter en note des cross-references à l'état dans lequel ils vont publier leurs deux contributions. Mais je crois qu'il ne faut pas aller plus loin. En effet, aussi longtemps que les contributions de DG et de DB demeurent inédites (comme nos quatre réponses), il est impossible d'y référer de manière objective. Chacun est cependant libre de mentionner l'existence d'une discussion entre nous sur ce sujet.

2. Que faire de la troisième contribution de DG ?

Etant donné que j'ai reçu une contribution de DG en vue de la 3e étape écrite que j'envisageais comme possible (solution 3), *je propose* de la communiquer dès maintenant à ET et à JL en suggérant *que nous répondions tous les trois à DG avant fin 1983.* Avoir à réagir sur un même texte peut aider à clarifier les points de vue, aussi bien dans la perspective de l'option A que dans celle de l'option B. *Que ET et JL me disent s'ils sont d'accord* sur ce point. S'ils ne sont pas tous deux d'accord sur ce point, je garde cette dernière contribution de DG jusqu'à ce que ET et JL se rencontrent à Salamanque et se mettent d'accord sur l'une des solutions suivantes :
1) ou bien nous réalisons chacun indépendamment des autres la 3e étape écrite telle que je la proposais dans ma lettre du 29.12.82.
2) ou bien nous prenons connaissance, tous trois, de la 3e contribution de DG à simple titre informatif.

Le 10 août 1983, je leur écrivis encore :
Merci d'avoir répondu à ma lettre du 12/5/83.

Deux d'entre vous (ET et JL) sont favorables à mon option A, alors que DG préfère nettement l'option B.

Aucun d'entre vous n'ayant fait objection au *modus procedendi* que j'avais proposé, j'en conclus que nous choisissons l'option A et je vous invite à venir ici pour un colloque de 3 jours, du 20 au 23 août 1984. Au cas où l'un d'entre vous ne serait pas libre à ces dates, dites-moi aussi si vous seriez libres la semaine suivante (du 27 au 30).

ET, JL (et DB) sont prêts à réagir avant le 31 déc. (ou un peu après : JL) par écrit sur la 3e contribution de DG (que je leur communique par ce courrier). Je rappelle que j'avais proposé d'écrire directement à DG. Je serais reconnaissant à DG de communiquer à chacun des "réacteurs" une photocopie des deux autres réactions qui lui ont été adressées. Cela pourra faciliter notre rencontre de 1984.

Le 5 février 1984, je leur écrivis enfin :
Excusez-moi d'avoir attendu si longtemps pour vous écrire à nouveau depuis août. J'attendais d'avoir reçu vos trois réponses à ma lettre du 10 août dernier. Quoique n'en ayant reçu directement que deux, je crois nécessaire de fixer définitivement nos projets de rencontre pour l'été prochain.

A. D'après ce que je sais directement ou indirectement de vos réactions, je considère que vous pouvez vous trouver ici du 20 au 23 août prochains. Si ce n'est pas le cas, écrivez-moi d'urgence. Si donc vous ne recevez rien de moi avant la fin de février, considérez que cette date est définitivement fixée.

De mon côté, je considère
1) que vous êtes décidés tous les trois à être ici du 20 août au soir jusqu'au 23 août au soir (avec possibilité de rester un ou deux jours de plus, si cela arrange l'un ou l'autre d'entre vous),

2) que si l'un d'entre vous est retenu par un empêchement imprévu, il délègue à ceux qui seront ici le droit de décider du mode de publication des documents qui m'ont été envoyés et que je vous ai communiqués à propos de notre recherche commune.

B. Dans ma lettre du 10 août, je vous disais que "ET, JL (et DB) sont prêts à réagir avant le 31 déc. (ou un peu après : JL) par écrit sur la 3e contribution de DG".

Cependant, en une réponse du 28 août, ET m'a écrit ceci que je crois utile de vous communiquer : "What is more of a problem is to decide what exactly we shall discuss in Fribourg. I discussed this, too, with JL. I suggest that we shall start out to discuss the methodological background of each of our contributions, each one speaking for himself. In my case that would involve the other books I have dealt with in the past and the same refers to the other participants. Each of us will speak up, not necessarily from a written paper, and at some point in the discussion we will reach the story of David and Goliath. This could, I think, be very fruitful indeed. ... Because of this proposal I suggest not to discuss DG's reaction. I prefer to leave that to the meeting itself, even if this differs from my previously expressed views. I think that JL agrees with this, but he'll speak for himself." [J'espère ne pas avoir déformé les paroles de ET en les déchiffrant.]

Etant donné cette prise de position de ET (et de JL ?), je n'ai pas rédigé de réponse à la 3e contribution de DG. J'aimerais avoir les réactions de DG et de JL au "point de départ" proposé par ET pour notre rencontre de l'été prochain. De mon côté, je proposerais que chacun rédige (même brièvement) une contribution méthodologique (chacun l'apportant avec lui, mais des propositions écrites aidant à accrocher la discussion).

De fait, seul JL formula par écrit des 'Methodological Remarks' qu'il communiqua aux participants au début du colloque qu'ils tinrent à Fribourg du 20 au 23 août 1984. Lors de cette rencontre, l'entretien porta surtout sur les problèmes de méthode qui s'étaient fait jour à l'occasion de notre travail commun.

Il fut décidé que chacun rédigerait ensuite un dernier 'papier' où il tirerait les conclusions de notre séminaire de quatre ans.

Le 21 janvier 1985, ces quatre derniers papiers furent communiqués à tous les participants, chacun ayant la possibilité d'envoyer encore un 'appendice' si quelque chose lui paraissait manquer.

Nous publions ci-après :

D'abord la 3e contribution de DG (qui fut communiquée aux autres participants, le 10 août 1983).

Puis les remarques méthodologiques que JL communiqua aux autres au début du colloque de Fribourg.

Enfin les conclusions tirées, après le colloque, par chacun des quatre participants : Celle de ET dont la première partie (pp. 129-137) était déjà rédigée avant le colloque. Celles de DB et de DG.

Celle de JL qui servira d'épilogue à ce travail commun.

It has once again been both pleasurable and profitable to study the responses of my three colleagues to the initial Contributions. I will now attempt to comment on those three of the four issues raised by DB on which it is appropriate for me to comment.

I. THE METHODOLOGICAL ISSUES RAISED BY **ET**

I am particularly glad to have this opportunity of clarifying my position. I agree with ET more, perhaps, than he realises, and I am sorry if the order in which I attacked the problem in my Contribution has confused the issue.

ET in his Contribution dealt first with textual matters (pp. 19-39) and then with literary questions (pp. 39-43). In my Contribution I dealt first with literary questions (Sections I-IV) and then with textual matters (Section V). ET feels that my order exposes me to one serious weakness, undue subjectivity, and then to one serious fault, *petitio principii.* How valid are these criticisms ? I answer as follows :

A. The Presuppositions Behind My Order

1. My Response shows that I am still not as ready as my colleagues to state with certainty at what level the minuses/pluses came about. Sections I-IV, however, of my Contribution were based on the working hypothesis which I stated in *Textus* VII, 1969, 1 : "Given a peculiarity in the LXX, we may not be able to say definitely whether it is, or is not, founded on a Hebrew text differing from the MT. *But if for the argument's sake we suppose it is,* we can proceed to consider whether this supposed Hebrew Vorlage, or the MT, better represents the original story. And at this level decision is often possible".

Now ET feels that his translation-analysis proves that the short text of *G in I S. 17-18 is based on a short Hebrew text. I am not so sure that it proves it (see B below); but throughout Sections I-IV I assumed it, without argument or proof, as a working hypothesis. I even went further in ET's direction : as a working hypothesis I assumed, with ET, that *G and *M represented two *Hebrew versions* of the David-Goliath story. The advantage of adopting these hypotheses was that it allowed me to proceed at once to consider the two supposed "versions" of the story as stories (just as ET does in his second section, pp. 39-43), in order to determine, if possible, whether one version derived from the other by expansion or abbreviation, or whether

they were completely independent. My conclusion was that one version was a truncation of the other; and that, therefore, if the working hypothesis was true, that the two
versions were once represented in different Hebrew texts, the conclusion would be
that the shorter Hebrew text was a truncation of the longer Hebrew text.

Now admittedly this conclusion is the direct opposite of ET's; but I do not see how
my methodology involves significantly more subjectivism than ET's. Granted that many
of my literary arguments are subjective, but equally so are his (in his paper 39-43) —
indeed since his case in his Section II is argued in a very brief and summary manner, some
of his claims and conclusions seem (to me) to be somewhat more arbitrary than mine.

But be that as it may, I cannot see either how my order of approach to the problem this far led me to a *petitio principii*. My presupposition was that both "versions"
may have been represented by Hebrew texts; I did not suppose that my subsequent
argument proved that presupposition. All I was seeking to prove in Sections I-IV of
my Contribution was that even if the two "versions" once existed in two different
Hebrew texts, the shorter version was a truncation of the longer.

2.   Nor can I see that I fell into the trap of *petitio principii* when in Section V of
my Contribution I turned to textual matters. Having concluded in Sections I-IV
that one version was a truncation of the other, I proceeded to ask in Section V at what
level the truncation was most likely to have taken place, at the level of the Hebrew
or at the level of the Greek. This did admittedly involve questioning my original
working hypothesis, and in the end rejecting it. But that did not logically invalidate
the conclusion I reached in Sections I-IV. That conclusion was, I repeat, "even if the
two versions once existed in two Hebrews texts, the shorter version was a truncation
of the longer". The conclusion still stands even if further consideration makes it seem
likely that the two versions did not at one stage both exist in Hebrew texts.

I agree with ET that the shorter text was probably not the result either of the
translator's, or of some scribe's, activity. I consider it, however, to be the result of
abridgement, and that at a much more deliberate, exegetical and scholarly level,
whereas ET apparently is only prepared to envisage the possibility that an originally
short version has been added to at some stage in the literary process. Is this because
of some unspoken assumption on ET's part that literary works in antiquity always
evolved and grew by accretion ? If short texts could be lengthened, why should longer
texts not sometimes be shortened ? (See also DB Réponse p. 96, "Ajoutons que... :).

Be that as it may, I still think it is *possible* that the truncation took place at the
level of the Hebrew, though I hold it to be more likely that it took place at the level
of the Greek. But whatever conclusions we adopt on this issue, I think that what I
have said in my Response pp. 99ff bears repetition : we should not unduly limit in
advance the theoretical possibilities.

B.   The Strength (and Weakness) of ET's Case

The strength of ET's case is that decisions based on a study of translation-technique are less subjective than those based on literary criticism; but it is important to

distinguish between what ET has demonstrated beyond doubt, and the further deductions he has made with rather less certainty.

What his analysis of translation-technique has shown beyond all doubt is that what the translator translates, he translates reasonably faithfully and literally, i.e. he does not indulge in wild paraphrase or précis. But strictly speaking it does not logically follow from the observation that what he translates he translates literally and accurately, that he must therefore necessarily have translated the whole of the document before him. It may create a high probability that he did : it does not logically prove it.

This admittedly is a small point. Much more important is the consideration (see my Response p.99f) that if the translator had had before him a longer Hebrew text, and had translated it all faithfully and fully, and some later scholar subsequently truncated his translation, then a study of what was left of the translation would certainly reveal that the translator was faithful to the Hebrew as far as his translation-technique was concerned; but it would be quite false to deduce from the fact that the translation-technique was faithful, the conclusion that the translator must have had before him a short Hebrew text.

How likely is it, then, that the original Greek translation has been truncated by some subsequent critical scholar ? Well, ps.-Aristeas (Sections 310-311) anticipates the possibility of such a truncation, and purports to tell of a precaution taken against it; and the fragments of Demetrius show him aware of the *aporiai* in the Greek translation. Against this it will be argued that there is no extant Greek manuscript-evidence to show that there was ever a longer Old Greek text than we now have. And that is true. But it is also true that there is no extant Hebrew manuscript, Qumranic or other, that presents a short Hebrew text of our chapters. In this situation, if we were to dismiss in advance the possibility of subsequent truncation of the Greek; and if we were to allow only the possibility of a hypothetical short Hebrew text; then if starting from this assumption we argued that a study of the translation-technique of the Greek proved that the Greek was based on a short Hebrew text, would we not be in danger of a *petitio principii* ?

II. **JL**'s TREATMENT OF THE MERAB/MICHAL PASSAGES

Here my chief concern would be to enquire as to the validity of some of the axioms which JL lays down for the literary criticism of these passages.

A. Are the sections on Merab and Michal part of the story of David and Goliath ?

JL's answer to this question is no. The reason he gives is : "When one wishes to connect the gift of Saul's daughter with the promise in question [i.e. with the tripartite promise in 17,25, DG], then one should be able to show how the other aspects of the promise were kept." (p.89). How valid is this claim ?

It is, one might have thought, a very common thing in life and in literature that a man, X, being in difficulty of some kind, will make another man, Y, various promises if Y will do this or that, and then when Y, against all expectation, manages to do the set task, X conveniently forgets his promises or else partially or completely refuses to honour them. So, for instance, in the classical myth, Pelias, being afraid of Jason, promises that if Jason captures the Golden Fleece, Pelias will hand over the kingdom to him. Jason captures the Golden Fleece; but then Pelias refuses to hand over the kingdom.

Theoretically, then, it is conceivable that a biblical narrator should have wished to convey the idea that Saul, having made the tripartite promise of 17,25 thereafter went back on part or all of it. The question at issue for us is, how must such a narrator have gone about the telling of the story if he were going to make it evident to his readers that the portion which relates the failure to keep the promise is part of the same story as recorded the making of the promise ? Will it be enough if when it comes to the point where the promise should be fulfilled, the narrator describes at length and in detail how Part A of the promise was fulfilled only begrudgingly and after a false start, a withdrawal, and the adding of further, seemingly impossible, conditions; and then, by making no further reference to the fulfilling of Parts B and C of the promise, leaves the reader to conclude that those two parts were not fulfilled ? JL answers No to this. He lays it down (p. 89), that the narrator must explicitly mention how all three parts of the promise were kept (or, presumably, not kept). If he does not explicitly say what happened to all the parts of the promise, the connection between the two parts of the narrative will be completely lost upon his readers.

To some of us this axiom would seem to be a recipe for a very dull and wooden narrative style. But this is a matter of taste, and therefore of personal preference. What I find disconcerting is what happens when one puts this axiom together with another axiom which he enunciates on p. 89 of his Response : "On the other hand, the occurrence of expressions or even sentences in several parts of a text does not necessarily prove the original unity of the narrative. The final editor may have used and re-used these terms and turnings in order to produce a better unity between several independent sections." Logically, JL's case is irrefutable; but put his two axioms together and apply them to our problem, and the result seems to be :

a) because 18,17ff mentions only Part A of the promise, and not Parts B and C, it cannot be considered part of the same narrative as 17,25;

b) even if 18,17ff mentioned all three parts of the promise, it still could not be regarded as necessarily part of the same narrative as 17,25.

On the basis of these two axioms few, perhaps no, ancient narratives (or modern ones either) could in strict logic be confidently regarded as literary unities. If we do regard them as unities, it must be on the grounds of personal taste and presupposition. Perhaps here, then, we can get no further than declaring our presuppositions. To me JL's presupposition seems to be that a biblical narrative must be presumed to be composite unless it is in strict logic proved otherwise — and the proof will be difficult, if not impossible. My presupposition would rather be that a biblical (or classical) narrative should be presumed to be a unity unless indisputable evidence is adduced for considering it composite.

B. Is it true that "the story does not present the stories of Saul's daughters as a fulfilment of the promise but rather as a part of Saul's plan to remove David" (JL Response p. 89) ?

Theoretically, the daughter-stories do not have to be *either* a fulfilment of the promise *or* a part of the removal-plan. They could be both. Real life can really be as complicated as that ! Whether they are, or are not, regarded as both will depend on the prior judgement as to whether 18,17ff is part of the same narrative as 17,25, or not. If one knows *on other grounds* that it is not, then it is fair enough to point out that 18,17ff does not explicitly mention the promise, but only the wish to remove David. If on the other hand 18,17ff were part of the same narrative as 17,25, it would be impossible to read 18,17ff as something completely unrelated to the promise of 17,25.

So here again, JL seems to me to be opting for one presupposition rather than another. A further example of this is his remark on p. 90 of his Response : "No similar context is given in 17,12. David enters the scene unexpectedly". One might protest, of course, that David's entry is not all that unexpected, since he has been mentioned a mere twelve verses earlier in 16,23 in such a way as might lead the reader confidently to expect his re-appearance (see my Contribution pp. 64ff). But this protest is ruled out in advance by JL's presupposition announced on p. 90 : "When one does not accept the MT of 1 Sam 17-18 as an original unit then..." (and if not 17-18, *a fortiori* not 16-18, presumably). In other words the non-acceptance of 17-18 as a literary unit is the prior judgement.

Now on p. 89f JL remarks that "the present MT version may be due to an editor who knew different stories about David and Saul's daughter(s). The LXX knew only the one on Michal. If his Vorlage had attested to Merab's story as well, the translator might not have omitted it in order to avoid the contradiction with 2 Sam 21,8. He might rather have changed Michal's name into Merab's in 21,8". My comment on this can be brief : first, DB (Réponse p. 96) no longer thinks that the *translator* would have omitted large portions of his Vorlage; and I have never thought it likely that the translator was responsible for the omissions. And secondly, my remarks on the danger involved in failing to consider the possibility that the omissions took place after the LXX was made (see above p. 116) apply here too.

III. COMMENT ON **DB**'s REFUTATIONS OF CAIRD's OBJECTIONS

A. A General Analogy

Though in matters of detail I disagree with DB, I support his general thesis, and I wish first to cite an analogous case which in several points supports DB against Caird.

It has been argued by Caird and others :

1. that the disputed sections in the David-Goliath story contain some details which are not inconsistent with the rest of the story, and these cannot be said to have

been omitted from the Septuagint for harmonistic reasons (Caird : Objection 1.).

2. that we cannot think it likely that an editor would have made harmonistic omissions if he did not do it consistently (Caird : Objections 2 and 3).

3. that the size of the alleged harmonistic omissions is unique and makes harmonistic omission an unlikely explanation.

As an analogous case I cite the complete absence from OGr. of the summary of Jeroboam's reign and the announcement of his successor : "And the rest of the acts of Jeroboam ... and Nadab his son reigned in his stead". In the MT this stands at I Kings 14,19-20. A summary of this kind is standard in this position throughout the Books of Kings, and the LXX normally has such summaries : cf. I K. 14,29-31; 15,7-8; 15,31-32; 16,14; 16,20; 16,27-28. Where KR duplicates OGr. a summary is found in both (though not equal in extent) : see I K. 16,28c-h and I K. 22,45-51.

1. First notice the length of the summary omitted by OGr at I K. 14,19-20. It consists of two longish verses, easily the equivalent of many of the omissions in I S. 17-18. Cf. DB's answer to Caird's 3rd Objection, Contribution pp. 52s.

2. Notice that the summary would not itself conflict with anything in the context of the LXX. The reason for its omission is as follows : it forms the last two verses of the long paragraph I K. 14,1-20. The first 18 verses of that paragraph tell of the visit of Jeroboam's wife to the prophet Ahijah; but in the LXX this same story has already been told in the course of the duplicate Jeroboam story inserted at I K. 12, 24a-z (it occupies 24g-n), and the story at 14,1-18 conflicts in several important respects with the story as told in 12,24g-n. The story of 14,1-18 was therefore omitted for harmonistic reasons; but when it was omitted it unintentionally dragged with it the last two verses of the paragraph which had nothing to do with the Ahijah story.

This is the same kind of point as DB makes in his Contribution p. 51.

3. Notice that the LXX in I K. is not consistent. It omits the Ahijah story from ch. 14 because that story would duplicate, and conflict with, the story in 12,24g-n. But at 12,24a-f and o-z it retains (or inserts) a story of Jeroboam's rise to power which duplicates, and conflicts with, the story of his rise to power given at 11,43-12,24. It is important to notice that this kind of atomistic and inconsistent critical activity is what we find both in the Talmud and Midrashim, and in scholars like Demetrius.

4. Notice that these points 1-3 all apply equally whether the omissions (and additions) in I K. 11-14 were made at the level of the Hebrew, at the level of the translators, or at the level of the subsequent critics and editors of the Greek translation.

B. Some Details in DB's Refutations

1. In his answer to Caird's Objection 2 (Contribution p. 51f) DB argues that *G has eliminated inconsistency. I hold (see my Contribution p. 56) that there was no inconsistency to start with. In the second instance cited by DB, it seems to me that αἴρων τὰ σκεύη does mean 'armour-bearer' and not just 'coolie' : cf. 2 S. 18,15 and 23,37(36). A mere coolie would surely not be mentioned in the list in 23,17. But, as is

evident from 3. above, I do not think it necessary to claim that the harmonistic omission has been carried out consistently throughout the whole book. The Merab/Michal question is a case in point. If the omission of the Merab section from ch. 18 is meant to harmonise ch. 18 with 2 S. 21,8, the fact remains that 2 S. 6,23 and 2 S. 3,14-16 appear to conflict with 2 S. 21,8 in one way or another, and yet *G does not omit these passages.

2. On DB's observation (Contribution p. 53) that many of *G's omissions concern "simples répétitions inutiles", I would comment by referring to my Contribution pp. 75ff. The point with many of these small and seemingly useless repetitions is that while at first sight they do seem to be needless, and their omission sometimes even appears superficially to obviate apparent difficulties, closer study shows that their presence was necessary for the precise thought-flow in their context, and that their omission is harmful and secondary.

3. I agree totally with DB's answer to Caird's Objection 4 (DB, Contribution pp. 53f).

4. What I think about Caird's Objections 5 and 6 will already be apparent from my Contribution.

DAVID AND GOLIATH IN THE HEBREW AND GREEK TEXTS

I learned much from my distinguished colleagues : from the predominantly textcritical approach of ET, the mainly literary historical remarks of DB and the chiefly rhetorical critical observations of DG. The differences in their respective methods appear to lead to divergent conclusions. Therefore, some methodological consideration may be to the point.

Although textual and literary criticism ought to be clearly distinguished from each other, they should not be separated. They are complementary. This is especially the case when major differences occur between the textual witnesses. There appears to be a growing consensus on this point not only in our papers on the David and Goliath story but also in other scholarly work. We may perhaps refer to the recent research on the topic by J. Trebolle Barrera [1]. It should be clear that, when we use the term literary criticism, we use it in its larger meaning, implying all kinds of historical criticism analysing 'the biblical books up to the stage where they reached their final form' [2] as well as rhetorical criticism and structuralism analysing nothing but the final form.

Discussions may arise concerning the sequence in which the respective critical methods should be applied. It is probably preferable to start with textual criticism. Indeed, when one tries to define the relation between different forms of a text, *in casu* the story of David and Goliath, one deals with the history of the text. Such a historical study is not the first aim of rhetorical criticism or of structuralism. These methods may find rhetorical and structural qualities in the text at any stage of its development or of its transmission. These qualities may have improved or deteriorated in the course of the history of the text. One form of the text, for instance the Hebrew, may have better rhetorical qualities then the other, i.e. the Greek. However this assesment does not allow direct conclusions concerning the historical priority of one form over the other. On the other hand historical literary criticism tries to reconstruct the earliest and most hypothetical stages in the history of the text whereas textual criticism focuses on its latest and partly still extant forms. One must admit that textual criticism most often leads to the reconstruction of a no longer existing 'original text'. Its conclusions are often hypothetical. Nevertheless, literary criticism is to be based on a 'critical text', i.e. a text which has been submitted to a textcritical analysis. For these reasons textual criticism seems to offer the best entrance to the study of the textual phenomena in question.

121

Methodological Remarks

Whatever method is chosen as a starting point, one should first record the formal or factual characteristics of the text. Judgements of value or evaluations should be postponed as long as possible, since at this stage the risk of subjectivity is higher [3].

I. TEXTUAL CRITICISM

a) First of all, the textual witnesses both of the Greek and of the Hebrew versions should be weighed carefully. Everybody agrees upon this. However, in cases such as the David and Goliath story, one might all too easily neglect this part of the investigation since the data seem to be well known and no new information seems to be available. It is true, the new data are not overabundant. In as far as the Hebrew text is concerned, the excavations of Qumran produced no more than a scrap of 1 Sam 18,17-18 and a longer segment of 1 Sam 17,3-6. Nevertheless the Qumranic fragments may prove to be relevant especially when they are considered in a larger context. Indeed, the fragment of 1 Sam 17,3-6 belongs to a scroll 4Q1Sam-a representing a non-massoretic type of text. As for the Greek text no new data seem to have been discovered recently. The version of Hippolytus remains interesting but it should not be overburdened. Perhaps the iconographical lead procured by the 'David plates' from Cyprus should be followed somewhat further. These plates which probably reflect a short text similar to the Hippolytus version are obviously inspired by older models [4].

b) When the witnesses are duly recorded one should turn to a characterisation of the translation techniques used in the section under discussion and in its context. This step is fully developed in E. Tov's Handbook [5] and in his papers on 1 Sam 17-18. A critical note may be brought up concerning the evaluation of 'semitisms' [6].

A first conclusion of this step in the inquiry is that the section in question is translated rather literally. A second conclusion is slightly more hypothetical. Since the translation is rather literal it is unlikely that the translator would have omitted larger sections which were found in his Vorlage. The absence of omissions in 1 Sam (LXX) comparable in length with the 'minuses' in 1 Sam 17-18, confirms this point. One might object refering to the 'minus' 1 Sam 13,1 (LXX). However it is not at all certain that this 'minus' is an omission [7]. Thus we may accept as a probability that the 'minuses' in 1 Sam 17-18 are not due to the translator but rather to his Vorlage. We have to admit that 'probability' does not mean 'certainly'. Other data will have to weaken or to strengthen the argument.

c) After having traced the Septuagint back to its Vorlage, as far as possible, one should turn to a comparison of the MT with the Septuagint and with its hypothetical Vorlage, in order to reconstruct the 'original form' of the text. However, here two preliminary problems arise. The first one concerns the identification of the 'original form' and the second the relation between textual and literary criticism.

What is the 'original form' of the O.T. ? With E. Tov one may identify it with its finished composition [8]. However, when do we have a finished composition of a biblical text ? In the given example, is it the shorter or the longer one ? Where are the criteria ? One may be inclined to prefer that form of the text which explains the other. In the David and Goliath case one may suggest that the Septuagint or its Vorlage omitted some sections because of harmonising and pedantic tendencies. In this view the MT stands closer to the original form. Or one may be convinced that the MT in a midrashic way expanded on the Vorlage of the LXX. In both cases the argument is built on the presupposition that only one finished composition can be accepted. But, is this a necessary and correct presupposition ? Several forms of the same Book of the Bible appear to have functioned alongside each other in the congregation of Qumran [9]. A decisive factor in this situation is the recognition of the respective texts or forms of the text by the religious community to which they belong.

Applied to the David and Goliath story this means that both the Septuagint and the Massoretic text may have preserved 'a final form' of the narrative.

This leads us to a second preliminary question : are these different 'forms' of the text to be considered as distinct editorial compositions or simply as successive products of the transmission of the text ? In the David and Goliath case the divergences between the Greek and the Hebrew texts are so important that they can hardly be adscribed to accidental errors of scribes or translators. They must be due to deliberate interventions. If this is true it will be hard to decide whether these took place in the course of the formation of the text or of its transmission. Theoretically, literary criticism deals with the formation of the text and textual criticism with the finished compositions and their transmission. In practice, the borderline between both areas tends to blur. Moreover the methods used on both levels largely coincide, once the probability of accidental errors is outruled.

II. LITERARY AND TEXTUAL CRITICISM

How shall one proceed in the evaluation of cases where two forms of the text show major differences ? In general, formal criteria should be given precedence over arguments based on possible biases in the context of the text or on its artistic qualities. Among the formal criteria we may mention patterns and literary genres as well as the vocabulary of the text and its context.

a) Stories or parts of them are often constructed according to fixed forms or patterns [10]. Features disturbing these patterns may be significant and reveal traces of the history of the text. In 1 Sam 17,12ff several characteristics can be found of a pattern similar to the one in Judges 13,1ff; 1 Sam 1,1ff and especially in 1 Sam 9,1ff. The formal correspondances are striking.

$$X \text{ שמו } ... \text{ יש מ } -$$
$$\text{ולו בן } -$$
$$\text{ויאמר } X \text{ אל } Y \text{ בנו } -$$
$$\text{קח נא } -$$

In the introductory sections both of 1 Sam 9,1ff and of 1 Sam 17,12ff not only the terminology but also the sequence of the data are almost identic. One of the special characteristics of these sections is that they do not presuppose an earlier introduction. They begin an independant story bringing a young hero on the scene [11]. This means that the narrative in 1 Sam 17,12ff does not presuppose the data given in 1 Sam 16,1ff and in 17,1ff. Obviously the text of 1 Sam 17,12ff has been tampered with in order to adapt its story to the pericopes prefixed to it or with which it had been combined [12].

Similar formal remarks can be made concerning 17,1-11 and its relation with 17,32ff. As far as Goliath and his taunt is concerned a comparison with biblical parallels, especially with the Rabshakeh, and his speech in 2 Kings 18.19 should be preferred over a comparison with the 'classical heroes'. The striking similarities in the terminology strenghten the connections between the two cases (comp. 2 Kings 18,7 with 1 Sam 18,(5)14-15 and 2 Kings 19,4.16 with 1 Sam 17,(26)36). It should be noted that the interruption of Goliath's speech in 1 Sam 17,43 LXX is not exceptional. The Rabshakeh is equally interrupted by his opponents (2 Kings 18,26ff).

b) The contacts with the context are important. They offer objective data. However the threat of subjectivity menaces their interpretation. In the case of a lengthy 'plus' one should check whether or not its terminology is in agreement with that of its context and whether or not it presupposes its context. One should also consider the textual unit to which the 'plus' belongs and see whether the context of this unit presupposes the longer or the shorter form of the unit.

The evaluation of the correspondences in the terminology is difficult. They may be due to the topic or to the unity of the authorship or to the editorial adaptation of an insert to its context. The latter interpretation is most likely to be preferred when repetitions occur which disturb or interrupt the flow of the narrative. Thus 17,12-13 repeats the information concerning the eight sons of Jesse, given already in 16,10-11. In 17,12ff this information disturbs the logic of the story which asks for four sons only.

On the other hand some of the expressions in 17,12-31 agree very well with those of 17,32-54. In both sections David is presented as a boy and pastor. Goliath is typified as the uncircumcised Philistine who defies the armees of the living God both in 17,26 and in 17,36. According to DB the conclusion must be that 17,32-54 was composed as the continuation of 17,12-31. Moreover, the editor of 16,1-14 seems to have borrowed materials both from 17,12-31 (the names of the elder brothers) and from 17,32-54 (the description of David, ruddy and handsome). According to DB this proves that the editor of 16,1-14 found 17,12-54 as a unity. However, it should be noted that the description of David in 16,12 does not fit the context very well. It may not be part of the original story according to which the Lord does not look on the outward appearance : 16,7. The core of the story of 17,12ff may have mentioned the name of the oldest brother of David only. The names in 17,13 may have been inserted in order to strengthen the link with the context. Verse 17,13 is certainly redundant and overburdened. As for the description of the Philistine in 17,26 and 36 its original 'Sitz' may have been in 17,36 in the version preserved in the LXX [13]. From there it may have been inserted into 17,26.

The disagreements in the terminology of the 'plus' and of its context may be more relevant. However, differences in the terminology are not necessarily disagreements. When in our example the author uses המעגלה in v. 17,20 referring to Israel's 'encampment' whereas elsewhere he uses המערכת or מחנה, this may be a synonym and nothing more. However, when in v. 23 the Philistine 'comes up' (עלה) out of the ranks of the Philistines, this hardly fits the scene described in 17,1-11 where both armees are encamped on two sides of a valley and one has to come down out of his own ranks to set out towards the enemy (ירד v. 4).

Before these complex data are evaluated a further analysis of the language and terminology should be given.

c) In the comparison of two divergent textforms the exploration of the early or late character of the Hebrew language is important. If the Hebrew idioms used in a text prove to be late, then this text must be a late composition. The variants in the Greek version may then easily preserve traces of an older or alternative phase in composition rather than a reworking or a free translation. S.R. Driver detects several characteristics of late Hebrew in 1 Sam 17.18. Of course, in this context, 'late' is an ambiguous notion. In Driver's view it appears to refer to the Hebrew of Chronicles, Ezra, Nehemiah and of 'late' Psalms [14]. A. Rofé further developed this argument in an article which was not available to me.

Most of the symptoms betraying a late Hebrew signaled by S.R. Driver occur in 17,32ff : מעל ל... in 17,39; הארץ & plural verb in 17,46; יהושיע with its retention of the ה in 17,47; שאול המלך in 18,6 [15].

These data suggest that at least 1 Sam 17,32ff does not belong to the early layers of the Book of Samuel, or, that the section in question has been reworked at a late stage of the redaction.

At this stage of the inquiry a hypothesis could be formulated allowing all or most of the data to fall into place. In our example the data appear to suggest that 17,12ff in the MT preserved the beginning of a story on David's accession to the court of Saul. It is probably older than its present context. The scene of the anointment in 16,1ff is likely to be a younger prophetic introduction to the story. Together with 17,1-11.32ff it looks like an alternative presentation of the David story. The MT combined both forms of the narrative; the Septuagint preserved the younger alternative only. In a further stage one may then try to demonstrate that the redactor for the massoretic text type did a very skilfull job. To me this seems to be a question of taste. One may also try to prove that the Septuagint did not simply preserve an alternative form of the text but rather truncated its longer form. For our problem this step in the precedure could be important as a counterproof.

d) We should repeat here that the rhetorical qualities of a text are not necessarily a criterium of its originality. The original author may have been more 'clumsy' than a later more skilfull redactor, or vice versa. The proof of a truncation by a redactor, translator or copyist will have to be based on formal criteria. Let us take 1 Sam 18,5 as an example. According to DG this is the first occurence of a refrain with as theme : David's increasing popularity [16]. Its three occurences present a picture to the completion of which all three are necessary. There is no hint of unnecessary repetitiousness that might suggest that an originally shorter account has been filled out by an expansionist addition. Thus DG. One may accept that verses 6.16.30 display some sort of a refrain. Is this a sufficient reason to conclude that they are part of an original composition ? DG gives the impression that there is an escalation in the repeated refrains describing David's 'ever increasing popularity', or at least that the three refrains are necessarily complementary. Both assertions seem to be rather subjective. Turning to more formal matters we notice that according to DG the 'men of war' in v. 5 presumably refers to the elite troops. A comparison with the other attestations of this expressions shows clearly that it simply denotes all the soldiers and not the elite troops. (Num 31,49; Deut 2,14.16; Josh 5,4.6; 6,3; 1 Sam 18,5; 1 Kings 9,22; 2 Kings 25,4.19; Jer 38,4; 39,4; 41,3.16; 49,26; 51,22; 52,25; Joel 4,9.) More intriguing is the fact that this phrase appears to occur in late texts only. A further analysis would argue in favour of a postexilic date of all of these texts. The idiom expressing David's success, also in 1 Sam 18,5, finds its most literal parallel in the dtr summary of Hezekiah's deeds and their evaluation in 2 Kings 18,7 : בכל אשר ... ישכיל. This appears to confirm the late date of composition of 1 Sam 18,5. The summary in 2 Kings 18,7 deals with the correct relation between Jhwh and the king as well as with the resulting successful life of the king. A similar pattern may be found in Jos 1,7.8; 1 Sam 18,14.15; 1 Kings 2,3 and perhaps in Is 52,13 and Jer 10, 21. In each of these cases the verb השכיל is used in order to express the success of a leader based on a correct relation with Jhwh. In 1 Sam 18,5 this pattern is slightly distorted. The relation between Jhwh and his king is replaced by the relation between king Saul and his officer David. David is successful not directly in what he does but in what he is sent to do. The editor probably adapted the pattern which he found in 18,14.15 in order to link verses 17,55-58 and 18,2 (or 18,1-4) with the context in which he wished to insert them.

This brief attempt towards a counterproof, based on DG's observations concerning 1 Sam 18,5, and its examination relying on formal criteria, does not contradict the earlier argumentation. The verse in question is part of a late editorial composition taken up in the MT. The artistic evaluation of this composition does not offer any arguments in favour of its priority.

Concluding these methodological remarks we suggest that in cases where major differences occur between the Septuagint and the MT :
1. Textcritical and literary critical methods should complement each other;
2. Formal criteria should be given precedence over criteria based on matters of contents.

Following this procedure one may reach a firm conclusion concerning the history of the formation and of the transmission of the text. This conclusion does not necessarily lead to a choice, giving preference to one text, for example the Septuagint, over the other. Both the MT and the LXX, or its Vorlage, are final texts with typical characteristics. Both have been accepted by and functioned in religious communities. There is no reason to discard one and to keep the other. A comparison could be made here with the synoptic gospels.

NOTES

1   See the interesting investigations by J.C. Trebolle-Barrera, Salomon Y Jeroboam (1 R 2-12,14). (Bibliotheca Salmanticensis), Salamanca, Jerusalem, 1980; Redaction, Recension, and Midrash in the Books of Kings, Bulletin of the IOSCS nr. 15 (1982) 12-35. And more recently : La primitiva confesión de fe Yahvista (1 Re 18,36-37). De la critica textual a la teologia biblica, Salmanticensis 31 (1984) 181-205; Jehù y Joàs. Texto y composición literaria de 2 Reyes 9-11, Valencia, 1984, with further bibliography.

2   See E. Tov, The Text-critical Use of the Septuagint in Biblical Research. (Jerusalem Bibl. Studies, 3), Jerusalem, 1981, p. 33.

3   Compare with J. Trebolle-Barrera, Salomon y Jeroboam, p. 36ff., esp. p. 42.

4   See The Story of David & Goliath in Hebrew & Greek, note 28.

5   See the reference in note 2.

6   Retroverted 'pluses' of the Greek text may reveal 'semitisms'. One might be inclined to appreciate these phenomena as proofs of a Hebrew Vorlage differing from the MT. However, this argument is a rather weak one. Indeed, the translator's Greek style may have been influenced by the Hebrew language even when he was freely composing. Moreover, when translators added inserts to the text they often took their inspiration from the context. The result was that their own Greek could hardly be distinguished from their translation-Greek. Comp. our Second Thoughts on David & Goliath, p. 88.

7   Similar chronological remarks indicating the age of a king when he began to reign and the number of years he reigned over his country are to be found in 2 Sam 2,10 (Ishbosheth, Saul's son); 2 Sam 5,4 (David); 1 Kings 14,21; 22,42; 2 Kings 8,17.26; 12,1; 14,2; 15,2.33; 16,2; 18,2; 21,1.19; 22,1; 23,31.36; 24,8.18 (kings of Judah). For the kings of Israel a different formula is used in which the age of the king is not given. It is possible that the notes on Saul in 1 Sam 13,1, on Ishbosheth in 2 Sam 2,10 and on David in 2 Sam 5,4 were coined after the stereotype formula used for the Southern kings in 1 Kings 14,21 etc.

8   Op. cit., p. 31.

9   See E. Tov, A Modern Textual Outlook Based on the Qumran Scrolls. (HUCA, 53.) Cincinnati, 1982, pp. 11-27.

10   See J. Trebolle-Barrera, Redaction, Recension, and Midrash in the Books of Kings, Bulletin of the IOSCS nr. 15 (1982) p. 14ff. and the other works mentioned in note 1.

11   An other special feature of the story in 1 Sam 17,12ff is the test of the hero and his reward. A similar pattern can be found in Judges 1,12; Joshua 15,16. The king or chief promises to give (נתן) his daughter to the one who slays (נכה) the enemy. Once the deed accomplished, the daughter is given (נתן). In the David and Goliath story the major elements of this pattern are to be found in 1 Sam 17,25 and in 18,17. Notice the use of the verbs נתן and נכה.

12 Notice that both the stories of 1 Sam 9,1ff and of 17,12ff have been reworked in function of the royal anointing of the hero. Comp. L. Schmidt, Menschlichen Erfolg und Jahwes Initiative, Neukirchen, 1970, p. 63ff.; F. Crüsemann, Der Widerstand gegen das Königtum, Neukirchen, 1978, p. 57.

12. Compare with DG's first paper, p. 73ff.

13 In verse 36 the LXX has the longer text and is more convergent with v. 26. The shorter version of the MT can easily be explained as a case of *parablepsis*. Comp. N. Peters, Beiträge zur Text und Literarkritik sowie zur Erklärung der Bücher Samuel, Freiburg im Breisgau, 1899, p. 13.

14 S.R. Driver, Notes on the Hebrew Text and the Topography of the Books of Samuel, Oxford, 1913, pp. 146ff.

15 Further 'late' elements are : כיום ביום in 18,10; מלפני in 18,12; אשר for the usual כי in 18,15.

16 See DG's first paper, p. 71f.

THE STORY OF DAVID AND GOLIATH IN THE MT AND LXX

A. WRITTEN BEFORE THE MEETING (WITH MINOR CHANGES)

As some of you have said in the past, we are probably closer to each other's views than I thought we are. Now is the time to find this out, and there is no better way to do so than to turn to a description of our respective methods. Sometimes we are aware of our methods, but often we are not. Sometimes one only gets to formulating his methods when he sees the descriptions of others, and the disagreement with their views turns out to be the best guide to such a description. I don't know exactly what it implies to describe your own method, but we can at least do our best to do so.

I wand to stress how much I have enjoyed our common enterprise. In a scholarly world in which our colleagues are used to do their own thing in the splendid isolation of their studies it is rare that four colleagues should address exactly the same topic in order to better understand the topic, themselves and their colleagues.

Often we are not aware of our own methodological presuppositions, and therefore it would be a good idea to examine some issues in which such presuppositions come to light. I believe that this is the case with the *sequence* of the components of our discussion. After all, we agree with regard to the facts, but we discuss them in a different sequence, and it seems to me that this very sequence determines our conclusions.

Johan and I started off by discussing the text-critical problem, and while each of us has different emphases, we thought both that it was important to commence with this aspect. In this sequence, in which I started with the text-critical issues, I stressed the importance of the analysis of translation technique. Only afterwards we turned to the literary analysis of the story in its two versions, that is, MT and the LXX. David, on the other hand started off with the literary analysis, and this applies also to Dominique. In the subsequent discussion, the very sequence of the analysis became an issue of discussion, addressed in great detail by David in the second series of responses, or, if you wish, in the third series of contributions.

David writes : "I agree with ET more, perhaps, than he realises, and I am sorry if the order in my Contribution has confused the issue."

He then continues : "ET in his Contribution dealt first with textual matters (pp. 19-39) and then with literary questions (pp. 39-43). In my Contribution I dealt first with literary questions (sections I-IV) and then with textual matters (section V). ET feels that my order exposes me to one serious weakness, undue subjectivity, and then to one serious fault, *petitio principii*. How valid are these criticisms ?"

David claims that my argumentation is equally subjective as his. But he realizes that there is somewhat more *objectivity* involved in my procedure since I start from the data themselves, from what may be called "the hard facts". At the same time David knows, as all of us do, that in this area of the humanities there is hardly any real objectivity. All our work is subjective, but I claim that some analyses are more subjective than others, or, if you wish, some are more objective than others. I should not deceive myself, also my own work is subjective. Maybe I should not have used this term. Maybe I also should not have used the term *petitio principii*. I do believe that circular reasoning is involved in the reasoning of my colleagues with whom I disagree, but at the same time I know that also in my own argumentation there is circular reasoning, Afterwards I will refer to my own hidden assumptions. Among other things I agree with Dominique that the very use of the terms "version 1" and "version 2" carries a circular reasoning with regard to the literary evidence, but this is a minor point, since the two blocks are called version 1 and version 2 at a later stage in the discussion. I want to find out what the hidden presuppositions are behind the views with which I disagree, and also behind the views I espouse myself.

I do believe that it is incorrect to start with a literary analysis in sections in which such an analysis is based on textual evidence. I think it matters very much to determine with which evidence or analysis one starts to tackle the issues. It actually determines the *results* of the analysis. In my view it is absolutely mandatory to start the analysis with the textual evidence, and I will soon say why. At the same time I cannot guarantee that my own conclusions are correct just because I choose a sequence which I consider correct. The conclusions may very well be incorrect or imprecise. I, too, have some axiomatic beliefs which guide my thinking, and I am grateful to my colleagues for pointing them out. Of some of these beliefs I was not aware previously.

What I shall say from now onwards is probably some kind of "credo", and it reflects my own approach, rather than a polemic against the views of others. For me the evidence regarding the story of David and Goliath fits in a certain framework, viz., that of large-scale differences between textual witnesses bearing or possibly bearing on literary criticism. In fact, if I formulate the issue in this way we probably all agree, because I have only said that these witnesses *may* bear on literary criticism. Now, the doubts behind this formulation precisely reflect the problems involved. If these data bear on the literary criticism of the *Hebrew* Bible, they could be very important indeed for the Hebrew Bible, and if they don't, they could still be important, but only for the Greek Bible, and that would hardly be called "literary criticism". Now there is only one way to find out whether they bear on the Hebrew or the Greek Bible, that is to analyze the nature of the *documents* in which they are found, the MT and LXX.

130

I might add that this issue is related to other, similar situations in which textual evidence relates to the literary analysis of the *Hebrew* Bible. It so happens that I have dealt with quite a few of such issues in my Grinfield lectures at Oxford University. My approach to the story of David and Goliath is also reflected in my treatment of other large-scale differences between MT and the LXX : the differences between the long MT text of Jeremiah and its short Septuagint text, the long MT text of Ezekiel and the somewhat shorter text of the LXX, the differences between the MT and LXX of Joshua, and several content transpositions between the MT and LXX. All of these were approached similarly and in a way the conclusions are similar, that is, the short or different LXX text was taken to reflect a deviating Hebrew text, and that Hebrew text was explained as reflecting a stage in the development of the Hebrew book. Now, the fact that I can point to similar conclusions in parallel instances is not necessarily good. I may be caught here in a difficult situation, for I have a theory, and theories are dangerous. I may have fallen in the pit which I have dug for myself, for if one has a theory one is often bound to explain additional instances according to that existing theory. This is possible, but I think I have been sufficiently aware of these difficulties for not all instances are explained in the same way. It is the approach which is identical in all these cases, and not necessarily the results. Besides, I can point to at least one issue which I have solved differently. All of you know of the so-called "Miscellanies" in 1 Kings 2 (3 Reigns 2), and David knows more about them than anyone else (see his *Relics of Ancient Exegesis*). Now, at one point in my research I had hoped, so to speak, that these large-scale differences, too, reflect significant differences between MT and the LXX. If that would be the case, they could be added to the aforementioned list, and they, too could have reflected a stage in the development of the Hebrew Bible. Upon studying the Miscellanies, however, I was unable to explain them as bearing on the Hebrew Bible, and, in fact, I am unable to explain them at all. I refer to my article in *Textus* 11 (1984), 89-118. In this case, I believe, I did not fall in a trap, as I explained the evidence differently from the other instances. The approach, however, was identical since I started off discussing the textual evidence. Also in other instances I followed this approach, yet reached completely different conclusions. Thus, it is quite clear to me that the large-scale differences between the LXX and MT of Job do not bear on the literary analysis of that book. Starting from the textual evidence relating to the book of Job, one first has to evaluate the nature of the Greek evidence, and will then soon reach the conclusion that this Greek translation reflects a very free rendering of the Hebrew. Within that free rendering it is understandable, *post factum*, that the translator also omitted large sections of the Hebrew. This situation is very interesting for analyzing the approach of the translator, but *not* for an analysis of the Hebrew text. I realized that the short text of the LXX of Job is not always logical, so that the actions of the translator are not even understandable. It would have been very interesting if the LXX would witness to a shorter text of the book of Job, but this simply cannot be proven. Again, I should like to emphasize that we use the same approach for different texts, viz. start off from the textual evidence, yet reach different types of conlusions in each case.

Why then do I stress so much the *sequence* of the analysis ? Why should we start with the textual evidence for the story of David and Goliath ? I think we should always start to deal with textual evidence because the different versions of the story of David and Goliath have been transmitted to us in textual sources. As long as we don't know enough about the nature of the textual sources, we have no means of evaluating their contents. The contents of the stories in MT and LXX are the topic of much controversy, and this insecurity will remain, so the only more secure yardstick we have is an analysis of the nature of the texts themselves. If I may be allowed to make an unusual comparison, let me refer to the following. Upon comparison of a biblical story with its counterpart in the Midrash or Josephus or Medieval legends, naturally you would never dream of saying that the post-biblical data bear on the biblical story itself. The post-biblical data bear solely on the *exegesis* of the biblical story, because we know that the Midrash, Josephus and the Medieval stories were composed after the completion of the Bible. Now, in the case of the LXX the relation between the MT and LXX is not known when we set out to study the issues. The data in the LXX are relevant to the contents of the biblical story, but possibly they refer only to its exegesis. In the latter case we do not have to be involved at all in literary analysis, for that would not be relevant. The literary analysis of the story applies only to one or more written formulations of the story in Hebrew. To be engaged in a literary analysis of the LXX may not be so helpful, for you don't know whether you analyze a story originally written in Hebrew or in Greek.

There is more involved. Here, too, I have to admit to an axiomatic view. For me the MT is *not* the central text with which all other texts are collated. I know that in textual studies MT is usually taken as the central text to which all other texts are compared, but I consider this a mere convention devised in order to enable an easy analysis of the variants. After all, the MT is readily available, it is the central text of the Jewish community, and it is in Hebrew. But all of this does not imply that for scholars MT should be the central text as well. It has been recognized that in many instances the LXX reflects a text which is more original than that of the MT. Therefore the LXX, and, in fact, all textual evidence has to be taken into consideration seriously at the time of the textual examination, and equal rights are to be granted to all ancient texts. This equality implies that the textual sources are not to be consulted merely when the MT is considered to be faulty or difficult, as is often done by scholars, but from the outset *all* textual witnesses need be consulted, for one does not know in advance in which textual witness the so-called original text is found. We are again talking only about Hebrew texts or texts that can be retroverted into Hebrew from one of the versional languages. All this leads to the procedure suggested by us that at the outset the nature of the MT and LXX needs to be analyzed first for its text-critical value.

To the reasons given above let me add another one in favor of examining the textual evidence first.

I don't know whether I should call this a practical reason or an axiomatic one. In our discussion we frequently refer to arguments appealing to *logic*. It is unavoidable and, in fact, desirable that we should use logical arguments since the internal dynamics of the story is the main criterion for our analysis. On the one hand it is desirable to refer to logics, but on the other we immediately realize the limitations of such argumentation. What seems a logical sequence to one scholar is not necessarily logical for another one. In view of this it may not be the best course to start the analysis with argumentations referring to logics. But there is more involved.

Question : Is it at all correct to start the analysis with data referring to arguments on the logical level ? Does this not imply that stories are necessarily logical, and follow a certain logical sequence of events ? The major difficulty in this regard is, in my view, the fact that many biblical stories, or parts of stories simply are *not* logical. If I say "logical" or "not logical" I naturally imply "by my modern standards". I mean the following. The biblical books, and especially narratives developed during a long period, often layer after layer. Sometimes two different accounts were juxtaposed, or inserted in each other, and such actions were bound to create unlogical sequences. There are many such unlogical sequences in the Bible. My main point here is : How and why should we make the reference to logics such an important part of our comparison of two versions if the Bible itself contains so many unlogical sequences ?

Judges 1 starts off with the words "After the death of Joshua the people of Israel inquired of the Lord, 'Wo shall go up first for us against the Canaanites, to fight against them ?'" In a way this heading is not problematic since we know from the preceding book that Joshua had died and was already buried (Jos. 24,29-30). On the other hand the heading is utterly strange in view of chapter 2 of the same book in which Joshua acts, then dies and afterwards is buried (Jdg. 2,6-10). Is it not unusual, to say the least, that the heading of the book refers to the death of Joshua, and in the next chapter he is active and only afterwards he dies ?

In so many other chapters the composite nature of the text creates unlogical sequences in major details. Obvious examples for me are Deut. 27 and Jer. 19, but there are many others.

For the ancients none of these stories created difficulties in the same way as they do for us. They wrote and read by different standards. When the editor combined two elements, he did not think about what we call logics. In conclusion, since the Hebrew Bible contains so many unlogical sequences, it would not be fruitful to refer to that criterion in the beginning of an analysis. After all, possibly the version which has the unlogical sequence is more original than another version of the story. Besides, reference to logics is very subjective. Therefore, the most fruitful approach is to start with the evidence itself. If that evidence yields an unlikely or unlogical story we must accept that story as it is and explain its place in the context.

No solution solves all the problems, and this should be remembered. I, too, had to account for elements in the two versions which are not original. They were explained as subsequent harmonizations. Furthermore, version 2 is not complete. But every decision is a matter of priorities. Should we first try to solve literary issues as in the papers of Dominique and David, or should we first untie the textual problems ?

Conclusion

I urge to accept MT as it is, with all its inconsistencies, as the result of editorial activity. The editor of MT may be called unwise, or uncoordinated, but there existed such editors, and this goes against the arguments of David and Dominique.

I now want to refer to the possibility that the Greek translator or his Vorlage truncated the original long version. The term "truncation" was introduced into the discussion by David.

The main argument for this view is probably a *negative* one on the literary level. It is contended by our colleagues that the assumption of the two versions, such as suggested by me, is not logical, coherent or correct. Among other things it is said that version 2 could not have existed separately. Although I do not accept the details, I agree that this is a reasonable and acceptable argumentation. At the same time I sense that there is too much "sitting on the fence", especially in the first and second reactions of my colleagues. This applies to the assertion that the truncation took place *either* in Hebrew or in Greek. Dominique now agrees that this truncation probably took place on the Hebrew level, and according to David this at least is a possibility. If in any point we come close to each other it would be here. For if two of us (David, Dominique) assume that the Hebrew of MT has been truncated to the short form of the LXX's Vorlage and two others (Johan, Emanuel) describe the same procedure the other way round, we have come close to each other. We will also have learned much from each other. If this is our minimal basis of agreement, I still have some criticisms :

I see no reason for assuming that the presumed truncation took place at the level of Greek revisers. To the best of my knowledge there are no parallels for such an assumption.

Now, with regard to the truncation on the Hebrew level, the idea does not sound acceptable to me, but I sense that we are moving here in the area of beliefs and feelings. David was right when he said in his third contribution (p. 115) :

"ET apparently is only prepared to envisage the possibility that an originally short version has been added to at some stage in the literary process". It seems to me that our general knowledge about the literary history of the books leads to the assumption that biblical books developed by way of expansion and not by way of shortening. Many examples can be given to support the contention that stories were expanded. At the same time, I am sure, some examples can be given of originally longer stories which were truncated. On a large scale this also happened in the book of Chronicles vis-à-vis its sources. So are we back to square one ? I don't think so. In my view the solution to this problem lies in the question whether or not the biblical story is *composite*. If the story is *not* composite, there is equal chance that the short form was created by truncation or that the long form was created by expansion. But if we recognize that the story in its present form in the Bible is composite, the situation changes. For in that case the assumption of an expansion becomes much more likely. Let us assume for a moment that we all agree that the story in the MT is composite. In that case two possibilities present themselves. A complicated solution would be to assume that the composite story (MT) consists of a combination of versions 1 and 2 and that a short form of version 1 is actually attested (thus Dominique). That short form was created by truncation of the longer story and thus *coincidentally* agrees with one of the original components of the story. In my view that description requires too many assumptions and it also reckons with a large margin of coincidence. A second, less complicated solution would be that the short version, version 1, which is attested in the LXX reflects an original component of the book, subsequently enlarged in MT. That supposition is more simple, although it may be problematic on another level. For it presupposes that the LXX reflects some very early material. That assumption, in my view, is not too difficult, since also in other books of the Bible has the LXX been proven to contain early material.

It thus seems to me that the decision between the possibility of the truncation and that of the expansion actually lies in the recognition whether or not the story is composite. This assumption has been taken for granted by Johan and myself, not by way of axiom, but arguments have been brought forward to that point. A counter-claim was forwarded by Dominique and especially David to prove that the story was homogeneous and logical and that the thought-flow was natural. In my view the decision between the two possibilities, that of the truncation and the expansion thus lies in the analysis of this point.

So far on the issue of the sequence of the discussion. I now want to devote some words to another issue, the analysis of *translation technique*. I have nothing to add to the data themselves. The data show, as far as I am concerned that the translator is relatively literal. There is a certain assumption behind the very use of these data, viz., that the translation is taken as a whole, as one unit. One of my assumptions — you may call this axiomatic — is that translators who are considered quite literal are not expected to add or omit long sections. Now, this assumption may be right or wrong. I cannot prove the assumption, nor can it be refuted. It is one of those assumptions appealing to logics. I cannot prove the assumption, as I said, but the least I could do is to use the data which are at my disposal in our computerized data base, available in Jerusalem and Philadelphia, and named by Kraft and myself Computer Assisted Tools for Septuagint Studies, or CATSS. The computer search underlined what we already guessed, but the details themselves are quite convincing. If you make a list of all the minuses of the LXX in 1 Samuel, the differences between chapters 17-18 and the remaining chapters are very striking. I listed the numbers of words of MT lacking in the LXX throughout 1 Samuel, and it so happens that in each chapter roughly twenty words are not represented in the LXX. In some chapters only one or two words are lacking, but in others 15, 20, or 30, and in one case (ch. 2) 60 words of MT. Strikingly different are chapters 17 and 18. In ch. 17, 402 words are lacking and in ch. 18, 216 words. If we want to be more precise we should actually also count the numbers of words in each chapter, so that exact percentages can be calculated. I want to make the following point : If we ascribe the minuses to the translator himself, how did it happen that only in these chapters he went so much astray ? Is it logical to assume that only in these chapters the translator took these liberties ? Or would we rather say that the Vorlage of the translation happened to be shorter in these chapters ?

Conclusion

I now append a table of the *number* of words of MT lacking in the chapters of 1 Sam., together with data on the pluses of the LXX (see below).

Chapter	Minuses of LXX	Pluses of LXX
1	22	76
2	60	80
3	16	31
4	19	31
5	11	50
6	21	23
7	1	11
8	3	9
9	15	18
10	9	37
11	7	14
12	5	20
13	12	29
14	21	84
15	9	39
16	15	11
17	402	29
18	216	8
19	19	11
20	22	27
21	8	18
22	15	16
23	30	25
24	8	15
25	24	19
26	16	9
27	9	10
28	12	12
29	12	20
30	22	31
31	7	3

The above list also records the pluses of the LXX in 1 Samuel. Like in the case of the minuses, we counted the Greek words in accordance with the underlying Hebrew words, that is, a combination like ἐν τῷ οἴκῳ αὐτοῦ is counted as one word since presumably it reflects only one Hebrew word, בביתו When counting in this manner, an average of 20-80 words is added in the individual chapters of the LXX of 1 Samuel. I did not detect a correlation between the pluses and minuses in 1 Samuel, and in the chapters under consideration, 17-18, the number of the pluses is 29 for ch. 17 and 8 for ch. 18.

I have made a similar investigation for the other books of the LXX, including percentages, but they are not relevant to the present discussion.

Finally, I think our analysis and subsequent discussion has made it necessary for each of us to find out what the hidden assumptions are behind the thinking of each of us. Some may have a natural inclination towards a shorter text. Others may have a natural inclination towards MT.

B. POST-SCRIPT

In our meeting in Fribourg, Dominique has guided our discussion on matters of method. The discussion would not have continued fruitfully if we would not have turned first to these issues. For our analysis it is very important to determine what the nature, aims, and limitations of textual criticism are, what our conception of the early stages (Urtext ?) of the text is, what the notion of a canon implies, and what the relation is between literary and textual criticism. Only afterwards we returned to the limited topic of the story of David and Goliath.

It seems that we have come closer to each other, both in the two series of reactions and in the meeting in Fribourg. The analysis of the translation technique has become accepted, so that the translator has not been blamed any longer for shortening the Vorlage. At the same time, David is still open for the suggestion that a subsequent Greek reviser shortened the text. Both David and Dominique now take as their point of departure the view that the Greek faithfully represents a short Hebrew text which itself was shortened from the proto-Masoretic text. At the same time, Johan and Emanuel prefer to reckon with the possibility that the short Hebrew text represents the original form of the story. Indeed, we work with presuppositions. One recognizes a preference of Johan and Emanuel for shorter texts and an almost axiomatic preference for starting the discussion with textual data rather than literary analysis. Dominique and David probably prefer taking MT as their point of departure, and hence they take the long version of MT as the original form of the story. For David MT reflects a homogeneous story.

It may very well be that we cannot come closer to each other because of these different inclinations. The situation would probably have been different had we agreed with regard to the literary analysis of the story, in particular with regard to its composite nature. However, the discussion has taught us that different views prevail.

In matters such as these, literary and textual analysis are very closely related to each other. It seems to me that systematic discussion of several complicated issues such as the story of David and Goliath will eventually yield a better understanding of the relationship between the aims, goals, and limitations of these two disciplines.

APRES NOTRE RENCONTRE

J'ai préféré attendre que notre rencontre ait eu lieu
1) pour rédiger quelques notes sur la manière dont, après nos entretiens, je répondrais à notre question initiale et
2) pour formuler quelques conclusions méthodologiques que j'ai dégagées à la fois de cette expérience de travail en commun et d'autres recherches que j'ai dû avancer en même temps.

I. POST-SCRIPTUM SUR DAVID ET GOLIATH

A. Rappelons d'abord la constatation dont nous sommes partis : pour 1 Sam 17-18, à peu près 44 o/o du texte contenu dans le *M manque dans le *G.

B. Notre travail commun a permis de nuancer la problématique :

1) L'analyse textuelle détaillée d'Emanuel a montré que le traducteur du *G ancien est d'ordinaire fidèle à sa Vorlage. On ne saurait donc admettre aisément qu'en ces chapitres, et là seulement, il ait pris la liberté de mutiler largement le texte de sa Vorlage.

2) L'analyse littéraire très fine que David a donnée du *M a montré que son rédacteur a construit son récit selon des principes de composition qui réapparaissent en d'autres oeuvres classiques. Nous risquons donc de formuler des jugements anachroniques lorsque nous considérons certaines juxtapositions, répétitions ou contrastes comme des maladresses permettant de déceler les retouches d'un glossateur inintelligent.

3) On peut considérer aussi comme admis par tous qu'une bonne partie de la matière textuelle manquant dans le *G est au moins aussi ancienne que la matière textuelle commune au *M et au *G, et qu'elle est même plus ancienne qu'une partie de cette matière commune.

C. La constatation faite sous B1 engagera ceux qui estiment que la forme brève est une mutilation de la forme longue à attribuer cette initiative à un érudit intervenant en fonction de principes distincts de ceux qui s'imposaient au rédacteur de la forme longue, cette intervention pouvant, en principe, avoir eu lieu ou bien sur l'hébreu, avant la traduction grecque, ou bien sur le grec, à une époque antérieure aux plus anciens témoins qui nous en ont été conservés.

La constatation faite sous B2 dissuadera ceux qui estiment que la forme longue est issue d'ajouts faits à la forme brève de situer ces ajouts à une époque récente.

La constatation faite sous B3 nous oblige à nous demander s'il existe d'autres cas où une nouvelle 'édition' d'un livre biblique ajoute ou omet des matériaux vraiment anciens.

D. En d'autres livres, il arrive en effet que certains 'plus' étendus soient interprétés par la critique comme des ajouts. Mais, en général, ils contiennent des matériaux nettement plus jeunes que le contexte en lequel ils sont insérés et, à ce titre, ils ne nous fournissent pas de parallèles satisfaisants. La plupart des 'plus' que les Chroniques présentent par rapport à Samuel-Rois ou que la forme *M de Jérémie offre par rapport à sa forme *G sont en effet plus jeunes que leur contexte. C'est également le cas de l'expansion caractérisant l'Esdras A des grecs par rapport à Esdras-Néhémie ou des ajouts qu'offrent les formes grecques de Daniel ou d'Esther. C'est aussi le cas des miscellanées du troisième livre grec des Règnes.

Il arrive, par contre, que des omissions portent sur des matériaux au moins aussi anciens que ce qui les entoure. C'est le cas en Job où le traducteur grec a omis des passages anciens et difficiles. Mais la liberté avec laquelle ce traducteur a travaillé nous interdit de le comparer avec le traducteur grec du premier livre de Samuel.

Le cas qui me semble le plus éclairant est celui du rédacteur des Chroniques omettant, pour des motifs vraisemblablement théologiques, les matériaux très anciens que Samuel-Rois lui offrait sur la faute de David et les drames qui la suivirent. Cela montre qu'une omission d'importants matériaux très anciens est possible dans une nouvelle 'édition' d'un livre historique.

E. Je continue à considérer comme trop étroit le dilemme qui obligerait à opter ou bien pour une origine composite de la forme longue, ou bien pour une origine de la forme brève par voie de mutilation. Je vois des arguments sérieux pour que nous devions associer ces deux hypothèses. Il me semble que Johan est d'accord là-dessus.

Au niveau de l'histoire des traditions, je continue à estimer qu'aussi géniale qu'ait pu être l'oeuvre du rédacteur de la forme longue, elle intègre plusieurs vieux récits traditionnels qui ont probablement été d'abord transmis de façon autonome. C'est à propos de l'entrée de David en relation avec Saül que la pluralité des récits apparaît le plus clairement.

Je considère aussi que les 'plus' de la forme longue (que le *M nous atteste) par rapport à la forme brève (que le *G nous atteste) ne sauraient s'expliquer par l'ajout de données anciennes (transmises jusque-là de façon autonome) à un récit déjà constitué (que le *M et le *G nous attestent en des formes très proches). David nous a montré que tout l'ensemble est trop finement construit pour que ce puisse être le résultat du placage d'ajouts sur un récit déjà construit. D'autre part, je crois avoir montré dans ma contribution initiale que certains détails que le *M et le *G ont en commun ne s'expliquent de façon satisfaisante que comme des préparations ou des rappels se référant à des données qui figurent dans les 'plus' du *M (cf. pp. 49s et 53s de ma contribution).

F. Quelle que soit l'hypothèse dont nous ferons usage pour expliquer le cas exceptionnel des chapitres 17-18, elle se heurtera au fait qu'il s'agit là dans les livres de Samuel d'un cas de 'plus' (ou de 'moins') d'une ampleur unique. Il faudra donc rattacher ce cas unique à une caractéristique unique qu'offrent ces récits. Or, si nous renonçons à expliquer la forme longue comme un placage d'ajouts effectué sur la forme brève, il me semble que l'on peut expliquer la forme brève comme une suite de mutilations de la forme longue provoquée par une caractéristique unique que la forme longue offre à l'endroit exact où a lieu la première de ces mutilations.

En effet, pour un lecteur qui, lisant ce livre depuis le début, a la connaissance de ce qui précède, c'est en 17,12 qu'il rencontre pour la première fois l'exposé formel de données qui lui ont déjà été exposées peu avant : que Jessé est de Bethléem (16,1), qu'il avait huit fils (16,10s) et que David est son fils (16,11-13); puis, en 17,13, on entend lui apprendre encore des choses qu'il sait déjà : que le fils aîné de Jessé s'appelle Eliab (cf. 16,6), le deuxième Abinadab (cf. 16,8) et le troisième Shamma (cf. 16,9).

Prêtons à ce lecteur une double intention qui n'a rien d'invraisemblable : d'abord celle d'éviter les répétitions qui lui paraissent inutiles et la mention de données qui lui semblent inadmissibles, puis celle de mettre en valeur l'accès de David à la royauté.

On comprend alors que 17,12a lui paraisse être une répétition inutile, ainsi que 17,13b. Ayant commencé, pour ce motif, une omission après 17,11, il parcourt des yeux la suite en cherchant où raccrocher son récit d'une manière qui fasse aisément suite à 17,11. Il est naturel qu'il le reprenne en 17,32 qui répond le mieux à cette condition.

La deuxième omission, par ordre d'ampleur décroissante, est celle qui va de 17,55 à 18,6a. Or c'est justement en 17,55 que notre lecteur va rencontrer la première donnée qui lui paraisse inadmissible : que ni Saül ni Abner ne sache de qui David est le fils. En effet, David a déjà été présenté à Saül comme fils de Jessé (16,18) et Saül est déjà en relations avec Jessé à propos de David (16,22). Ayant donc commencé une nouvelle omission après 17,54, il parcourt la suite et il est normal que ce soit 18,6b qui lui offre l'événement qui fait le plus aisément suite à 17,54.

Toujours par ordre d'ampleur décroissante, les trois omissions suivantes sont 18,17-19; 18,10-11 et 18,29b-30. Toutes entrent dans la catégorie des répétitions que notre lecteur-abréviateur était en droit de juger inutiles. On peut se demander cependant pourquoi, dans les deux premiers cas, il a supprimé le premier terme du doublet apparent et conservé le second. Cela tient au fait que le second terme de chacun de ces doublets apparents était plus difficile à omettre, car plus fortement soudé à son contexte. En effet, le projet de mariage de David avec Merab échouera. On peut donc l'omettre sans mutiler aussi gravement le récit qu'on le ferait en essayant d'omettre la tractation matrimoniale analogue à propos de Mikal, tractation qui, ayant abouti, conditionne la suite du récit (19,11-17; 2 S 3,13s; 6,16-23). De même, on peut éliminer le premier jet de lance de Saül contre David (18,10s) parce qu'il n'a pas de conséquence immédiate dans les épisodes qui suivent. Mais ce n'est pas le cas du second jet de lance (19,9s), puisqu'il a pour suite la fuite de David qui est racontée juste après (19,11-18). Quant au petit sommaire sur les succès de David en 18,29b-30, notre lecteur a pu juger qu'il faisait double emploi avec le sommaire analogue qui avait précédé en 18,13-16.

G. Dans l'hypothèse où la forme brève serait issue de mutilations, il est possible d'expliquer, comme on le voit, ces mutilations caractéristiques à partir de quelques critères simples. Mais il faut répondre alors à deux objections :

1) Pourquoi l'abréviateur a-t-il omis des petits récits (comme les trois derniers que nous avons mentionnés) qui pouvaient lui paraître répétitifs, mais a-t-il laissé dans le livre de grands récits qui pourraient tout aussi aisément faire figure de doublets, comme les deux désobéissances de Saül ou les deux fois où David épargna Saül ? En réponse à cette objection, il suffit de noter que, lorsqu'un recenseur intervient, en fonction de quelque critère que ce soit, pour retoucher le texte biblique (ou, en notre cas, pour l'abréger), il ne se résigne d'ordinaire à intervenir que dans une situation qui lui semble particulièrement urgente (ce qui fut le cas pour les deux premières grandes mutilations), puis il continue d'intervenir pour de plus petites interventions, en quelques cas moins caractéristiques, durant un certain temps encore, avant de cesser ses interventions. J'ai déjà eu souvent l'occasion de remarquer cette manière de procéder pour d'autres recenseurs, par exemple ceux du groupe kaige.

2) N'est-il pas surprenant que l'entrée en scène de l'abréviateur supposé ait lieu au moment précis (après 17,11) où commence un récit auquel la plupart des critiques reconnaissent une origine distincte de celle(s) des récits qui le précèdent ? On estimera que ce hasard défie la vraisemblance et que mieux vaut admettre que ce récit, absent de la forme brève, a été ajouté pour constituer la forme longue.

Rappelons d'abord ici une fois de plus les difficultés que nous avons soulevées contre l'hypothèse d'un développement par placage relativement tardif d'éléments jusque-là autonomes. Puis, pour répondre à l'objection du hasard improbable, il suffit d'admettre que, avant les critiques littéraires de l'époque moderne et contemporaine, d'autres lecteurs ont pu avoir conscience des indices d'hétérogénéité que présentent ces récits et intervenir en fonction des principes qui gouvernaient leur conception de ce que doit être une Ecriture Sainte.

II. CONCLUSIONS METHODOLOGIQUES SUR L'ARTICULATION DE LA CRITIQUE LITTERAIRE AVEC LA CRITIQUE TEXTUELLE ET LA CRITIQUE CANONIQUE

Notre travail commun a été pour moi l'occasion de constater, une fois de plus, que nous ne mettons pas les mêmes choses sous les mêmes mots. Je n'entends pas édicter un vocabulaire. Notre rencontre ne suffisait d'ailleurs pas pour aboutir à des définitions précises. Pourtant, il me semble utile de formuler certaines distinctions.

Au cours de notre rencontre et des contributions écrites qui l'ont précédée, il a été discuté en effet de l'ordre de succession des investigations portant sur la critique textuelle et sur la critique littéraire. C'est pourquoi j'ai estimé utile de dégager de là quelques vues sur ce qu'est la critique textuelle (A) et sur la manière dont les développements textuels s'articulent avec les développements littéraires (B).

Conclusion

Je voudrais également reprendre deux distinctions qui ont été proposées au cours de nos discussions. D'abord celle qui a été faite entre certains développements littéraires qui ont joué un rôle dans la constitution d'une forme textuelle et d'autres développements littéraires qui se situent comme des interprétations d'une forme textuelle préexistante (C). Une distinction a été faite aussi entre Ecriture Sainte et Ecriture Canonique (D).

A partir de ces distinctions, je voudrais apporter une conclusion théorique et une conclusion pratique, la première portant sur ce qu'est la canonicité (E) et la deuxième sur ce que doit viser une édition critique de la Bible (F).

Dans tous ces domaines, je formulerai des suggestions que je ne puis argumenter dans le cadre d'un bref 'papier' dont le but est seulement de ne pas laisser sombrer dans l'oubli certaines idées suscitées par notre brève rencontre.

A. Il peut être utile de distinguer la "critique textuelle sur témoins" (CTT) et l'"analyse textuelle génétique" (ATG).

La CTT suppose que l'on dispose de plusieurs exemplaires d'une même édition d'un certain texte. Elle visera à établir la forme la plus authentique de cette édition à partir de ces témoins immédiats (manuscrits dans la même langue) ou médiats (traductions, citations). Elle ne fera appel à la conjecture qu'au cas où ces témoins divergent à partir d'une base commune qui peut être clairement reconstituée par le simple recoupement de leurs témoignages.

L'ATG prendra pour point de départ un certain texte (ou bien stabilisé et diffusé en une édition, ou bien attesté par un témoin isolé). A partir de ce texte, elle essaiera d'inférer les accidents textuels qu'il a subis au cours de sa filière de transmission antérieure. L'ATG vise à analyser une forme textuelle. Elle ne vise pas (comme la CTT) à en établir une. Elle travaillera normalement par voie de conjecture.

B. Au cours de sa filière de transmission, un texte peut subir, en des phases successives, des accidents textuels et des développements littéraires. Ainsi, l'épopée de Gilgamesh a subi des développements littéraires successifs ou simultanés en plusieurs langues et plusieurs témoins textuels ont existé de certaines de ces recensions, donnant par là-même occasion à une CTT. Il faut également qualifier de littéraires les développements qui séparent les Chroniques de Samuel-Rois, chacune de ces deux oeuvres littéraire pouvant faire l'objet d'une ATG à partir du texte des éditions qui en ont été données.

Une modification pourra être qualifiée de 'littéraire' dans la mesure où elle émane d'une intervention humaine plus ou moins consciente et intentionnelle. On la qualifiera de 'textuelle' dans la mesure où elle consiste en un accident subi par le texte. Le 'littéraire' et le 'textuel' peuvent s'interpénétrer étroitement. Ainsi, lorsqu'un copiste veut rendre un sens à un texte devenu incohérent du fait d'un homéotéleuton, il restaurera par quelques retouches intentionnelles le texte accidentellement mutilé. Cette initiative 'littéraire' est étroitement liée à l'accident 'textuel' qui l'a précédée. Ou bien, lorsqu'un vocalisateur essaie de trouver une prononciation donnant sens à un mot qu'un copiste a défiguré par une permutation de consonnes, il fait oeuvre 'littéraire' pour tirer un sens de ce texte corrompu par un accident 'textuel' (voir, à ce propos, ma contribution en FS Wevers, Mississauga 1984, 21-40).

142

C. Il est légitime de distinguer les interventions littéraires qui aboutissent à constituer un texte de celles qui visent à interpréter un texte. Une activité littéraire sera considérée comme 'constitutive' dans la mesure où elle se trouve aboutir à un texte stabilisé. Elle sera considérée comme 'interprétative' dans la mesure où elle part d'un texte stabilisé. Les retouches intentionnelles que le Chroniste a apportées au texte de Samuel-Rois constituent une activité littéraire qui est à la fois 'interprétative' de Samuel-Rois et 'constitutive' de Chroniques.

Or la stabilisation textuelle est un événement culturel qu'il faut situer dans un contexte socio-politique que la critique canonique a pour tâche d'analyser. Il se peut que des cristallisations successives stabilisant un texte soient séparées par des dégels où le texte qui avait été stabilisé revient à un état de fluidité littéraire. Ainsi, le 'livre de la Torah' qui inspira la réforme de Josias avait, aux yeux des réformateurs, valeur de norme intangible. Plus tard, après l'effondrement des structures politico-religieuses du royaume de Juda, il ne sera plus qu'un élément dans le remalaxage qui aboutira à la constitution du Pentateuque d'Esdras sous l'autorité du Dieu des Cieux et du Roi des Perses.

D. Il peut être opportun de distinguer une Ecriture Sainte d'une Ecriture Canonique. La première est considérée comme 'Sainte' dans la mesure où elle a valeur de parole de Dieu pour ses dépositaires. La seconde est 'Canonique' dans la mesure où elle a été imposée comme normative par le pouvoir qui codifie la religion.

Les Ecritures Canoniques se stabilisent en se diffusant par édition à partir d'exemplaires authentifiés, alors que tombent en désuétude les formes non-authentiques.

Une Ecriture Sainte peut constituer un patrimoine tenu en dépôt par une école relativement close au sein de laquelle cette Ecriture évolue par ajouts, par retouches ou par omissions pour maintenir actuel le message divin qu'elle transmet et qui doit garder sa valeur pour d'autres générations. C'est en cet état d'Ecriture Sainte que la Torah parmi les prêtres ou le livre d'Isaïe au sein de son école ont pu franchir la faille de l'exil et du retour.

Ce qui constitue l'essentiel de notre Deutéronome fut d'abord Ecriture Sainte parmi des prêtres avant de devenir Ecriture Canonique (sous l'autorité de Josias), puis de redevenir Ecriture Sainte (après l'écroulement de l'autorité canonisante) et d'être canonisé à nouveau (sous une autorité politico-religieuse nouvelle, au cinquième siècle).

Une oeuvre littéraire profane ne présente pas les mêmes nécessités d'actualisation qu'une Ecriture Sainte qui doit continuer à dire la même chose, au nom de Dieu, en des circonstances et des mentalités qui changent. C'est la nécessité d'actualiser une Ecriture Sainte qui imposera à ses dépositaires des omissions, des ajouts ou des retouches qui peuvent être importants et étendus.

Ces modifications importantes seront interdites dans le cas d'une Ecriture Canonique dont l'autorité canonisante maintient l'identité en référence à son état authentifié. La possibilité de modifier ne se maintient que sous forme marginale par des tiqquné sopherim ou grâce à la différence subsistant entre tradition d'écriture (ketib) et tradition de lecture (qeré), ou enfin à l'occasion des traductions qui peuvent aller du décalque à la paraphrase.

E. Le cas le plus typique de canonisation (et ce qui en constitue le premier analogué) est ce qui eut lieu au scriptorium du Temple, puis dans l'Ecole pharisienne jusque vers 100 après J.-C. (voir, à ce propos, ma contribution à 'Le canon de l'A.T.', Genève 1984).

La Septante alexandrine a combattu (voir la lettre d'Aristée) pour sauver sa canonicité ptolémaïque en face d'efforts de recension prenant pour référence la forme du Pentateuque hébreu considérée comme normative à Jérusalem.

Chaque livre ou groupe de livres a accédé à la canonicité par des voies et à des époques différentes, 'Jabné' n'étant qu'un point final (sauf pour Esther dont la canonisation populaire a été homologuée après coup).

Les Deutéro-canoniques et la Septante extérieure au Pentateuque ont eu une canonisation polycentrique.

Il est souvent impossible de dire si les formes textuelles que l'on serait tenté de qualifier comme 'aberrantes' ont été semi-canoniques en certaines communautés.

F. Une édition critique de la Bible doit viser un texte canonisé, c'est-à-dire une édition qui a exercé la fonction de 'Bible' pour une communauté historiquement et sociologiquement identifiable.

Dans le cas de l'hébreu, deux possibilités se présentent :

1) Ou bien une édition diplomatique commentée d'un témoin du Texte Massorétique tibérien classique. On obtient ainsi une forme considérée comme authentique à la fois dans les milieux rabbanites et dans les milieux karaïtes les plus cultivés, au Xe siècle de notre ère, c'est-à-dire au terme de l'effort des Massorètes et juste avant l'âge d'or de la philologie hébraïque.

2) Ou bien une reconstitution approximative du type textuel protomassorétique. En se fondant sur le témoignage combiné du texte massorétique, des recensions origénienne et antiochienne du Grec, de Théodotion-Aquila-Symmaque, de la Vulgate, de la Peshitto et du Targum, on peut viser, avec un certain flou (tenant à son unification imparfaite et à la déficience de nos témoins), le type textuel correspondant aux traditions de lecture les plus autorisées du texte consonantique que le rabbinat essaya de standardiser après la répression de la première révolte contre Rome.

Le mieux serait :
d'éditer un témoin de référence du texte tibérien classique et de lui joindre trois apparats :
— un apparat massorétique (de CTT) constitué essentiellement par les autres témoins tibériens classiques, mais intégrant aussi les quelques données utiles que pourraient fournir d'autres traditions contemporaines ou postérieures,
— un apparat protomassorétique (à mi-chemin entre CTT et ATG) visant la base à partir de laquelle divergent les témoins énumérés ci-dessus,
— un apparat d'ATG décelant par référence à d'autres traditions textuelles (le Grec ancien, Qumrân, etc.) ou par voie de conjecture celles des modifications antérieures à la stabilisation protomassorétique qui relèvent d'accidents textuels.

DAVID — GOLIATH PROJECT : STAGE FOUR

I.

For my final contribution I should like to examine in some greater depth the idea that *G represents an early stage of chs. 17-18 and *M a later stage. My approach to the problem will once more be via what my colleagues will doubtless call rhetorical criticism and structuralism as distinct from historical literary criticism. Two preliminary remarks may therefore be in order.

First let me make clear exactly what I am doing in this essay and what my presuppositions are. As my colleagues will know I am not fully convinced that Emanuel has proved that *G represents faithfully a Hebrew text that differed from *M in all those respects in which *G differs from *M. On the other hand Emanuel has made out a very strong case for his point of view; so as the starting point for my present essay I adopt his view as a working hypothesis. On this understanding *G faithfully represents a short Hebrew text; my aim is to investigate how likely it is that this short Hebrew text represents an early stage in the literary (not textual) development of ch. 17-18, and *M a later, expanded stage (1).

Secondly let me admit that rhetorical criticism relies to some great extent on subjective literary judgments. But then let me point out that historical literary criticism likewise depends to some considerable extent on equally subjective literary judgments. True, attempts to discern the various sources used in the historical books have endeavoured to rely on the more objective criteria of vocabulary, morphology, stock phrases, and literary formulae and have tried to relate sources and redactions to objective, historical events, movements and personages. But not seldom the detection of more than one source in a narrative has depended on the detection of alleged discrepancies, contradictions, disjunctions, interruptions and incoherences in the thought-flow of the narrative in question; and of course the very existence of these alleged discrepancies etc. is sometimes, indeed quite frequently, itself the product of a subjective literary judgment. See, for example, my Contribution (p. 56) and Dominique's subsequent remarks in his Réponse (p. 96). And when historical literary criticism goes further and conjectures external motives (2) for its conjectural redactions, it quite plainly is relying on highly subjective judgments (3). Now from time to time it happens that rhetorical criticism finds itself at odds with historical literary criticism because the latter wishes to say that two features in a narrative are discrepant or contradictious or that a passage is a disruptive insertion, where the former sees nothing but a coherent and carefully developed thought-flow. Bot these judgments are literary

145

judgments; my simple point is that the former is not necessarily any less subjective than the latter simply because the former is the product of historical literary criticism. Indeed until rhetorical criticism has had its opportunity to discern and demonstrate the thought-flow of a narrative, it can be dangerous for historical literary criticism to go looking for discrepancies and disruptions in order to detect the diverse sources underlying the narrative.

II.

To examine the likelihood that *G represents an earlier stage than *M in the literary development of ch. 17-18, I wish now to take as a test-case the two different treatments that we find in *M and *G of the end of the David-Goliath story (4). In *G the battle against the Philistines, in which the fight between David and Goliath is the centre-piece, ends at 17,51-54 with the decapitation of Goliath, the rout of the Philistines, and David's carrying of the head of the giant to Jerusalem and the putting of the giant's armour in his tent. In the next paragraph, 18,6ff, David has left the battle-field and is returning (home ? to the palace ?) when the women come out to meet him and celebrate his praise.

In *M the announcement at 17,54 is clearly proleptic, and throughout 17,55-18,5, except for the last verse, which acts as a summary general statement and conclusion, we are still on the battle-field. At 17,55-56 we have a flash-back to the moment when David left Saul's presence to go out to face the giant and then at 17,57-18,4 we have an account of what happened when after the battle David returned to the king's presence, still on the field of battle, with the giant's head in his hand. Moreover what happened then was vastly more significant than the mere victory over the giant taken by itself would have been. Not only did Saul take David permanently into the royal entourage (18,2) and give him a commission in the army (18,5), but — and this is the highlight of the passage — Jonathan, filled with admiration and love for David, made a covenant with him, stripped himself of his robe and gave it to David along with his tunic, sword and belt (18,3-4).

According to *M this was a spontaneous and emotional reaction on Jonathan's part immediately after the excitement and relief of David's unexpected and brilliant victory; but since the later narrative is going to show that Jonathan never subsequently regretted or withdrew from, but rather confirmed, the implications of the symbolic gestures which he made on the battle-field, it would be difficult to exaggerate the symbolic significance of those gestures. The narrative of 13,3 and ch. 14 has made it clear that up to this point Jonathan had been not only crown-prince but also Israel's leading single-combat hero. In giving David his hero's armour and weapons he was acknowledging David's military superiority as a hero; in "loving" David and making a covenant with him he was taking the first steps in ceding to David the political right of succession to the kingship of Israel (5). Now while David's felling and mortal wounding of the giant without the use of a sword (17,50) forms the brilliant climax to that run of the narrative which deals with the choice-of-weapons theme (see my Contribution 69-70), this scene between David, Saul and Jonathan while still on the battle-field is obviously intended to form the climax to the whole of the battle-story. It is to be noted that Saul and Jonathan's reaction in this climax is altogether positive.

Now *G, as we have already noticed, lacks the passage 17,55-18,5, and the effect is to give us a very different story from *M. In *G the climax of the battle as a whole is simply David's victory over the giant and Israel's subsequent rout of the Philistines. There is no meeting between David, Saul and Jonathan on the field of battle after the fight, and there is no account of Saul's positive reaction to David's victory. His first recorded reaction of any kind is on their return from the battle-field (18,6-9) and it is negative as are all his subsequent reactions (6). Moreover no reaction on Jonathan's part is recorded, indeed no mention is made of Jonathan at all, until at 19,2 we are told somewhat incidentally that Jonathan loved David without being told explicitly why.

I have already commented on the inherent unlikelihood of *G's version of the story in this regard (Contribution p. 78). What I propose to do now, therefore, is to put the question into the wider context of the macro-structure of the book. I want to examine the major divisions of the narrative, and within those major divisions the principal movements of thought, and the way in which the minor and major climaxes are themselves marked and how they in turn mark the progress of the book's thought-flow at the macro-level. We can then see to what extent *G shares with *M these compositional and structural features throughout 1 Sa.; and then when we find, as we shall, that *G shares the same compositional and structural features, the same principal movements, the same minor and major climaxes as *M all the way through the book except in chs. 17-18, we can ask whether *G's arrangement of the principal movements of thought and its treatment of the minor and major climaxes in chs. 17-18 are best understood as an early stage in the evolution of the work that eventually became 1 Sa., or whether some other explanation of its special features is to be preferred.

III.

We take first the sweep of the narrative from 1,1-15,35. In this part of the book *G shares with *M all the same macro-structural features (7). These chapters are made up of two well defined sections. The first, from 1,1-7,17, is the story of the birth and consecration of Samuel and of his part in Israel's recovery from the religious and political decline which the nation suffered under Eli and his sons. It comes to its major climax with the account of Israel's dramatic victory over the Philistines at Mizpeh (7,2-14), and the section is then rounded off with a general summary-statement of Samuel's ministry (7,15-17).

When ch. 8 opens we obviously begin another section. Samuel is now old (8,1) and his sons, who serve as judges in his place, are corrupt (8,2-3). The people therefore demand a king. This is an utterly new departure; and the rest of the section is devoted to the story of Samuel's protest, of the choice and appointment of Saul as king, and then of his disobediences until at the major climax of the section God finally rejects Saul. Then the section is rounded off with unyielding finality : "And Samuel did not go to see Saul any more until the day he died... and the Lord repented that he had made Saul king over Israel" (15,35).

Now let us notice one of the devices which is used to give the thought-flow in each section a certain coherence, namely the placing of vividly similar and/or contrasting ideas near the beginning and near the end of each section.

Section I.	Section II.
1. In the first movement as a result result of Hannah's prayers Samuel is born and Hannah in her song of praise finally prophesies : "those who oppose the Lord will be shattered. *He will thunder against them from heaven..."* (2,10).	1. In the first movement God tells Samuel : "Listen to the voice of the people... for they have not rejected you, *but they have rejected me, that I should not be king* over them" (8,7)
2. In the last movement as a result of Samuel's intercessions the *Lord thunders with a great thunder* against the Philistines and they are smitten down before Israel (7,8-10).	2. In the last movement Samuel tells Saul : "Because you have rejected the word of the Lord, *he has also rejected you from being king"* (15,23).

Let us just remind ourselves that so far *G shares these compositional features with *M.

Now let us examine the principal movements of thought and the chief minor and major climaxes in both these sections.

Section I. Part A

Movement 1. (1,1-2,10). The foreground is altogether dominated by Hannah's distress, prayer for a son, vow, the birth of Samuel, his consecration and Hannah's song of praise. In the background is Eli as a rather imperceptive priest whose misjudgment of Hannah is eventually proved wrong.

Movement 2. (2,11-36). Here the focus is reversed. In the foreground are the wicked behaviour of Eli's sons, Eli's ineffectual attempts to reprove them, and the denunciation of Eli by a man of God for his failure to restrain his sons. In the background (2,18-21) are the pure service of the innocent child Samuel and the devoted piety of his mother.

Movement 3. (3,1-21). In this movement the two major themes of the first two movements come together and reach their climax. Samuel has his first experience of the voice of God coming to him live, so to speak, and is from then on established and known as a prophet (3,19-21). So Hannah's faith and exercises receive their final vindication. Simultaneously final sentence is passed on Eli's indulgent irresponsibility and his sons' wickedness through the prophecy given to Samuel which establishes him as a prophet who hears the living voice of God.

At this point then we have reached a climax. This is not, of course, the end of the section. The narrative-flow must proceed to show how the sentence delivered in Movement 3 is actually carried out. The climax in Movement 3, therefore, is a minor climax. We should notice, however, because we shall need this observation later on, that the matter of the voice of God coming to Samuel (and Samuel's response) in the night to pronounce judgment on Eli and his sons is not some incidental feature. It forms the very heart of the climax.

Section I. Part B.

Movement 1. (4,1-22). The threatened judgment is executed. As a result of the wickedness of Eli's sons and the people's superstitious use of the ark, the Philistines defeat Israel and capture the ark. The ark seems to be ineffectual.

Movement 2. (5,1-7,1). Among the Philistines the ark proves to be very effectual while for its sake God smites the Philistines and their god with humiliating sufferings. The Philistines return the ark to Israel where also severe judgment attends its mishandling.

Movement 3. (7,2-17). As a result of Israel's eventual penitence and contrition led by Samuel and Samuel's intercessions and sacrifices, God intervenes by thunder out of heaven to give Israel a resounding victory over the Philistines.

With this victory we have the climax of Part B. But we have more : with this long-lived (7,13) recovery of Israel, in things both spiritual and military, we have reached the high-point of Samuel's career. At the beginning of Part A Israel's condition was at its nadir; now it is at its zenith. We have reached the major climax of the section. Once more, however, we should notice that God's thundering out of heaven in Movement 3 is not an incidental detail : it lies at the heart of the major climax. We may now turn to

Section II. Part A.

Movement 1. (8,1-22). The people demand a king. Samuel is distressed, and God is grieved but nonetheless instructs Samuel to warn the people of their folly but under protest to accede to their demand.

Movement 2. (9,1-11,13). Saul is singled out, anointed, presented to the people as king, accepted by most, but resented by some until his victory over Ammon puts his worth beyond doubt and he is universally recognized as king.

Movement 3. (11,14-12,25). The renewal of the kingdom. Samuel reverts to the theme of the first movement and protests strongly against the people's folly in demanding a king. But he now carries that theme forward by assuring the people that in spite of this folly God will go along with them and bless them and their king if only they will from now on obey him. With this we have reached a high point : the people's king is accepted by God and all could be well. After this there is nothing but decline as the king proceeds from one disobedience and folly to another. But for the moment we are at the high-point and the minor climax of the section. We should notice that at the heart of this climax (12,16-19) lies a demonstration of the people's wickedness designed to encourage them not to rebel again. It takes the form of God sending thunder and rain in the middle of harvest.

Conclusion

Section II. Part B.

Movement 1. (13,1-23). This movement tells of certain of Saul's skirmishes and of one expected battle with the Philistines which in the end did not eventuate but which nevertheless proved disastrous for Saul because he disobeyed the word of the Lord and was told that his kingdom would not continue (13,13-14).

Movement 2. (14,1-52). Another battle with the Philistines, this time successful thanks to Jonathan. But now things go topsy-turvy, for Jonathan breaks a ban imposed by Saul (which he had not heard) and Saul demands that he shall be exectued for this disobedience. Saul is ignominiously over-ruled by the people.

Movement 3. (15,1-35). Saul once more disobeys God's word and for this rebellion he is finally rejected by God and abandoned by Samuel. We have reached the major climax of Section II, and we should notice that it is marked by God's speaking to Samuel and Samuel's crying to God all night (15,11).

Both Section I and II, then, are marked by the same structural pattern and the same rhythm of movements. Especially interesting is the way the minor and major climaxes are marked :

Section I.	Section II.
Minor climax : voices in the night. The Lord calls Samuel; Samuel responds; the Lord announces judgment on Eli's house; Samuel tells Eli the verdict.	*Minor climax :* thunder by day, sent by God in answer to Samuel's call to convict Israel of sin and dissuade them from further rebellion.
Major climax : thunder by day, sent in answer to Samuel's prayers to defeat the Philistines and give Israel victory.	*Major climax :* voices in the night, as God announces his judgment on Saul and Samuel cries to God all night. Samuel tells Saul the verdict.

These literary features are not accidental. The fact that they are shared by *G and *M shows that both *G and *M owe these features to the same organising mind operating at the same stage in the literary development of 1 Sa.

IV.

We turn now to the sweep of narrative that runs from 16,1 to 26,25, that is from David's anointing to his last meeting with Saul (at 27,1 he goes for the second time and semi-permanently to the Philistines). It covers three more major sections of the book. Section III runs from David's anointing (16,1-13) to the point where, in spite of Saul's private and surreptitious attempts to kill him or to get him killed, David becomes a member of the royal family by marriage to Saul's daughter, Michal (18,17-30). Section IV runs from Saul's first issuing of public orders that David is to be killed (19,1) to David's escape and flight to the Philistine king, Achish (21,10-15). Section V runs from David's return from the Philistines to various cities of Judah (22,1ff) to his final meeting with Saul (26,1-25). We shall not need to go beyond Section V. Since

SECTION III 16,1-18,30

A

1. 16,1-13. David is secretly anointed as king, in spite of Samuel's fear that if Saul discovers it he will kill Samuel.

2. 16,14-23. David is summoned to the king's house as harpist. Saul loves him greatly.

3. 17,1-18,5. David defeats Goliath. In love and admiration for him JONATHAN MAKES A COVENANT WITH DAVID. JONATHAN STRIPS HIMSELF OF ROBE, TUNIC AND WEAPONS AND GIVES THEM TO DAVID. Saul takes David into his entourage and gives him a commission.

B

1. 18,6-9. On the return of David and Saul from the field of battle, the women praise David more than Saul. Saul becomes jealous and suspicious.

2. 18,10-16. Saul in a sudden fit tries to spear David. David twice avoids death. Saul becomes afraid of David and removes him from his immediate entourage. David's popularity with the people increases.

3. 18,17-30. Saul attempts to lure David to his death by offering him marriage to first Merab, then Michal. He asks an unreasonable brideprice; but David pays it and gains his bride BY SLAYING 200 PHILISTINES. AND WHENEVER THE PHILISTINE PRINCES CAME OUT, DAVID BEHAVED HIMSELF MORE WISELY THAN ALL SAUL'S SERVANTS (18,27-30).

SECTION IV 19,1-21,15

A

1. 19,1-10. Saul issues public orders that David is to be killed. Jonathan induces temporary repentance in Saul; but when David is again successful against the Philistines, Saul becomes frenzied again and tries to spear him. David escapes.

2. 19,11-17. Saul orders David to be killed. Michal saves David by a ruse. David escapes.

3. 19,18-24. David flees to Samuel. Saul pursues him intent on killing him; but when he comes near Samuel the Spirit of God comes on Saul and SAUL STRIPS HIMSELF AND LIES DOWN NAKED ALL DAY AND NIGHT.

B

1. 20,1-42. Jonathan decides to test Saul's attitude to David, after making a covenant with David's house. At Jonathan's request David swears an oath. Jonathan discovers that David will have to depart. The story of the arrows.

2. 21,1-9. David flees to Ahimelech the priest. He is given the shewbread to eat and Goliath's sword.

3. 21,10-15. David flees to the Philistine king, Achish. When the Philistines recognize him as the slayer of Goliath, David takes fright and PRETENDS TO BE MAD. ACHISH DECIDES HE HAS ENOUGH MAD MEN ALREADY WITHOUT WELCOMING ANOTHER. He refuses David entry to his house.

SECTION V 22,1-26,25

A

1. 22,1-23. David escapes from Philistines and returns to Judah. Saul's servants refuse, but Doeg complies with, Saul's command to slay the priests for alleged complicity with David.

2. 23,1-13. David saves Keilah from the Philistines; but he is advised that the men of Keilah will hand him over to Saul. David escapes.

3. 23,14-29. David comes to Ziph. JONATHAN COMES SECRETLY TO DAVID, ENCOURAGES HIM TO THINK THAT DAVID WILL BE KING AND JONATHAN HIS DEPUTY. JONATHAN MAKES A COVENANT WITH DAVID; but then returns home. The Ziphites summon Saul; only a raid by the Philistines saves David.

B

1. 24,1-22. David spares Saul's life in the cave. At Saul's request David swears an oath not to destroy Saul's family after Saul's death.

2. 25,1-44. David is restrained from vengeance by Abigail's wisdom, and spares the life of the fool, Nabal.

3. 26,1-25. David once more spares Saul's life. David curses those who have stirred up Saul against him and have driven him out to foreign nations and gods. SAUL CONFESSES : I HAVE PLAYED THE FOOL AND HAVE ERRED EXCEEDINGLY (26,21).

the disputed climax to the story of the battle with Goliath comes in Section III, a study of Sections I to V will show us how *G and *M behave in two sections either side of the disputed section and give us a basis for comparison in Section III.

Now it is my contention that in *M Sections III, IV and V show the same structural patterns, the same rhythm of movements and the same way of managing and marking minor and major climaxes as do Sections I and II. But it would be tedious and out of proportion with the scope of this present essay for me to describe all this in detail as I did for Sections I and II. I propose, therefore, to set out what I conceive to be *M's arrangement in brief tabular form, using capital letters to call attention to interesting and significant features which mark the minor and major climaxes. Then after the table we can come to a few comments and a comparison of *G's scheme with *M's.

If this, then, is *M's scheme we may report at once that *G has the same sectioning as *M. In Sections IV and V moreover it has the same number of principal movements and the same minor and major climaxes as *M. We need not stay, therefore, to examine the logic that lies behind this common selection and arrangement of material and themes in these two sections.

But since in Section III *G disagrees violently with *M, let us first look at the logic behind *M's arrangement. The section has two climaxes because it wants to relate the two necessary steps in David's securing legitimate succession to the throne. The first is that the crown-prince Jonathan should acknowledge his superiority and willingly cede to David his right of succession. The second is that David should be incorporated into the royal house by marriage to one of the king's daughters. David's victory over Goliath accomplishes the first step; his success in killing 200 Philistines accomplishes the second.

Next let us look at the three minor and major climaxes. Jonathan's voluntary stripping of himself at III.A.3 contrasts vividly with Saul's involuntary and ignominious stripping of himself at IV.A.3. Again at V.A.3 Jonathan's covenant with David makes explicit what his symbolic gestures and covenant at III.A.3 had implicitly foreshadowed.

Again David's "wise", that is shrewd and successful, tactics against the Philistines that are the key to his royal marriage at III.B.3 contrast vividly and sadly with his temporary lapse into feigned madness among the Philistines at IV.B.3. Even so, David's feigned madness is nowhere near so sad as unrepentant Saul's confession of utter folly at V.B.3.

*M's structure, number of principal movements and above all its minor and major climaxes in Section III make admirable sense in themselves and fit in to the structural and compositional patterns of all the other sections we have examined.

*G's scheme in Section III, however, is ruinous. At III.B.2 it has only the remnants of a movement, scarce enough to be classed as a separate movement since it lacks 18,10-11 (8). It thus disturbs the rhythm of movements which both it and *M have in all the other sections.

Then its entire lack of the Jonathan episode from the minor climax at III.A.3 removes the first necessary step towards the legitimization of David's right to succession. It simultaneously leaves this minor climax with nothing in common with the other minor climaxes in Sections IV and V.

Conclusion

Finally *G's omission of 18,30 leaves its major climax at III.B.3 with nothing in common with the major climaxes in Sections IV and V.

Now if *G did not have the same structural and compositional patterns as *M in all the other sections, its own peculiar scheme in Section III might be taken as evidence that it represented an early stage in the evolution of 1 Sa. which had not quite achieved the fullness and completeness subsequently arrived at in *M. But when *G has *M's full scheme in all the other sections, its peculiar omissions in Section III proclaim it as a self-evident wreck of the fuller scheme. How and for what reasons that wreckage came about, I have discussed in my Contribution.

NOTES

1   Throughout 1 Sa. *G and *M have such a vast amount of material in common that it seems to me to go without saying that *G and *M in ch. 17 and 18 cannot be thought to represent two completely different and independent accounts of the David-Goliath story.

2   By 'external' I mean motives such as religious reform, political sympathies or desire for propaganda that are supposed to have motivated successive redactors, as distinct from internal literary consideration for the coherence of the composition and thought-flow of the narrative.

3   For further remarks on this score see the present writer's 'The composition of the Book of Judges' Eretz-Israel, XVI, Jerusalem, 1982, 71*-72*.

4   I have already dealt with this passage at various places in my Contribution (pp. 60-61, 63, 71-74, 78-82). I still adhere to the position for which I argued in those passages, with one minor modification : I now wish to argue that the progression presented by 17,55-18,30 in *M should be analysed into four paragraphs rather than three as I originally suggested. For the rest I am not about to go over again the matters discussed in my Contribution. I wish now to examine the end of the David-Goliath story in the light of the way in which *M and *G handle the major and minor climaxes in the rest of the book.

5   Cf. P. Kyle McCarter, Jr., 1 Samuel, Anchor Bible, p. 305, and the literature there cited. For the irony of this scene see my Contribution p. 61.

6   Even those subsequent reactions which appear on the surface to be positive are either negatively motivated or else turn out to be unstable and short-lived.

7   There are of course numerous differences at the micro-level.

8   Its translation "suniôn" at 18,14 gives to the Hebrew verb the connotation of "wisdom" which we wish to give the same Hebrew root at 18,30.

EPILOGUE

1. The four participants in the "Joint Venture" had, and still have, more or less diverging solutions to the problems they intended to disentangle.

A hasty reader of the reports may discern two camps from the outset. To him it may seem clear that Dominique and David defend the MT, whereas Johan and Emanuel favour the LXX. This first appreciation is not entirely false. However, lots of nuances should be added.

A closer evaluation shows that one of the basic points of difference between the approaches is their starting point. Emanuel's and Johan's point of departure is the level of textual criticism with its factual evidence, whereas that of Dominique and David is that of literary criticism with its more hypothetical judgments. The roads further diverge, no longer two by two but individually : David discovers in the MT of 1 Sam 17-18 and artistically composed and well balanced unit, misunderstood by the Septuagint. The LXX-version truncated the original text* and simplified it in a pedantic manner. Thus one could say that David approaches the MT with what today is called the rhetorical critical method, paying attention to the final text and not to the history of its formation. Dominique, on the other hand, is much more interested in the literary growth of the text, discerning between several sources combined by an editor. According to him, the final text of the MT is not a harmonious unity. The Septuagint, based directly of indirectly on the Hebrew preserved in the MT, tries to eliminate some of its incongruencies. Emanuel's approach is of yet a different kind. Setting out from text-critical data he analyses the translation technique of the Septuagint in 1 Sam 17-18. He emphasises its literalness and concludes that the translator cannot have omitted large sections of the text. He must have found the short text in his Vorlage. Rather briefly he then turns to the questions concerning the nature of the short text, leaving the realm of textual criticism for that of literary criticism. In his argumentation, the shorter text is the older one. Johan also begins with text-critical observations, and reaches similar conclusions on that level. However, he then goes deeper into the literary critical questions, emphasising the difference in the literary genre between 1 Sam 17,1-11.32ff and 1 Sam 17,12-31. In 1 Sam 17,12ff he discovers the incipit of an older and originally independent story of David and Goliath. These data suggest a complex history of the growth of the text of which the Septuagint and the MT offer two diverging final editorial compositions.

-----
* Note de l'éditeur : *Sur ce point, David a apporté une dernière précision :* "I hold that if the truncation arose at the Greek level, it more probably arose as a result of subsequent scholarly criticism on the part of Jews like Demetrius, and not at the level of the translators."

2. The discussions in Fribourg did not simply repeat the written dialogue. First the participants exchanged information concerning their personal background and interests revealing biases, and explaining their particular approach. Dominique is completely immerged in the Hebrew Old Testament Text Project of the UBS. His work with the Hebrew manuscripts of the Bible and with the early Jewish commentators and grammarians orients him towards the Massoretic text and increases his respect for it. David feels and thinks as a classicist. He is convinced that individual authors composed the great classics, such as Homer, and that, as long as the contrary cannot be proven, similar individual minds must be responsible for the biblical books. Emanuel is specialised in textual criticism and the Septuagint. His work with the Hebrew University Bible Project and with the computer has given him a growing interest in the factual evidence. He is aware of the long period of literary formation and development of the Biblical texts but is in need of factual evidence to prove the theory. Johan belongs to what one could call the more common type of exegete, working with historical critical methods. His interest in the Redaktionsgeschichte draws his attention to the final text and to the borderlines between literary and textual criticism.

After this opening round, the perspectives were widened from another point of view. More general methodological questions were brought to the fore, concerning the character of the Greek translation and its role in textual criticism, as well as questions concerning the aims of textual criticism and the nature of the 'final text'. When Old Testament textual critics try to establish 'the final text' of the Bible, what do they mean by that ? The participants agreed that for several biblical books more than one text must have existed. To a certain extent the final character of such a text depended on its functioning and its acceptance by a religious community. This observation led to a discussion concerning the impact of the canon and to the appraisal of the MT and the LXX as two different canonical forms of the text.

Returning to the particular case of 1 Sam 17-18 a certain agreement was reached regarding the literalness of the Greek translation and the short character of its Vorlage. Already on this level David had some hesitation. No unanimity could be found in the answers to the next problem : Are the differences between the shorter and the longer text to be explained on the level of the formation of the text or on the level of its transmission ? The present author remains convinced that the origins of the divergences are to be sought on the editorial level. Both the Vorlage of the MT and of the Septuagint combined several stories of David and Goliath.

The Vorlage of the Septuagint collected fewer data than the MT. The major problem is that the material missing in the LXX and in its Vorlage appears to be the oldest. However its version in the MT betrays several traces of editorial reworking and adaptation to the context. Its characteristics of a folk or fairy tale may offer a key to the problem. Some editors may have judged the story unfit for the official and religious records of David's deeds, while others may have thought differently. Whatever the conclusion may be, it should be clear that both versions, the MT and the LXX are valuable ones and stand in their own right. The one should not be corrected by the other. This rule should be applied to all cases in which the differences between the MT and the LXX are not to be explained as accidental errors.

Durant ces quatre années, nous avons essayé, à l'occasion de cette recherche, de travailler vraiment ensemble, chacun de nous quatre ayant la même part d'initiative, mon rôle étant seulement de coordonner notre tâche commune.

Lorsque j'ai été chargé d'éditer les divers documents de travail qui en émanèrent, il a été convenu que je résumerais les règles que nous avions établies et les choix que nous avions faits. J'ai préféré reproduire ici toutes les circulaires sur la base desquelles ces choix furent faits et dans lesquelles les règles résultant de ces choix ont été formulées. On pourra suivre ainsi les diverses étapes de notre travail commun telles qu'elles se sont déroulées.

Je m'excuse d'avoir dû, comme je le craignais, attendre plus d'un an avant de publier ces documents.

Je remercie Bernadette Schacher, secrétaire scientifique de l'Institut Biblique, à qui l'on doit la typographie et la présentation de cet ouvrage.

A mon collègue Othmar Keel et au Conseil de l'Université de Fribourg, nous devons l'accueil de cette publication dans la série OBO.

6 avril 1986

Dominique Barthélemy

ORBIS BIBLICUS ET ORIENTALIS

Bd. 1   OTTO RICKENBACHER: *Weisheitsperikopen bei Ben Sira*. X–214–15* Seiten. 1973. Vergriffen.

Bd. 2   FRANZ SCHNIDER: *Jesus der Prophet*. 298 Seiten. 1973. Vergriffen.

Bd. 3   PAUL ZINGG: *Das Wachsen der Kirche*. Beiträge zur Frage der lukanischen Redaktion und Theologie. 345 Seiten. 1974. Vergriffen.

Bd. 4   KARL JAROŠ: *Die Stellung des Elobisten zur kanaanäischen Religion*. 294 Seiten, 12 Abbildungen. 1982. 2. verbesserte und überarbeitete Auflage.

Bd. 5   OTHMAR KEEL: *Wirkmächtige Siegeszeichen im Alten Testament*. Ikonographische Studien zu Jos 8, 18–26; Ex 17, 8–13; 2 Kön 13, 14–19 und 1 Kön 22, 11. 232 Seiten, 78 Abbildungen. 1974. Vergriffen.

Bd. 6   VITUS HUONDER: *Israel Sohn Gottes*. Zur Deutung eines alttestamentlichen Themas in der jüdischen Exegese des Mittelalters. 231 Seiten. 1975.

Bd. 7   RAINER SCHMITT: *Exodus und Passa*. Ihr Zusammenhang im Alten Testament. 124 Seiten. 1982. 2. neubearbeitete Auflage.

Bd. 8   ADRIAN SCHENKER: *Hexaplarische Psalmenbruchstücke*. Die hexaplarischen Psalmenfragmente der Handschriften Vaticanus graecus 752 und Canonicianus graecus 62. Einleitung, Ausgabe, Erläuterung. XXVIII–446 Seiten. 1975.

Bd. 9   BEAT ZUBER: *Vier Studien zu den Ursprüngen Israels*. Die Sinaifrage und Probleme der Volks- und Traditionsbildung. 152 Seiten. 1976. Vergriffen.

Bd. 10 EDUARDO ARENS: *The (4:έ-Sayings in the Synoptic Tradition*. A Historico-critical Investigation. 370 Seiten. 1976.

Bd. 11 KARL JAROŠ: *Sichem*. Eine archäologische und religionsgeschichtliche Studie, mit besonderer Berücksichtigung von Jos 24. 280 Seiten, 193 Abbildungen. 1976.

Bd. 11a KARL JAROŠ/BRIGITTE DECKERT: *Studien zur Sichem-Area*. 81 Seiten, 23 Abbildungen. 1977.

Bd. 12 WALTER BÜHLMANN: *Vom rechten Reden und Schweigen*. Studien zu Proverbien 10–31. 371 Seiten. 1976.

Bd. 13 IVO MEYER: *Jeremia und die falschen Propheten*. 155 Seiten. 1977.

Bd. 14 OTHMAR KEEL: *Vögel als Boten*. Studien zu Ps 68, 12–14, Gen 8, 6–12, Koh 10, 20 und dem Aussenden von Botenvögeln in Ägypten. – Mit einem Beitrag von Urs Winter zu Ps 56, 1 und zur Ikonographie der Göttin mit der Taube. 164 Seiten, 44 Abbildungen. 1977.

Bd. 15 MARIE-LOUISE GUBLER: *Die frühesten Deutungen des Todes Jesu*. Eine motivgeschichtliche Darstellung aufgrund der neueren exegetischen Forschung. XVI–424 Seiten. 1977. Vergriffen.

Bd. 16 JEAN ZUMSTEIN: *La condition du croyant dans l'Evangile selon Matthieu*. 467 pages. 1977. Epuisé.

Bd. 17 FRANZ SCHNIDER: *Die verlorenen Söhne*. Strukturanalytische und historisch-kritische Untersuchungen zu Lk 15. 105 Seiten. 1977.

Bd. 18 HEINRICH VALENTIN: *Aaron*. Eine Studie zur vor-priesterschriftlichen Aaron-Überlieferung. VIII–441 Seiten. 1978.

Bd. 19 MASSÉO CALOZ: *Etude sur la LXX origénienne du Psautier*. Les relations entre les leçons des Psaumes du Manuscrit Coislin 44, les Fragments des Hexaples et le texte du Psautier Gallican. 480 pages. 1978.

Bd. 20 RAPHAEL GIVEON: *The Impact of Egypt on Canaan*. Iconographical and Related Studies. 156 Seiten, 73 Abbildungen. 1978.

Bd. 21 DOMINIQUE BARTHÉLEMY: *Etudes d'histoire du texte de l'Ancien Testament*. XXV–419 pages. 1978.

Bd. 22/1 CESLAS SPICQ: *Notes de Lexicographie néo-testamentaire*. Tome I: p. 1–524. 1978. Epuisé.

Bd. 22/2 CESLAS SPICQ: *Notes de Lexicographie néo-testamentaire*. Tome II: p. 525–980. 1978. Epuisé.

Bd. 22/3 CESLAS SPICQ: *Notes de Lexicographie néo-testamentaire*. Supplément. 698 pages. 1982.

Bd. 23 BRIAN M. NOLAN: *The royal Son of God*. The Christology of Matthew 1–2 in the Setting of the Gospel. 282 Seiten. 1979.

Bd. 24 KLAUS KIESOW: *Exodustexte im Jesajabuch*. Literarkritische und motivgeschichtliche Analysen. 221 Seiten. 1979.

Bd. 25/1 MICHAEL LATTKE: *Die Oden Salomos in ihrer Bedeutung für Neues Testament und Gnosis*. Band I. Ausführliche Handschriftenbeschreibung. Edition mit deutscher Parallel-Übersetzung. Hermeneutischer Anhang zur gnostischen Interpretation der Oden Salomos in der Pistis Sophia. XI–237 Seiten. 1979.

Bd. 25/1a MICHAEL LATTKE: *Die Oden Salomos in ihrer Bedeutung für Neues Testament und Gnosis*. Band Ia. Der syrische Text der Edition in Estrangela Faksimile des griechischen Papyrus Bodmer XI. 68 Seiten. 1980.

Bd. 25/2 MICHAEL LATTKE: *Die Oden Salomos in ihrer Bedeutung für Neues Testament und Gnosis*. Band II. Vollständige Wortkonkordanz zur handschriftlichen, griechischen, koptischen, lateinischen und syrischen Überlieferung der Oden Salomos. Mit einem Faksimile des Kodex N. XVI–201 Seiten. 1979.

Bd. 25/3 MICHAEL LATTKE: *Die Oden Salomos in ihrer Bedeutung für Neues Testament und Gnosis*. Band III. XXXIV–478 Seiten. 1986.

Bd. 26 MAX KÜCHLER: *Frühjüdische Weisheitstraditionen*. Zum Fortgang weisheitlichen Denkens im Bereich des frühjüdischen Jahweglaubens. 703 Seiten. 1979.

Bd. 27 JOSEF M. OESCH: *Petucha und Setuma*. Untersuchungen zu einer überlieferten Gliederung im hebräischen Text des Alten Testaments. XX–392–37* Seiten. 1979.

Bd. 28 ERIK HORNUNG/OTHMAR KEEL (Herausgeber): *Studien zu altägyptischen Lebenslehren*. 394 Seiten. 1979.

Bd. 29 HERMANN ALEXANDER SCHLÖGL: *Der Gott Tatenen*. Nach Texten und Bildern des Neuen Reiches. 216 Seiten, 14 Abbildungen. 1980.

Bd. 30 JOHANN JAKOB STAMM: *Beiträge zur Hebräischen und Altorientalischen Namenkunde.* XVI–264 Seiten. 1980.

Bd. 31 HELMUT UTZSCHNEIDER: *Hosea – Prophet vor dem Ende.* Zum Verhältnis von Geschichte und Institution in der alttestamentlichen Prophetie. 260 Seiten. 1980.

Bd. 32 PETER WEIMAR: *Die Berufung des Mose.* Literaturwissenschaftliche Analyse von Exodus 2, 23–5, 5. 402 Seiten. 1980.

Bd. 33 OTHMAR KEEL: *Das Böcklein in der Milch seiner Mutter und Verwandtes.* Im Lichte eines altorientalischen Bildmotivs. 163 Seiten, 141 Abbildungen. 1980.

Bd. 34 PIERRE AUFFRET: *Hymnes d'Egypte et d'Israël.* Etudes de structures littéraires. 316 pages, 1 illustration. 1981.

Bd. 35 ARIE VAN DER KOOIJ: *Die alten Textzeugen des Jesajabuches.* Ein Beitrag zur Textgeschichte des Alten Testaments. 388 Seiten. 1981.

Bd. 36 CARMEL McCARTHY: *The Tiqqune Sopherim and Other Theological Corrections in the Masoretic Text of the Old Testament.* 280 Seiten. 1981.

Bd. 37 BARBARA L. BEGELSBACHER-FISCHER: *Untersuchungen zur Götterwelt des Alten Reiches im Spiegel der Privatgräber der IV. und V. Dynastie.* 336 Seiten. 1981.

Bd. 38 MÉLANGES DOMINIQUE BARTHÉLEMY. Etudes bibliques offertes à l'occasion de son 60? anniversaire. Edités par Pierre Casetti, Othmar Keel et Adrian Schenker. 724 pages, 31 illustrations. 1981.

Bd. 39 ANDRÉ LEMAIRE: *Les écoles et la formation de la Bible dans l'ancien Israël.* 142 pages, 14 illustrations. 1981.

Bd. 40 JOSEPH HENNINGER: *Arabica Sacra.* Aufsätze zur Religionsgeschichte Arabiens und seiner Randgebiete. Contributions à l'histoire religieuse de l'Arabie et de ses régions limitrophes. 347 Seiten. 1981.

Bd. 41 DANIEL VON ALLMEN: *La famille de Dieu.* La symbolique familiale dans le paulinisme. LXVII–330 pages, 27 planches. 1981.

Bd. 42 ADRIAN SCHENKER: *Der Mächtige im Schmelzofen des Mitleids.* Eine Interpretation von 2 Sam 24. 92 Seiten. 1982.

Bd. 43 PAUL DESELAERS: *Das Buch Tobit.* Studien zu seiner Entstehung, Komposition und Theologie. 532 Seiten + Übersetzung 16 Seiten. 1982.

Bd. 44 PIERRE CASETTI: *Gibt es ein Leben vor dem Tod?* Eine Auslegung von Psalm 49. 315 Seiten. 1982.

Bd. 45 FRANK-LOTHAR HOSSFELD: *Der Dekalog.* Seine späten Fassungen, die originale Komposition und seine Vorstufen. 308 Seiten. 1982.

Bd. 46 ERIK HORNUNG: *Der ägyptische Mythos von der Himmelskuh.* Eine Ätiologie des Unvollkommenen. Unter Mitarbeit von Andreas Brodbeck, Hermann Schlögl und Elisabeth Staehelin und mit einem Beitrag von Gerhard Fecht. XII–129 Seiten, 10 Abbildungen. 1982.

Bd. 47 PIERRE CHERIX: *Le Concept de Notre Grande Puissance (CG VI, 4).* Texte, remarques philologiques, traduction et notes. XIV–95 pages. 1982.

Bd. 48   JAN ASSMANN/WALTER BURKERT/FRITZ STOLZ: *Funktionen und Leistungen des Mythos.* Drei altorientalische Beispiele. 118 Seiten, 17 Abbildungen. 1982.

Bd. 49   PIERRE AUFFRET: *La sagesse a bâti sa maison.* Etudes de structures littéraires dans l'Ancien Testament et spécialement dans les psaumes. 580 pages. 1982.

Bd. 50/1 DOMINIQUE BARTHÉLEMY: *Critique textuelle de l'Ancien Testament.* 1. Josué, Juges, Ruth, Samuel, Rois, Chroniques, Esdras, Néhémie, Esther. Rapport final du Comité pour l'analyse textuelle de l'Ancien Testament hébreu institué par l'Alliance Biblique Universelle, établi en coopération avec Alexander R. Hulst †, Norbert Lohfink, William D. McHardy, H. Peter Rüger, coéditeur, James A. Sanders, coéditeur. 812 pages. 1982.

Bd. 50/2 DOMINIQUE BARTHÉLEMY: *Critique textuelle de l'Ancien Testament.* 2. Isaïe, Jérémie, Lamentations. Rapport final du Comité pour l'analyse textuelle de l'Ancien Testament hébreu institué par l'Alliance Biblique Universelle, établi en coopération avec Alexander R. Hulst †, Norbert Lohfink, William D. McHardy, H. Peter Rüger, coéditeur, James A. Sanders, coéditeur. 1112 pages. 1986.

Bd. 51   JAN ASSMANN: *Re und Amun.* Die Krise des polytheistischen Weltbilds im Ägypten der 18.–20. Dynastie. XII–309 Seiten. 1983.

Bd. 52   MIRIAM LICHTHEIM: *Late Egyptian Wisdom Literature in the International Context.* A Study of Demotic Instructions. X–240 Seiten. 1983.

Bd. 53   URS WINTER: *Frau und Göttin.* Exegetische und ikonographische Studien zum weiblichen Gottesbild im Alten Israel und in dessen Umwelt. XVIII–928 Seiten, 520 Abbildungen. 1983.

Bd. 54   PAUL MAIBERGER: *Topographische und historische Untersuchungen zum Sinaiproblem.* Worauf beruht die Identifizierung des Ǧabal Mūsā mit dem Sinai? 189 Seiten, 13 Tafeln. 1984.

Bd. 55   PETER FREI/KLAUS KOCH: *Reichsidee und Reichsorganisation im Perserreich.* 119 Seiten, 17 Abbildungen. 1984

Bd. 56   HANS-PETER MÜLLER: *Vergleich und Metapher im Hohenlied.* 59 Seiten. 1984.

Bd. 57   STEPHEN PISANO: *Additions or Omissions in the Books of Samuel.* The Significant Pluses and Minuses in the Massoretic, LXX and Qumran Texts. XIV–295 Seiten. 1984.

Bd. 58   ODO CAMPONOVO: *Königtum, Königsherrschaft und Reich Gottes in den Frühjüdischen Schriften.* XVI–492 Seiten. 1984.

Bd. 59   JAMES KARL HOFFMEIER: *Sacred in the Vocabulary of Ancient Egypt.* The Term *DSR,* with Special Reference to Dynasties I–XX. XXIV–281 Seiten, 24 Figuren. 1985.

Bd. 60   CHRISTIAN HERRMANN: *Formen für ägyptische Fayencen.* Katalog der Sammlung des Biblischen Instituts der Universität Freiburg Schweiz und einer Privatsammlung. XXVIII-199 Seiten. 1985.

Bd. 61   HELMUT ENGEL: *Die Susanna-Erzählung.* Einleitung, Übersetzung und Kommentar zum Septuaginta-Text und zur Theodition-Bearbeitung. 205 Seiten + Anhang 11 Seiten. 1985.

Bd. 62   ERNST KUTSCH: *Die chronologischen Daten des Ezechielbuches*. 82 Seiten. 1985.

Bd. 63   MANFRED HUTTER: *Altorientalische Vorstellungen von der Unterwelt*. Literar- und religionsgeschichtliche Überlegungen zu «Nergal und Ereškigal». VIII–187 Seiten. 1985.

Bd. 64   HELGA WEIPPERT/KLAUS SEYBOLD/MANFRED WEIPPERT: *Beiträge zur prophetischen Bildsprache in Israel und Assyrien*. IX–93 Seiten. 1985.

Bd. 65   ABDEL-AZIZ FAHMY SADEK: *Contribution à l'étude de l'Amdouat*. Les variantes tardives du Livre de l'Amdouat dans les papyrus du Musée du Caire. XVI–400 pages, 175 illustrations. 1985.

Bd. 66   HANS-PETER STÄHLI: *Solare Elemente im Jahweglauben des Alten Testamentes*. X–60 Seiten. 1985.

Bd. 67   OTHMAR KEEL/SILVIA SCHROER: *Studien zu den Stempelsiegeln aus Palästina/Israel*. Band I. 115 Seiten, 103 Abbildungen. 1985.

Bd. 68   WALTER BEYERLIN: *Weisheitliche Vergewisserung mit Bezug auf den Zionskult*. Studien zum 125. Psalm. 96 Seiten. 1985.

Bd. 69   RAPHAEL VENTURA: *Living in a City of the Dead*. A Selection of Topographical and Administrative Terms in the Documents of the Theban Necropolis. XII–232 Seiten. 1986.

Bd. 70   CLEMENS LOCHER: *Die Ehre einer Frau in Israel*. Exegetische und rechtsvergleichende Studien zu Dtn 22, 13–21. XVIII–464 Seiten. 1986.

Bd. 71   HANS-PETER MATHYS: *Liebe deinen Nächsten wie dich selbst*. Untersuchungen zum alttestamentlichen Gebot der Nächstenliebe (Lev 19, 18). XIV–196 Seiten. 1986.

Bd. 72   FRIEDRICH ABITZ: *Ramses III. in den Gräbern seiner Söhne*. 156 Seiten. 1986.

Bd. 73   DOMINIQUE BARTHÉLEMY/DAVID W. GOODING/JOHAN LUST/EMANUEL TOV: *The Story of David and Goliath*. 160 Seiten. 1986.